PINHOLES IN THE NIGHT

Pinholes in the Night

ESSENTIAL POEMS FROM LATIN AMERICA

Selected by Raúl Zurita
Edited by Forrest Gander

Poetry Foundation's Harriet Monroe Poetry Institute
Ilya Kaminsky, *Poets in the World* series editor

 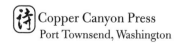 Copper Canyon Press
Port Townsend, Washington

 Copper Canyon Press

Pinholes in the Night: Essential Poems from Latin America is a copublication of
The Poetry Foundation and Copper Canyon Press, as part of the *Poets in the World*
series created by The Poetry Foundation's Harriet Monroe Poetry Institute.

Cover art: Juan Dolhare, *Latinoamerica or Series of Individualisms or Individualisms
in a Series.* Oil on canvas, 59 × 78 inches.

Copper Canyon Press is in residence at Fort Worden State Park in Port Townsend,
Washington, under the auspices of Centrum. Centrum is a gathering place for artists
and creative thinkers from around the world, students of all ages and backgrounds,
and audiences seeking extraordinary cultural enrichment.

LIBRARY OF CONGRESS CATALOGING-IN-PUBLICATION DATA
[Pinholes in the night : essential poems from Latin America / selected by Raúl Zurita ;
edited by Forrest Gander.
pages cm
ISBN 978-1-55659-450-2 (pbk.: alk. paper)
1. Latin American poetry—Translations into English. I. Zurita, Raúl. II. Gander,
Forrest, 1956–
PQ7087.E5P56 2013
861.008'098—dc23

2013020595

9 8 7 6 5 4 3 2 FIRST PRINTING
Copper Canyon Press
Post Office Box 271
Port Townsend, Washington 98368
www.coppercanyonpress.org

A Antonio Cisneros, mi amigo
In Memoriam

Percibo lo secreto, lo oculto:
¡Oh ustedes señores!
Así somos, somos mortales,
De cuatro en cuatro nosotros los hombres,
habremos de irnos,
todos tendremos que morir en la tierra

Como una pintura
nos iremos borrando.
Como una flor
nos iremos secando
aquí sobre la tierra.

Como vestidura de plumaje de ave zacuán,
de la preciosa ave de cuello de hule,
nos iremos acabando
Nos vamos a su casa.
Medítenlo, señores,
águilas y tigres,
aunque fueran de jade,
aunque fueran de oro
también allá irán,
al lugar de los descarnados

Tendremos que desaparecer
nadie habrá de quedar.
¿A dónde iremos que la muerte no exista?
Pero, ¿por eso viviré llorando?

Percibo lo secreto, lo oculto:
¡oh ustedes señores!
Así somos nosotros mortales
de cuatro en cuatro nosotros los hombres
todos tendremos que irnos
todos tendremos que morir aquí en la tierra.

—NEZAHUALCÓYOTL
TRANSLATED INTO SPANISH BY MIGUEL LEÓN-PORTILLA

I sense the secret, the dark truth:
Oh my brothers!
Being mortal, being men,
four by four, all of us
have to pack ourselves off,
have to die on the earth.

Like a painting
we will fade.
Like a flower
we'll dry up
here in the dirt.

Like a cape made from the feathers of a zacuan,
from that rare rubbernecked bird,
we start to come apart
the moment we leave the house.
Consider this, my friends:
eagles and tigers,
though made from jade,
though made from gold,
come to the same end,
to the same rotten place.

All of us must disappear,
none is given to stay.
Where can we go where there is no death?
And this is why we lug ourselves around weeping?

I sense the secret, the dark truth:
Oh my brothers!
Being mortal, being men,
four by four, all of us
have to pack ourselves off,
have to die on the earth.

—NEZAHUALCÓYOTL,
TRANSLATED INTO ENGLISH BY FORREST GANDER

CONTENTS

INTRODUCTION

This anthology of eighteen poems reflects my personal taste and represents, for me, the greatest poems written in Castilian in America. The selection begins, however, with a poem written before the imposition of Castilian. Translated from Nahuatl into Spanish by Miguel León-Portilla, it is a song by Nezahualcóyotl (1402–1472), king of the ancient Mexican city-state of Tetzcuco, and its subject is death and the brevity of life:

> All of us must disappear,
> none is given to stay.
> Where can we go where there is no death?

My selection ends, as if poetry were never more than an eternal return, with a poem by Gonzalo Millán, "Life." Along with José Watanabe's "Guardian of Ice," "Life" functions as the contemporary Latin American expression of Nezahualcóyotl's inaugural song. So in a relentless crescendo, "Life" begins by describing the birth and flowering of everything that lives—trees and plants, animals and birds—and it ends by embracing all of it:

> Lizards grow new tails
> when they lose their old ones,
> and when crabs lose their pincers and legs
> they grow new pincers and legs.
> Wounds on men and animals scar over;
> broken bones mend on their own.

The poem abruptly breaks off, there's a space, and then come three of the most powerful lines written in our poetry:

> Cells, organs, tissues wear out.
> Life forces wane.
> Death is the end of life.

Although there are many other more than remarkable Latin American poems, they nevertheless seem to me, despite their achievements, subsidiaries of these I've selected. One poem by each of the nineteen poets. For most of the poets, the choice of the poem was obvious, but in the cases of Gabriela Mistral, César Vallejo, and Pablo Neruda, the job was practically impossible and at the same time fascinating. The question was: what poem, had it not been written, would have rendered the author another author and Latin American poetry something else? I would have liked to include examples of the immensity of poetry written in Portuguese by poets such as Carlos Drummond de Andrade, Joâo Cabral de Melo Neto, Ferreira Gullar (with his "Poema Sujo"), Lédo Ivo. I would have liked to include the complete 600 pages of one of the major poems of our time, *Gran Sertón: Veredas* by Joâo Guimarâes Rosa, a novel that suspends the barriers between genres in ways comparable to James Joyce's *Ulysses,* Hermann Broch's *The Death of Virgil,* Faulkner's *The Sound and the Fury,* or Juan Rulfo's *The Plain in Flames* and *Pedro Páramo,* and so becomes one of the pinnacles of the language, but of course, that would have called for a second list that exceeded my purpose. In any case, placed against the work I've collected here, I asked myself what other poem, or fragment of a poem, or what single line written by any poet I didn't include could stand with dignity against the poems of Gabriela Mistral, César Vallejo, Vicente Huidobro, Pablo de Rokha, Jorge Luis Borges, Pablo Neruda, or "Letter to My Mother" by Juan Gelman. The only thing I could consider on par or even superior to them would be "You Don't Hear Dogs Barking," a tale by Juan Rulfo from *The Plain in Flames* which is, along with other stories in the book, one of the finest poems of the twentieth century in any language.

What follows are some brief notes about each of the selections.

☙☙☙

"The Fugue" by Gabriela Mistral (Montenegro, Valle de Elqui, Chile, 1889– New York, 1957) whose real name was Lucila Godoy Alcayaga, is the signal poetic record of the Latin American landscape transfigured by dream, memory, and death. Published in *Tala* (Slash), 1938, a book composed in nine parts, one of which, "America," includes the poems "Cordillera" and "Tropical Sun," "The Fugue" foreshadows what will be, twelve years later, Neruda's *Canto general.* "The Fugue" is a startling, hallucinatory elegy that opens the book's first section, "Death of My Mother." It shows us a landscape, an actual landscape, cliffs along the Elqui, a river stretching below an endless succession of mountains in which the figure of the mother appears repeatedly, always in the nearest one. The mother materializes in one mountain, then another, and then another, without ever coalescing into wholeness. So we come to understand that what we call nature, geography, and landscape are nothing but huge white canvases we fill with our passion for life, with our misery, joy, or nostalgia. The mountains in the poem by Gabriela Mistral are inaccessible because the life of the past is beyond us, because death, which is the face of someone who has been loved, who is dead and appears in dreams or in memory, never lets us in, because it is a figure like the mountains in which the mother emerges, forever outside language.

‡‡‡

Altazor by Vicente Huidobro (Santiago, Chile, 1893–Cartagana, Chile, 1948) represents the major effort in Latin American poetry to build a work associated with the European avant-garde of the early twentieth century; it radically tore itself from the straitjacket of Spanish poetry that, from Quevedo and the baroque of Góngora, imposed an academic formalism so severe it lacked any capacity for renewal. Beyond the romantic movement, Spain didn't undergo the kind of aesthetic explosion that took place in France, Italy, and the United States. Without a Baudelaire, a Rimbaud, a Whitman, or a Leopardi, it depended on its former colonies to broaden the horizon of Castilian, that language for which American poetry seemed to feel resentment, as we see in César Vallejo's *Trilce,* and claustrophobia, as we see in the avant-garde ambitions of Vicente Huidobro who, in *Non Serviam,* a 1922 manifesto, after asserting that "the poet is a little god," introduces his program called "poetic creationism." Huidobro demands that the poet must not mimic nature but create his/her own universe. As is often the case with manifestos, its precepts are surpassed by his best poems. *Altazor*'s theme is double. On the one hand, and this is what precludes any criticism, *Altazor* is an extraordinary experimental work, its formal freedom unmatched, that cuts against the linearity of conventional poetry; its theme is the slow descent by parachute of someone, Altazor, who knows where he is falling but doesn't know from where he falls and whose final disintegration matches the disintegration of the whole world being represented. Secondly, perhaps more crucial for the understanding of Latin American history, *Altazor,* one of the most remarkable poems in the Castilian language, a language imposed on Latin America by conquest, is paradoxically a poem of the destruction of that language. Dividing the poem into seven songs plus a preface, Huidobro begins the first canto in a masterful, almost ostentatious language that he mines for all its sonorities, its magnificent images and metaphors, its rhythmic and metric possibilities. The second canto represents one of the most enduring love poems produced in the last century, but by the third canto, Huidobro refers to the language we speak as a dead language. As the poem progresses, the language is transformed, metamorphosed, ruptured right through to the end of Canto VII, where the idiom is absolutely pulverized, as if to show us that the poem, the true poem, only begins when the book ends, and it is the reader who must raise, from the crushed remains of the dead languages we speak, a fresh language.

⚐⚐⚐

Spain, Take This Cup from Me, a book-length poem by César Vallejo (Santiago de Chuco, Peru, 1892–Paris, France, 1938), was published in 1939, a year after his death, in the eponymous book, and its importance, along with Pablo Neruda's "The Heights of Macchu Picchu," surpasses every literary categorization in demonstrating for us the impossibility of separating history from our very particular history as speakers of an imposed language. In the poems of Vallejo's *Trilce* (1922) words seem nailed together over a relentless shriek; lines are shredded by a broken syntax full of archaisms and neologisms, exclamation points, ellipses, words set apart in capital letters or separated into syllables, as if everything were laid out in positions of permanent torture and poems were physical bodies, hooded, about to die. In contrast to *Altazor* in which Vicente Huidobro shatters language according to the dictates of an avant-garde that guides the poet's choices, agendas, and productions, in *Trilce* Vallejo shatters language in obedience to a kind of existential tension, an extreme anxiety that feels like expressionism and through which the poems are demolished because the subject, at one with the poems, is demolished. With Vallejo, we sense poems exploding from within, spewing out bits of viscera, organs, bones, and they can't fail to show the signs of their agony. It will be the reader who comes to travel along those lines one by one, giving a little space to the words, unpinning each from the others, reordering them so that the poems, at last, can live. The price is that it falls on the reader to bear the death the poems contain, but this is also the condition of our speech. The Spanish speakers of the Americas speak a language in which every sentence, syllable, and turn of phrase contains a memory of the infinite violence that prevailed, and so, in Vallejo, poems are dying bodies. They make clear, just as Huidobro does, but by opposite signs, the tortuous relationship to a language we admire because it is ours, it is the language we read and write, and yet at the same time it instills a deep grudge in us because its imposition signifies the death, marginalization, and misery of millions and millions of human beings in the biggest holocaust in history. Fifteen years after the appearance of *Trilce,* Vallejo wrote *Spain, Take This Cup from Me* in which, by focusing on the Spanish Civil War, he provides the keys to understanding *Trilce;* they are no more than the keys for comprehending the constant and dramatic spasms of Latin American history, its internal turbulence, and its endemic inability to build projects that have durance. The problem is at the heart of words. At the end of the third stanza of *Spain, Take This Cup from Me,* Vallejo observes that if Spain falls to Franco, we will have to go backward in language, descending level by level along the stair of the inherited alphabet until we arrive at the letter "in which shame is born." What César Vallejo is telling us is that through all these vast territories we travel in words, we'll never be happy because pain is encrusted on every particle of the language we speak.

⚶

"The Old Man's Song" by Pablo de Rokha (Licantén, Chile, 1894–Santiago, Chile, 1968, his real name was Hernan Díaz Loyola), published in 1961, is one of the most moving tragic poems written in Castilian. Displaying both a verbal power, comparable only to that of his archenemy Pablo Neruda, and an uncounterfeitable tone present through all his work from the adolescent *Versos de infancia* (Childhood verses), 1916, to the monumental *Mis grandes poemas* (My great poems), 1969, a compilation he prepared but which appeared posthumously, Rokhian poetry is an extreme attempt by an extreme poet to redefine the national. Beyond his monumental achievements and monumental blunders, Pablo de Rokha develops a cartography unequaled in its emotional force, its affections, sympathies, loathings, and repudiations, pushed to the limit, forged from a language in which prose is exposed in all its rawness even as it takes on the tragic and solemn intensity of great funerals, liturgies, oracles. Appealing to "gutter" slang, orgiastic and pregnant with speech, the work of Pablo de Rokha signified, in our language, the deepest cut by which, up to that point, poetry might be comprehended. Much more radically than Vicente Huidobro and decades before the revolutionary antipoetry of Nicanor Parra, De Rokha with *Los gemidos* (The wailing), published in 1922 (the same year that saw the publication of *Ulysses* by James Joyce, *The Waste Land* by T.S. Eliot and *Trilce* by César Vallejo) anticipated the major literary transformations to come in the literature of the last century: the fusion of poetry and prose, stream of consciousness, the deletion of punctuation. But the real beauty is that, like the work of Pablo Neruda, this new writing was not limited to an aesthetic proposal, as with Huidobro, except in as much as De Rokha proposes to refound a continent just as Neruda does in *Canto general,* with the difference being that this territory for Pablo de Rokha, as fervent an anti-imperialist as Neruda, is devastated by the omen of defeat and absolute ruination. It is an irreparable sadness that finally overwhelms Rokhian landscapes. De Rokha makes colossal, he reiterates the outrageous, stretching words as if the mission of those words were to bury the intolerable, bestowing on the real an eternity that exists only in the deep unreality of the poem. It's a fierce and wounding paradox that reveals defeat in "The Old Man's Song," but it's also a fierce and wounding paradox that such defeat underlies all writing and all existence. In his excess, in his monumentality, his limitations and exorbitant errors, Pablo de Rokha understood that fateful paradox for all of us. He committed suicide on September 10, 1968.

⚊⚊⚊

"Conjectural Poem" by Jorge Luis Borges (Buenos Aires, Argentina, 1899–Geneva Switzerland, 1986) appears to be quite distinct from the last two poems mentioned and yet its theme is not alien to them. As in the cases of "White Stone on a Black Stone," the poem where Vallejo announced his death, Pablo de Rokha's "The Old Man's Song," and the poem by Jaime Sabines, "A Few Words on the Death of Major Sabines," the core of this poem is identity in the face of death, or rather, the definitive identity bestowed by the imminence of the end, but with a radically contrasting effect. The entire oeuvre of Borges represents a successful attempt to bestow upon language a literary rank that language doggedly denies. In "Conjectural Poem," recalling the famous book *Civilization and Barbarism* by fellow Argentine Domingo Faustino Sarmiento, one of the characters, a certain Francisco Laprida, a man who dreams up another man, discovers his "destiny as a South American" just moments before being murdered. He is killed by gauchos, by the conquerors. Borges's poetry never reaches the prodigious linguistic dimension, the abyss of contradictions, or the depths of other major Hispano-American poems. It's not in his conception of the thing-made-literary (where, as noted in his poem "The Apocryphal Sermon," the worst sin is *emphasis*), but in his best poems, when they are released from the straitjacket of academic discussions, Borges achieves limpidness, a clarity, and lucidity unique in our language's poetry. A small final remark: Borges's "Conjectural Poem" is, from its very title, reiterating a paradox present in all his work, that every name is an alias because one is just one of many: "I who have been so many men / never was the one into whose arms Matilde Urbach swooned" he writes in one of his best-known poems, so that the true madness, the absolute craziness, isn't that someone wakes up in the morning as a cockroach, as in Kafka's famous story, but that you wake and for a few seconds you believe the completely implausible fact that that you are the same as you were. The verification of this metamorphosis is literature and every poem is an awakening.

In one of those awakenings, a celebrated writer who believes he is Borges, Francisco Laprida—who is about to be murdered by gauchos, the strangers—experiences an ineffable moment, an epiphany: it's the instant in which he comprehends his "destiny as a South American," which is to say he realizes that to be a South American is to accept that the only moment in which we come together in community is the moment of death.

The sockdolager—and here is the genius of this accumulation of blood, pervasive night, and blindness that we know as Borges—is that he shows us that every death is a murder. "Conjectural Poem" is profound and moving, but even at that, it isn't Borges's best poem. There's another. It also has a peculiarity that is, perhaps, its secret desire. The most South American of Borges's poems, the one in which he names his ancestors who fought in the War of Independence, wasn't written in Castilian but in English. If in "Conjectural Poem," Borges shows us that all death is murder, in this other poem, which he never rendered in Castilian, someone who was, maybe, or dreamed he was, a celebrated writer shows us that death is an imminent fact and therefore that every human being, even the most abject, has the right to ask for love. I'll print it here. This is the second of Borges's "Two English Poems":

> What can I hold you with?
> I offer you lean streets, desperate sunsets, the moon of the jagged suburbs.
> I offer you the bitterness of a man who has looked long and long at the lonely moon.
> I offer you my ancestors, my dead men, the ghosts that living men have honoured in marble: my father's father killed in the frontier of Buenos Aires, two bullets through his lungs, bearded and dead, wrapped by his soldiers in the hide of a cow; my mother's grandfather—just twentyfour—heading a charge of three hundred men in Perú, now ghosts on vanished horses.
> I offer you whatever insight my books may hold, whatever manliness or humour my life.
> I offer you the loyalty of a man who has never been loyal.
> I offer you that kernel of myself that I have saved, somehow—the central heart that deals not in words, traffics not with dreams, and is untouched by time, by joy, by adversities.
> I offer you the memory of a yellow rose seen at sunset, years before you were born.
> I offer you explanations of yourself, theories about yourself, authentic and surprising news of yourself.
> I can give you my loneliness, my darkness, the hunger of my heart; I am trying to bribe you with uncertainty, with danger, with defeat.

⚑⚑⚑

"The Heights of Macchu Picchu" by Pablo Neruda (whose real name was Neftali Reyes Basoalto, Parral, Chile, 1904–Santiago, Chile, 1973) is the greatest poem in the history of the Spanish language. To read it is to imagine that nothing exists outside the pulse of a few words, of certain stanzas and rhythms that loop around and around in your head with a throbbing that never ends. It belongs to that class of poems such as Book XXIV of *The Iliad,* the biblical Psalms, Shakespeare's *Sonnets,* and Whitman's

Leaves of Grass, works that seem to be telling us that we ourselves, the readers, are just a minor occasion of something written long before the human was invented. The sensation is not unlike experiencing the vastness of the Pacific or the peaks of the Andes. Poems like these remind us of those dimensions. Neither the period in which they were written matter nor the centuries whose generations engaged in writing them, such works are so full and overwhelming that the human is superseded by the presence of world, nature. This is what happens with "The Heights of Macchu Picchu" from *Canto general,* a book that often seems to exceed the limits of individual creation in approaching mythical stories. Neruda's poetry, if you will allow a hasty comparison, is something like the image of a river: its banks may widen or narrow, its current move faster or slower, and sometimes just a simple bend, a change of light, renders it unlike itself. It's that books such as *Twenty Love Poems and a Song of Despair, Residence on Earth,* and *Canto general* represent the river that Neruda's long and narrow country (Chile) does not have. *Canto general.* It takes two words: and in them the sum of lives, of stories, of names, of places, a poetry that is our river. Neruda is our Mississippi. In the currents of that river, the towns of a continent have understood love, the constantly renewed anguish of existence, and the variable winding paths of their history and the possibly better future. Latin America before Neruda is something else after Neruda. The crucial question, forever unresolved and recurrent in masterful poems is: if human beings are capable of producing art, poetry, how is it that at the same time they torture other human beings, that they slaughter them, rape them, exterminate them? Without poetry, it's possible that violence would be the norm, the steady state, but because poems exist, all violence is unjustifiable, is monstrous. I think that for Chile, for America in general, the first answer to that question was the long sixteenth-century epic poem, *La Araucana* by the Spanish soldier Alonso de Ercilla y Zúñiga, who spoke on behalf of the conquistadors and in the language they imposed. The second answer, 350 years later, was the response of *Canto general,* which presents the first major Latin American take on itself, its nature, and its history. This book opens with an image that can only be read as a response to Ercilla and the conquistadors. It is the beginning of the first poem of *Canto general,* "The Lamp on Earth": "Before the wig and the coat / There were rivers, arterial rivers ..." "The wig and coat" refer to the costumes of the

Spanish officers (civil servants, judges, officials) who came to America for the conquest. What Neruda tells us is that prior to their arrival in America, there was already a place (rivers, mountains, forests) countermanding Ercilla's vision of nature as nothing but background for the progress of the conquest, and that this nature precedes all human adventure as a constant reserve against oppression, conquest, or subjugation. Attention to the presence of landscape in Latin American poetry of the first half of the last century has evolved in such a way that it comes to express the full range of human emotions, linking geography and history into a single expression.

But the major mark of Neruda's work is most evident, as I mentioned, in the second poem of *Canto general.* "The Heights of Macchu Picchu" references the Inca citadel of Macchu Picchu, which remained largely unknown for more than three hundred years. "The Heights" is the assurance that poetry from south of the Rio Grande rises from a new world. The fact that it was written constitutes, in the respective histories of independence of the countries of that continent, something much more crucial than wars of liberation against Spain's dominion.

Actually, the poem needs to be heard aloud. It's as though a river were dragging a mountain of stones up to a point when, suddenly, the stones fall away precisely into the places where they were forever destined to be. Into each singular, perfect place. In extreme contradistinction to César Vallejo, Neruda's words suggest an absolute reconciliation of the imposed language and its speakers. *The Heights of Macchu Picchu* thus anticipates a future dream that was, perhaps, the dream of Alonso de Ercilla, when in an episode from *La Araucana,* this same poet, Ercilla, an on-duty soldier, helps the wife of one of his enemies to find, among the dead, her husband's body so that she can take it home to her village for a proper burial. From both sides of a curse that has never relented: the curse of violence between human beings, the curse of their massacres, their conquests, their submissions, the Spanish soldier Alonso de Ercilla intuited in the language of the invaders a peace, and a prediction that in times to come, their language would be welcome. Pablo Neruda in *Canto general* anticipates that vision of a language in which some might sing the felicity of those who speak it. This is finally the dream that Neruda expresses and how he gives to *Canto general* the dimension that defines foundational poems. In the last verses of "The Heights of Macchu Picchu," Neruda asks the dead to speak through his mouth, to return to speak, to return through him to the word: "Cling to my body like magnets / Hasten to my veins and to my mouth."

What's certain is that these verses have been fulfilled. What Neruda's detractors have a hard time understanding is that unceasingly, without end, those lines are fulfilling themselves: in designating himself the interpreter of the dead Incas, Neruda shows us that in speaking, no one is singular. That the act of speaking is the opportunity for those who have preceded us to return, to be granted words. To look, to feel, to hear is always to see through the eyes of our predecessors. A peak of the Andes or the Rockies is also the sum of the many eyes that have gazed on it and anyone who sees those peaks again is greeted by those bygone eyes. That's what is so moving about the world: every grain of dust, every weed, every piece of grass is the port of arrival for a river of the dead in which those who came before us find themselves and are given speech, sight, hearing; in short, by living our lives we give the dead an opportunity for new existence. "The Heights of Macchu Picchu" was written to grant such possibility to all the victims, the oppressed and marginalized, to find in poetry a new destiny in wait for them, one which had not been waiting before. Writing *Canto general,* Neruda couldn't know that his book would come to be the proof of the people who wrote it through him, who spoke themselves there, who had to endure yet another "general death"—the ignominious dictatorships and the monstrous sequence of assassinations and disappearances—and survive it. At the beginning of the conquest, a Spanish soldier unknowingly spoke to us of the disappeared of our time. These works aren't in the past because, in fact, no one is in the past. When we read a book, we put it in front of our eyes, not behind them, which is to say, more or less, that we open ourselves to a dimension of our future. As such, reading is a form of the future and for poetry the future also can be a phenomenon that occurred five hundred or a thousand years ago. Vast and terrible events such as wars, dictatorships or the Holocaust have, for the poem, an intensity equivalent to a drop of dew on a leaf in a forest of tea trees, of a butterfly zigzagging between flowers or the glint of a nascent tear behind a closed eye. For the poem, as for a life, the end of humanity or a new birth may already have taken place or is taking place constantly. The Pacific War, the destruction of Troy, the construction of the Great Wall of China, the conquest of America go on constantly inside our lives and in poetry.

"Soliloquy of the Individual" is one extraordinary example of the revolution accomplished by Nicanor Parra (San Fabian, Nuble Province, Chile, 1914) who, like Baudelaire with romanticism a century before, upturned and mocked an idealized vision of poetry and of the poet as someone special, set apart from ordinary people. Already "The Heights of Macchu Picchu" had carried poetry to a summit beyond the reach of emulators. There where Neruda was swimming (which calls to mind the time Joyce brought his daughter, who was suffering from mental problems, to Jung saying, "but she writes like me;" "Yes," came Jung's response, "but where you swim, she drowns"), his imitators drowned, and in that sense "Macchu Picchu" is a culmination that, at the same time marks a diminishment of the hymn from poetry's horizon, or at least its immediate horizon. This is what Nicanor Parra, founder of Antipoetry, understood: that he might restore to writing a vitality that Castilian hadn't seen since Francisco de Quevedo, using humor, orality, self-confidence, self-delusion, a task that fused high comedy with radical skepticism and disbelief. Against the portentousness of Neruda, Parra constructed a poetry of the ordinary, the everyday, of the antiheroic that nevertheless didn't avoid the issues of "great poetry," but approached them at a slant. This is what we see in "Soliloquy of the Individual" in *Poems and Antipoems* (1954), which along with being a kind of parodic emulation of *Canto general,* gives us a synopsis of everything that, up to this moment, calls itself Antipoetry.

Nine years after the appearance of *Poems and Antipoems,* in a book-length work called *Manifesto,* Nicanor Parra would declare, in a phrase that has become legendary, that "the poets have come down from Olympus," and he would impugn the poetry of his colossal predecessors:

We condemn
—And I say this with respect—
The poetry of the little god
The poetry of the sacred cow
The poetry of the raging bull

in a clear reference to Vicente Huidobro, Pablo Neruda, and Pablo de Rokha. The impressive thing is that for all its diametrically contrastive intentions, Antipoetry, in its dimension and scope, is no less impressive than the proposals of Parra's Chilean predecessors. His revolution is comparable to Joyce's when, in *Ulysses,* he realizes that the mythic journey of twenty years from the time Odysseus leaves his homeland to his return is exactly equivalent to the passage of a day for any man in a modern city who leaves his home in the morning and returns again at night. It's Parra's arrant rupture and the poem "Soliloquy of the Individual" is an example of this. So the overwhelming monumentality of Pablo Neruda, the cosmic trip of Huidobro's *Altazor* and the sometimes bombastic gigantism of Pablo de Rokha are sidestepped for a history of the world narrated by a subject, "the individual," any person who signifies that the entire history of humanity is the history of every single human being and is, therefore, meaningless in terms of the individual. Nicanor Parra invented a new freedom for poetry and his work stands at the head of the insurgence and is written into the future. He showed us the irrefutable democracy of speech, its shared attributes, making us realize that human beings, like their words, aren't divided by steep hierarchies but are equal. Antipoetry fulfilled itself in the task of freeing working words, those in which our lives are grounded day by day, from the submission imposed by sacred words. What his work proposes is a communitarian claim to the plurality of forces that, depleted, under alibis, enslaved, lie beneath the tyranny of ownership. Speech absorbs the "mighty" works, and these in turn are but particular modulations of the languages of tribes that rise into being and submerge again. Plato, Shakespeare, and Quevedo are flashes in that sea of speech with not a whit more prerogative than the back and forth of two washerwomen on the riverbank or two students in a bar. This is what Nicanor unveiled and his revolution is nothing less than that. At the start, prisoners of a shameful world, we think we're masters of what's being written, what's being spoken, and so we grow obsessed with copyright, individual authorship, to wit: profit. Nicanor Parra reminds us of the uncanceled image of a dream deferred: the dream of the end of privilege, that is, the dream of the end of loneliness.

iii

"When You Love What Do You Love?" is the most vaunted poem by Gonzalo Rojas (1917–2011), whose technical virtuosity is comparable only to Pablo Neruda's. Few poets can cover the range of registers that Rojas deploys. During the time of Antipoetry, Rojas incorporated forms of spoken language in a manner no less radical than Nicanor Parra. But unlike Parra who, true to the slogan from his 1963 manifesto—"the poets have come down from Olympus"—assumed that common speech was the only source for poetic or antipoetic work since it alone can give a true account of life, Rojas channeled multiple streams of diction. His poetics draws from the biblical Song of Songs, from Latin poets, from the dazzling Spanish poetry that culminated in 1600 in the so-called Golden Age, and from neighborhood vernacular. Into this plurality of languages, Rojas also assimilated the visions and movements of his predecessors: symbolist poetry, surrealism (which he tapped briefly), and then later he drew from Paul Celan. But above all other influences, there was César Vallejo from whom he took, and made more extreme, a particular mode of line break that stresses multiple meanings.

In Vallejo's work, the abrupt line breaks, the exclamation points, the ellipses, the capitalized words all lead to decidedly expressionist connotations that suggest a world of perpetual sacrifice. In Rojas, the contrary is true. His is essentially a poetry of desire in which the lineation doesn't assume any metric or visual unity but instead, cut off mid-sentence or after an article, for example, or in the middle of a word, contracting or dilating, follows the rhythms of breathing, an asthmatic gasping that characterizes most of his poetry with a kind of orgasmic intensity or peremtory eroticism, a figuration of sexuality produced by the eros between words and things.

In this sense, to read Gonzalo Rojas is to encounter the most intimate texture of a language, its very particular way of linking sounds with world. Along with Neruda, Rojas embodies a poetry of pleasure and desire in which the senses—smell, touch, sight—acquire a relevance that had been absent from Spanish poetry (which with almost no exceptions translated eroticism into mysticism), producing a sound that had not been heard before. But Rojas's new sound is also, as indicated by the last lines of "When You Love What Do You Love?" the sound of the old Paradise. And this is why his short poem stands as one of the great poems of desire bequeathed to us by modern poetry.

iii

"You Don't Hear Dogs Barking" appears among the stories of *The Plain in Flames,* a masterpiece far beyond the compartmentalizing literary jockeying that makes its author, Juan Rulfo (Sayula, Jalisco, Mexico, 1918–Mexico

City, 1986), Mexico's matchless poet and one of contemporary literature's best. As in his novel *Pedro Páramo*, Rulfo thematizes the Mexican desert, transforming it into a universal space of suffering, atonement, and pain, creating a language that, perhaps like Homer's Greek, was never actually used, even if people—that heterogeneous conjunction generally identified by their gestures, their tics, their modes of talking and arguing—recognized it as speech. A poem without redemption, its journey the anticipation of a defeat as universal as it is intimate, "You Don't Hear Dogs Barking" makes clear that misfortune is bound to be reiterated because beyond secular injustice, abuse, exploitation, and violence, its source, as Vallejo's poem also insists, springs from an imposed language. Few images in the history of art and literature match that of the old man carrying his dying son on his shoulders through the night. What this parable of defeat shows us is that the history of language, those 150 thousand years during which we've crisscrossed the earth exchanging grimaces, grunts, and words, is also a fable of misunderstanding: "And you didn't hear them, Ignacio?... You didn't help me even with that hope."

⚑⚑⚑

Oblivious to bombast, disinterested in the scramble for novelty, "Not Anymore," by Idea Vilariño (Montevideo, 1920–2009) is the most momentous example of how Latin American poetry has handled the ubiquitous theme of love and loss. As if the poem desired to disappear into what it names, each line bears the extremity of pain before which words succumb, making clear to us that extreme happiness, like extreme pain, is inexpressible and neither the embrace of two people who merge for an instant, nor the shout of irremediable separation imposed by death, nor utter heartbreak can be evinced within the confines of language. It is this limitation that comes so clear in Idea Vilariño's poem. Like Shakespeare's speaker's observation in sonnet 76, "Spending again what is already spent: / For as the sun is daily new and old, / So is my love still telling what is told," Vilariño's monologue is unique precisely because it is so common; it has been declared innumerable times and stamped into countless poems, songs, and stories with virtually the same words, because for all the poem's apparent simplicity, its repetitions reveal the spectacle of a desolation that attends all of us even while it promises the fullness of human experience.

We see, then, that poems exist because pain never can speak of pain,

pain is the *black hole* of language, all words are sucked up into its immediacy, and part of the force of Idea Vilariño's poem is that it makes clear that one of the most necessary conditions of all groundbreaking poetry is that it be written at the edge of death, at the precise boundary beyond which all language fails. The poem is the last glimmer of the speakable, the final glow of words before they are extinguished and absorbed, and at the same time, the poem is what emerges first from the unspoken. At the margins of death, the poem announces that the life and voice that are about to flicker out are just being born. "Not Anymore" is everything that can't be perceived in the other, everything that won't be created through the other and the sentences that declare that impossibility—quotidian, common, domestic—take on, in the poem's measure, the fullness of sacred revelations. The poem's finale, in its brevity and its irrevocable truth, is one of the biggest in the history of literature: "I won't see you die."

⸎

"Prayer for Marilyn Monroe" by Ernesto Cardenal (Granada, Nicaragua, 1925) is perhaps, after Neruda's "Poem xx," the most widely read poem in Latin America. Deeply marked by his experience as a Trappist monk, Cardenal is often concerned with the ineffable presence of God whom he curses, begs, and prays to, but at the same time, his poems are thoroughly penetrated by reality; by newspapers, movies, the Somoza dictatorship, billboards, and they seek meaning in neon letters, in automobile graveyards, in discarded cigarette packs. In short, Cardenal's God is a sixties God of Pop, pierced and suspended over a world "polluted with sin and radioactivity" as he writes in "Prayer for Marilyn Monroe." At the furthest end of the spectrum from metaphysical poetry, Ernesto Cardenal continues the legacy of the baroque bleeding Christ that Spanish Catholicism imported to America, but in a completely new mode, closer to the kind of atheistic luck-theology found in the antipoetry of Nicanor Parra than in the tormented religiosity of a God who fails, suffering, and is deposed in that agony of Vallejo's assemblage of body parts. It isn't the "I was born one day/ when God was ill" of Vallejo's *The Black Heralds,* nor is it the "I'll grow tired of your scent of supplications and sobs" from "The Request" by Gabriela Mistral (in *Desolación,* 1922), but something altogether distinct.

What Cardenal displaces is the idea of intimacy. While in Vallejo and Mistral, religiosity is generally ascribed to the self, in Cardenal God is sacred because he illuminates the materiality, the tangibility, of things: "You know our dreams better than the psychiatrists." Except in the case of a few poems, including some of his famous epigrams, we find that intimacy in Cardenal is always situated outside the self, modeling what he calls "exteriorism." Although it is based entirely, like Nicanor Parra's work, in vernacular speech, it is unlike Parra's in as much as Cardenal's exteriorism sucks in a historic and cosmic breath that Parra's antipoetry rejects. Three years after his "Prayer for Marilyn Monroe," Cardenal published another of his best-known poems, "Mayapán," and a year later, in 1968, *Homage to the American Indians*, the book in which he meant to steal the wind from Neruda's *Canto general* and "The Heights of Macchu Picchu." "Mayapán" advocates for "Tahuantinsuyo economics" in an homage that is really more of a refutation:

Neruda: no freedom
no social security
and not everything was perfect in the "Inca Paradise."

But in fact, the main rebuttal that *Homage to the American Indians* makes is not ideological but formal. Cardenal rebuts Neruda not with his own poetics but with the poetics of Ezra Pound. And indeed, in its constant references to the economy and exchange value, in its inclusion of facts and figures, its absorption with speech, its ceaseless fusion of past and present, its achievements rise into this finale:

The journey was to the beyond, not the Museum
but in the glass of the Museum
the dry hand of the mummy was still clutching
its sack of grain.

Homage to the American Indians can be read as one more canto in the immense structure of Pound's *Cantos,* one that hadn't been included before: the one concerned with American civilizations. Twenty years after *Homage,* in 1989, Cardenal published the principal work of his career so far, *Cosmic Canto,* which like the *De rerum natura* of Lucretius and *The Divine Comedy* of Dante, aims to merge science with poetry in a story of the drift of the universe following the big bang. It is also the story of the struggle to over-throw the Somoza dictatorship. It has incredible passages where it fuses the immensity of the cosmos with quotidian scenes that call to mind a line from "Prayer for Marilyn Monroe" that might be said to express his entire work: "alone like an astronaut up against the galactic night." "Prayer" isn't concerned with Inca economy or the derivation of the cosmos, but with something infinitely smaller and infinitely more transcendental: it's con-cerned with "a little shopgirl / who like any little shopgirl dreamed of being a movie star."

⁂

"A Few Words on the Death of Major Sabines," Jaime Sabines (Tuxila Gutiérrez, Chiapas, 1926–Mexico City, 1999) is a singular lonely expletive covering every sphere of existence and to read it is to experience, as though it were born in that very instant, a scream of pain, of anger, and helpless-ness, capable of dissolving everything, capable even of returning the uni-verse to its original chaos—if it weren't for the reader. The reader, in the piety of reading, is granted by the poem the possibility of transcendence into another body. The poet, disqualifying the reader, struggles to ignore this possibility: "Goddamn anyone who thinks this is a poem!" he shouts, reaching a paroxysm of suffering heard earlier in Cuco Sánchez songs like "Arrastrando la cobija" (Pull up the Blanket) and "Háblenme montes y valles" (Tell Me Mountains and Valleys) or in José Alfredo Jiménez com-positions, to name the best-known examples, but never heard before in the cautious and well-schooled poetry of Mexico.

Excessive, spilling into extreme forms of lewdness, Sabines's poem insults sickness, death, and God as never before. He commands tears and death to "fuck off," he calls cancer "Lord Asshole," says God is the "arm-less one with a hundred hands," an "old, deaf, childless man," a "pimp." The whirlwind of death stirred up from bones, vomit, liver, tears, Venetian blinds, calls to mind the poem "Only Death" from Pablo Neruda's *Resi-dence on Earth*. But beyond such parallels, for Sabines the bloody joke is trying to write poetry against the profligacy of death. Unlike Pablo de Rokha, Sabines isn't interested in the social realm, that apocalyptic lan-guage associating dignified death with the heroic dimension of popular wars, as we see in "The Old Man's Song," and in certain passages from Neruda's *Canto general,* and for that reason "A Few Words on the Death of Major Sabines" is left to the solitude of its own howl. It's a poem that permits every excess and overcomes them all by force of its own consequence, a consequence stemming from the poet who, in absolute solitude, connects the death of his father to a conspiracy involving the totality of existence: the sea, land, bones, rain, himself, and God as a senescent man who drools laughing at the destruction of what He created. So the ire and rebellion of the poet Jaime Sabines. He doesn't want to write a poem. He is ashamed —he says—to try to write these things, to hover over the death of his father like a scavenger bird. He refuses to be "God's errand boy," the collaborator in His dirty work. And yet, he can't help but involve himself to the point that the poem becomes less about the death of the father than about the death of the son, of the poet himself, who is willing to exchange his death for his father's life, begging a desolation no one can escape, but at the same time revealing to us that the only warning death gives us of our own death is the death of those we love.

⁂

"Letter to My Mother" by Juan Gelman (Buenos Aires, Argentina, 1930–Mexico City, 2014) is a singular poem, unique in any language's contemporary poetry. Masterfully constructed, it consists exclusively of a succession of interminable questions that a son poses to his mother after receiving a letter from her twenty days after her death. The questions open out like a spiral, encircling the passage of two lives, revealing familial scenes, memories, reproaches, outpourings of tenderness, places the two held in common, emigrations, creating a crescendo that touches the most fragile, numb, encrusted, and swollen realms of what we persist in calling *human.* With an imposing intensity that recalls Greek tragedies centered on mother figures—"The Libation Bearers" from Aeschylus's *The Oresteia* or Sophocles's *Electra,* in which the central motif, as in this Gelman poem, concerns detachment (of son from mother, of mother from son)—the poem unfolds in shocked grandeur, at once intimate, torn, inconsolable. Beyond showing us Whitman's maxim that each of us contains the whole of humanity—"I contradict myself, I contain multitudes," he asserts—this grandeur makes clear that the sentiments, each one of them, contain all sentiments, that words such as love, rejection, hatred, tenderness are nothing but the result of the twining of countless emotions that collide, splitting themselves to reveal, like icebergs, only their prominent tip. We are shaped by this series of visible peaks, and one of the most startling implications of the poem is that we ourselves are only vestiges of the unpronounceable. Thus the feeling of infinity that provokes "Letter to My Mother," in which each question opens another and this other opens to an abyss where all meanings collapse because the answers are either always scattered or never heard by us since they are infinitely anterior to the very questions that inspire them. The poem was written in 1968 and was published as a book a year later. Earlier, I mentioned the Greek tragedies; of course, there are multiple readings of a poem of this magnitude, but there is one thing for certain: if Sophocles or Aeschylus were authors in our day, they would have written a work like this one.

     ***

Hospital Británico is the last work of Hector Viel Temperley (Buenos Aires, Argentina, 1933–Buenos Aires, 1987). As with "The Old Man's Song," "Conjectural Poem," and "A Few Words on the Death of Major Sabines," *Hospital Británico* takes place against the background of death, its imminence. And yet it is utterly distinct from those other works even with regard to the idea of its author. To start with, it isn't the wailing imprecation of loneliness of Sabines who curses anyone who thinks that what he's writing about his father's death is a poem, nor is it the tragic loss of Pablo de Rokha who takes poetry to be the heroic expression of a war waged to the very end, despite the knowledge that it is lost from the start; it is at odds with the dazzling precision of Borges and it doesn't try to demystify the poem by creating an antipoetry. In short, it doesn't look like any other text, because it's a poem written in the margins of the poem. With Temperley, we don't encounter an author who writes; writing is the condition of suffering. The shredded attempts to anchor writing to the real; the obsession for dating the fragments that compose the poem, the name of which, *Hospital Británico*, references a real hospital in Buenos Aires. The poem's allusions to a bandaged head correspond with the fact that Temperley underwent brain surgery in that hospital, together with many other details that follow and, in their intermingling, are linked to vivid memories, the dead mother, a beach, the card with the image of Christus Pantokrator. Rather than adding up to a life, they whittle away at an insurmountable impossibility: that writing is pain. Suffering, pure suffering, comes out of the world and everything said or expressed is no more than a substitute shadow coming to tell us the only words we have to express extreme pain, that is to say: we have no words to express extreme pain.

The cry of suffering is the real limit of existence, aimed at everyone and no one. At the same time, it is the beforehand of language, the Inferno of what never actually arrives into words and if there were such words, if that nothing, that shadow stripped from the world and from language, actually succeeded in saying "I suffer," it would only be because it had reached, once again, the threshold of the scream and so had decided to participate once again in life, that is, in the purgatory of words. That's what *Hospital Británico* expresses. Written in a series of prose fragments that are situated before and after the brain operation that emerges as a central event, starting with the most recent entry to the poem: "Month of April, 1986" and continuing with a series of texts, the majority written in the year before the final entry, titled "British Hospital," "Pabellón Rosetto," "Christus Pantokrator," "Long corner of summer," "Your Face," "Your Body and Your Father," "My head is bandaged," "They have taken me from the World," "Freedom, summer," "Lies Dying," "Asleep on Your Lips," titles that are repeated many times before the oldest fragment, "In Order to Begin Again," dated 1969. But this isn't one of those classic stories that unwinds backward from the present toward the moment when you triggered the sequence of events leading to the present. Instead, it's a field littered with shrapnel from a head that has literally exploded, that has been trephined, strewing its own detritus among images of a sometimes extreme beauty, indescribable, beginning with the dedicatory phrase: "my mother is the smile, the freedom, the summer," where the mystical acquires features of a surreality often eerie, blue, crosshatched by multiple specific references, precise ones: the new wall that they painted white in The Rosetto Pavilion, the postcard with the iconic figure of Christ on which "Christus Pantokrator: 13th Century" is written, a long summer beach where the speaker appears with his mother, all of which are traces of life and, at the same time, forms on the border of their own dissolution because that biography, the desperate anxiety to, as we say, nail down what was real, is the shadow that comes to fill the void of the scream. What we read then is a trace, the trace left in the water by Charon's ferry as it hauls its cargo of dead to the other side.

iii

Diana's Tree is comprised of a series of brief stanzas, among the loveliest short poems written in Spanish, whose author, Alejandra Pizarnik (Buenos Aires, Argentina, 1936–Buenos Aires, 1972), writes in a style that is arguably the most imitated and admired by young Latin American poets. With a talent for imagery that has few equals, Pizarnik is heir to the best of surrealism—that of Paul Éluard and of Robert Desnos's *A la mystérieuse*—and yet her writing never surrenders to unnecessary obscurity or the fashionable "magicismo" practiced by more than a few authors from Latin America. Instead, Pizarnik's poetry, with a clarity that becomes piercing, illuminates the abysses of emotional sensitivity, desire, and absence that, pressing against our lives, touch the most exposed, fragile, and numb parts of humanity. Without ever abandoning her dreamy tone, by which she channels the porous face of the real, Pizarnik constructs in her work a biography of solitude and strangeness that, more than anything else, is the strangeness of being, the surprise of being suspended beneath an identity only the voice of another can define with a face, a form, a profile, as in "Solo un nombre" (Only a Name):

> Alejandra   Alejandra
> I am below
> Alejandra

What emerges is a world doubled upon itself, a self-awareness of life and love where the vividness of emotions attains a precision and power of synthesis that only mastery allows: "when you see the eyes / I have tattooed on mine." That is poem nineteen. It's about a journey on which beauty and farewell are merely faces of a neglect that bottoms out in the indescribable. "Diana's Tree" was published in 1962, and two extraordinary works followed it: *Extracción de la piedra de locura* (Extraction of the rock of madness) in 1968 and, in 1971, *El infierno musical* (The musical Hell), which was her last. But everything was already said: "explain with words of this world / that bore from me a boat elsewhere." That is the thirteenth poem. Alejandra Pizarnik committed suicide in Buenos Aires on September 25, 1972.

ⵌ

"Then, in the Waters of Conchán" by Antonio Cisneros (Lima, Peru, 1942–2012) summons the experience of a village, in the sands on the coast of Peru, whose people, the "poorest of the poor," behold in front of them a huge, dead whale floating in the sea. This poem ends Cisneros's book *Crónica del niño Jesús de Chilca* (Chronicle of the Christ child of Chilca), published in 1981, which—along with *The Plain in Flames* by Juan Rulfo—is the most penetrating portrait of poverty yet rendered in the poetry of Latin America. Unlike Rulfo, whose poem's characters meet situations and conflicts so intractable that not even death solves them (just as in *Pedro Páramo,* his prose masterpiece), Cisneros shows us, with magisterial intensity, a dimension of joy and celebration that has never before been expressed so succinctly.

His tone is unique. Descriptive and at the same time psalmodic. Lightweight yet cautionary. And among its many readings, it can be considered as a parable. The creator of a novel tonality, Cisneros published an essential book at the age of twenty-two. *Canto ceremonial contra un oso hormiguero* (Ceremonial song against an aardvark) won the Cuban Casa de las Américas Prize which was, at that time, the most prestigious and coveted Latin American poetry competition (showing, incidentally, that although unlikely, it's possible that a great poem can win a poetry contest).

With this book's publication, Cisneros began to exert a tremendous influence on a younger generation of American poets. His poetry—colloquial, rendered in a common tongue—lacks the programmatic burden of Antipoetry, giving it a freshness and breadth that paradoxically make it extremely receptive to the many-layered urban Castilian language of Peru.

However, not even his indubitable genius could presage the magnitude of the poems that Cisneros would write in what we call now, given the dry fact of his death, the second half of his life. Since the publication in 1978 of *El libro de Dios y de los húngaros* (The book of God and the Hungarians) in which he abandoned neither his calculated lightness, his brilliant associations, nor his humor, his poems gradually became more serious and more self-reflective in order to finally reveal that what he'd been writing since the beginning was a chronicle of his agony, and that poetry, whatever its subject, form or time, is forever the history of those curious creatures, maybe unique in all the universe, who write poems because they understand they are going to die. In the durable poetry of Antonio Cisneros, there is no pathos, just an ultimate revelation made clear in the last line of his last book: "But none of it is yours, you tedious diabetic. Shut up and learn. All you have are a few grams of insulin and a herd of tawny pigs." It was on the journey to such lines that Cisneros came into his most important poem, "Then in the Waters of Conchán." Written as a parable for our times, it is perhaps the only Latin American poem that might have been plucked from the Bible.

♁♁♁

"The Guardian of Ice" by José Watanabe (Laredo, Peru, 1946–Lima, 2007) was first published in *Cosas del cuerpo* (Things of the body), 1999, and twelve years after its publication, it is recognized as one of the prime examples of new Latin American poetry. A mestizo, a Peruvian, a poet, the son of an Indian mother snagged in her youth to work on a sugar plantation and a Japanese immigrant father, a painter, who taught José the art of haiku, Watanabe reveals—from his first book, *Álbum de familia* (Family album) 1971, to *Banderas detrás de la niebla* (Flags behind the fog), published the year before his death—his basic themes: his peasant childhood in Laredo, the memory of his dead brother, his time in hospitals, and scenes from the natural world as, for instance, in "The Praying Mantis." In that poem, describing how the male insect is devoured by the female in the act of copulating with her, Watanabe writes in a direct language, almost oral, which asserts, in the complete absence of temptation toward rhetoric, its capacity to extract, just as Juan Rulfo does in his proverbial prose, a tremendously powerful representative capacity that gives his poems the texture of parables. As we read what painfully since 2007 we must call his complete work, we see that Watanabe was sketching for us, in poem after poem, the portrait of someone who had wanted everyone, all of humanity to see what he was seeing, to hear what he heard, in order not to have to perform the bloody ritual of registering what only he could see, what no one else could hear, the condition only he could feel exactly like that, that way, with that particular intensity, in the moment when the pain subsides. We understand then why poetry is the loneliest of occupations, because the poet must assume, on behalf of all humanity, that no one will be there because to die is to allow everyone else, absolutely everyone else, to go on living. José Watanabe, watching the ice melt under the relentless sun, understood what Vallejo, Rulfo, The Pizarnik, and Millán understood: that poetry is the loneliness of the dying. So the poet is the guardian of ice.

☥☥☥

"Life" by Gonzalo Millán (Santiago, Chile 1947–Santiago, 2006). Composed a few decades before the arrival of Hernán Cortés to Mexico and the beginning of the conquest of America, the Nezahualcóyotl poem I quoted at the beginning of this introduction, part of what we now call Nahuatl poetry (although it isn't right to use the word "poetry" since the Nahuas didn't develop the concept of poetry conceived in the West, simply because they didn't need it), like testamentary texts or the Hindu *Mahabharata,* is one of the extraordinary creations of mankind. What broadly characterizes the songs of the ancient Nahuas is an essential wisdom, naturalness, and purity that seems to be unclouded by anything beyond its own material: this is also the case in the poetry of Gonzalo Millán. Five hundred years after Nezahualcóyotl's song, Millán writes a poem, "Life," that is its reflection, the singular work of a singular poet. Author of a seminal book, *La ciudad* (The city) 1979, which constitutes one of the cardinal literary reference points of the Chilean anti-dictatorship, Millán pushes beyond the stance of objectivity, with often devastating effects, to show us the sum of evidence for our world. Renewing Latin American poetry in a moment when poetry, after the explosion of Nicanor Parra's Antipoetry, seemed trapped in the margins of the trivial, *La ciudad* ratchets up the consequences derived from the conception of a wide-spanning poetry based on minimal elements arranged through small objective displacements of words and sounds that freeze-frame emotions and register what is visible to everyone, the fact that poetry returns to things precisely what poetry had almost given up: the overwhelming force and the strength of the obvious.

Dying prematurely, like the great companion of his generation, José

Watanabe, Gonzalo Millán, unlike Watanabe, pursued a poetry without an "I." His poem "Life" rises into a transparency, grandeur, and comeliness that makes apparent its kinship with Nahuatl songs, as though what we finally call poetry were nothing more than the relentless repetition of evidence:

> And after going along with your eyes closed
> through the guiding darkness,
> to open your eyes and see the
> darkness that leads us,
> to open your eyes and see the darkness that leads us
> with your eyes open and to close your eyes.

This is the final poem of the book *La ciudad.* In the distance, the horizon sits below an empty sky etched with that endlessly resonant line: "Death is the end of life." But it is likewise the beginning of all poetry.

Raúl Zurita's introduction was written in a fever-dream between serious surgeries with concern that it might constitute the final act of his life. He wrote the introduction from his hospital bed in one take without reference to books, quoting from memory.

PINHOLES IN THE NIGHT

LA FUGA

Madre mía, en el sueño
ando por paisajes cardenosos:
un monte negro que se contornea
siempre, para alcanzar el otro monte;
y en el que sigue estás tú vagamente,
pero siempre hay otro monte redondo
que circundar, para pagar el paso
al monte de tu gozo y de mi gozo.

Mas, a trechos tú misma vas haciendo
el camino de juegos y de expolios.
Vamos las dos sintiéndonos, sabiéndonos,
mas no podemos vernos en los ojos,
y no podemos trocarnos palabra,
cual la Eurídice y el Orfeo solos,
las dos cumpliendo un voto o un castigo,
ambas con pies y con acentos rotos.

Pero a veces no vas al lado mío:
te llevo en mí, en un peso angustioso
y amoroso a la vez, como pobre hijo
galeoto a su padre galeoto,
y hay que enhebrar los cerros repetidos,
sin decir el secreto doloroso:
que yo te llevo hurtada a dioses crueles
y que vamos a un Dios que es de nosotros.

Gabriela Mistral

(Chile, 1889–1957)

THE FUGUE

Mother, in the dream
I walk through bruised landscapes:
a black mountain that bends on
toward the other mountain; and I
can barely see you on the one
that follows, but there's always another
mountain to round, to pay the price
to the mountain of our joy.

But now and then you yourself
walk the path of games and ruin.
We go on close, continue aware,
but we can't look into each other's eyes,
and we can't talk,
like Orpheus alone and Eurydice alone,
each living out a promise or penance,
with broken accent and feet.

Sometimes you're not beside me:
you're in me, in a weight as anguished
as it is loving, like some poor galley-
slave son to his galley-slave father,
and we've got to weave through the hills,
without speaking the painful secret:
that I've stolen you from cruel gods
and that we go to a God of our own.

Y otras veces ni estás cerro adelante,
ni vas conmigo, ni vas en mi soplo:
te has disuelto con niebla en las montañas,
te has cedido al paisaje cardenoso.
Y me das unas voces de sarcasmo
desde tres puntos, y en dolor me rompo,
porque mi cuerpo es uno, el que me diste,
y tú eres un agua de cien ojos,
y eres un paisaje de mil brazos,
nunca más lo que son los amorosos:
un pecho vivo sobre un pecho vivo,
nudo de bronce ablandado en sollozo.

Y nunca estamos, nunca nos quedamos,
como dicen que quedan los gloriosos,
delante de su Dios, en dos anillos
de luz o en dos medallones absortos,
ensartados en un rayo de gloria
o acostados en un cauce de oro.

O te busco, y no sabes que te busco,
o vas conmigo, y no te veo el rostro;
o vas en mi por terrible convenio,
sin responderme con tu cuerpo sordo,
siempre por el rosario de los cerros,
que cobran sangre por entregar gozo,
y hacen danzar en torno a cada uno,
¡hasta el momento de la sien ardiendo,
del cascabel de la antigua demencia
y de la trampa en el vórtice rojo!

And other times you're not ahead,
or with me, or in my breath:
you've receded into the hills' mist,
you've given in to the bruised landscape.
And out of nowhere your voice
is sarcastic with me, and I break down
because my one body is the one you gave me,
and you're now water of a hundred eyes,
you're a landscape of a thousands arms,
that won't ever again be what lovers are:
living chest on living chest,
bronze knot eased in sobs.

And we're never there, we never stay,
like they say the glorious end up,
in front of their God, in two rings
of light, or two enraptured medallions,
skewered into a ray of glory
or lying flat in a golden riverbed.

Or I look for you, and you don't know,
or you're with me, and I can't see your face;
or you're in me because of an awful pact,
but don't answer with your deaf body,
always by those rosary hills,
that draw blood to grant joy,
and make us dance around each one,
until that moment your head's on fire,
the rattle of old dementia,
and snare within the red vortex!

De ALTAZOR

Prefacio

Nací a los treinta y tres años, el día de la muerte de Cristo; nací en el Equinoccio, bajo las hortensias y los aeroplanos del calor.

Tenía yo un profundo mirar de pichón, de túnel y de automóvil sentimental. Lanzaba suspiros de acróbata.

Mi padre era ciego y sus manos eran más admirables que la noche.

Amo la noche, sombrero de todos los días.

La noche, la noche del día, del día al día siguiente.

Mi madre hablaba como la aurora y como los dirigibles que van a caer. Tenía cabellos color de bandera y ojos llenos de navíos lejanos.

Una tarde, cogí mi paracaídas y dije: «Entre una estrella y dos golondrinas». He aquí la muerte que se acerca como la tierra al globo que cae.

Mi madre bordaba lágrimas desiertas en los primeros arcos–iris.

Y ahora mi paracaídas cae de sueño en sueño por los espacios de la muerte.

El primer día encontré un pájaro desconocido que me dijo: «Si yo fuese dromedario no tendría sed. ¿Qué hora es?». Bebió las gotas de rocío de mis cabellos, me lanzó tres miradas y media y se alejó diciendo: «Adiós», con su pañuelo soberbio.

Hacia las dos aquel día, encontré un precioso aeroplano, lleno de escamas y caracoles. Buscaba un rincón del cielo donde guarecerse de la lluvia.

Allá lejos, todos los barcos anclados, en la tinta de la aurora. De pronto, comenzaron a desprenderse, uno a uno, arrastrando como pabellón girones de aurora incontestable.

Junto con marcharse los últimos, la aurora desapareció tras algunas olas desmesuradamente infladas.

Entonces oí hablar al Creador, sin nombre, que es un simple hueco en el vacío, hermoso como un ombligo.

Vicente Huidobro (Chile, 1893–1948)

From ALTAZOR

Preface

I was born at the age of 33 on the day Christ died; I was born at the Equinox, under the hydrangeas and the aeroplanes in the heat.

I had the soulful gaze of a pigeon, a tunnel, a sentimental motorcar. I heaved sighs like an acrobat.

My father was blind and his hands were more wonderful than the night. I love the night, the hat of every day.

The night, the night of day, from one day to the next.

My mother spoke like the dawn, like blimps about to fall. Her hair was the color of a flag and her eyes were full of far-off ships.

One day, I gathered up my parachute and said: "Between two swallows and a star." Here death is coming closer like the earth to a falling balloon.

My mother embroidered abandoned tears on the first rainbows.

And now my parachute drops from dream to dream through the spaces of death.

On the first day I met an unknown bird who said: "If I were a camel I'd know no thirst. What time is it?" It drank the dewdrops in my hair, threw me 3½ glances and went off waving "Good-bye" with its pompous handkerchief.

At around two that afternoon, I met a charming aeroplane, full of fish-scales and shells. It was searching for some corner of the sky to take shelter from the rain.

There, far off, all the boats were anchored in the ink of dawn. One by one they came loose from their moorings, dragging pennants of indisputable dawn like the national colors.

As the last ones drifted off, dawn disappeared behind some immoderately swollen waves.

Then I heard the voice of the Creator, who is nameless, who is a simple hollow in space, lovely as a navel.

«Hice un gran ruido y este ruido formó el océano y las olas del océano.

»Este ruido irá siempre pegado a las olas del mar y las olas del mar irán siempre pegadas a él, como los sellos en las tarjetas postales.

»Después tejí un largo bramante de rayos luminosos para coser los días uno a uno; los días que tienen un oriente legítimo o reconstituido, pero indiscutible.

»Después tracé la geografía de la tierra y las líneas de la mano.

»Después bebí un poco de cognac (a causa de la hidrografía).

»Después creé la boca y los labios de la boca, para aprisionar las sonrisas equívocas y los dientes de la boca para vigilar las groserías que nos vienen a la boca.

»Creé la lengua de la boca que los hombres desviaron de su rol, haciéndola aprender a hablar... a ella, ella, la bella nadadora, desviada para siempre de su rol acuático y puramente acariciador».

Mi paracaídas empezó a caer vertiginosamente. Tal es la fuerza de atracción de la muerte y del sepulcro abierto.

Podéis creerlo, la tumba tiene más poder que los ojos de la amada. La tumba abierta con todos sus imanes. Y esto te lo digo a ti, a ti que cuando sonríes haces pensar en el comienzo del mundo.

Mi paracaídas se enredó en una estrella apagada que seguía su órbita concienzudamente, como si ignorara la inutilidad de sus esfuerzos.

Y aprovechando este reposo bien ganado, comencé a llenar con profundos pensamientos las casillas de mi tablero:

«Los verdaderos poemas son incendios. La poesía se propaga por todas partes, iluminando sus consumaciones con estremecimientos de placer o de agonía.

»Se debe escribir en una lengua que no sea materna.

»Los cuatro puntos cardinales son tres: el Sur y el Norte.

»Un poema es una cosa que será.

»Un poema es una cosa que nunca es, pero que debiera ser.

»Un poema es una cosa que nunca ha sido, que nunca podrá ser.

»Huye del sublime externo, si no quieres morir aplastado por el viento.

»Si yo no hiciera al menos una locura por año, me volvería loco».

Tomo mi paracaídas, y del borde de mi estrella en marcha, me lanzo a la atmósfera del último suspiro.

Ruedo interminablemente sobre las rocas de los sueños, ruedo entre las nubes de la muerte.

"I created a great crashing sound and that sound formed the oceans and the ocean waves.

"That sound will be stuck forever to the waves of the sea and the waves of the sea will be stuck forever to that sound, like stamps to a postcard.

"Then I braided a great cord of luminous rays to stitch each day to the next; the days with their original or reconstructed, yet undeniable dawns.

"Then I etched the geography of the earth and the lines of the hand.

"Then I drank a little cognac (for hydrographic reasons).

"Then I created the mouth, and the lips of the mouth to confine ambiguous smiles, and the teeth of the mouth to guard against the improprieties that come to our mouths.

"I created the tongue of the mouth which man diverted from its role to make it learn to speak... to her, to her, the beautiful swimmer, forever diverted from her aquatic and purely sensual role."

My parachute began to dizzyingly drop. Such is the force of the attraction of death, of the open grave.

Better believe it, the tomb has more power than a lover's eyes. The open tomb with all its charms. And I say it even to you, you whose smile inspires thoughts of the origin of the world.

My parachute caught on a burnt-out star conscientiously continuing its orbit, as if it didn't know the uselessness of such efforts.

And taking advantage of this well-earned rest, I began to fill the little squares of my chessboard with deep thoughts:

"True poems are fires. Poetry is propagating everywhere, its conquests lit with shivers of pleasure or pain.

"One should write in a language that is not the mother tongue.

"The four cardinal points are three: South and North.

"A poem is something that will be.

"A poem is something that never is, but ought to be.

"A poem is something that never has been, that never can be.

"Flee from the external sublime, if you don't want to die flattened by the wind.

"If I didn't do something crazy at least once a year I'd go crazy."

Grabbing my parachute, I leap from the edge of my speeding star into the stratosphere of the last sigh.

I wheel endlessly over the cliffs of dreams, I wheel through clouds of death.

Encuentro a la Virgen sentada en una rosa, y me dice:

»Mira mis manos: son transparentes como las bombillas eléctricas. ¿Ves los filamentos de donde corre la sangre de mi luz intacta?

»Mira mi aureola. Tiene algunas saltaduras, lo que prueba mi ancianidad.

»Soy la Virgen, la Virgen sin mancha de tinta humana, la única que no lo sea a medias, y soy la capitana de las otras once mil que estaban en verdad demasiado restauradas.

»Hablo una lengua que llena los corazones según la ley de las nubes comunicantes.

»Digo siempre adiós, y me quedo.

»Amame, hijo mío, pues adoro tu poesía y te enseñaré proezas aéreas.

»Tengo tanta necesidad de ternura, besa mis cabellos, los he lavado esta mañana en las nubes del alba y ahora quiero dormirme sobre el colchón de la neblina intermitente.

»Mis miradas son un alambre en el horizonte para el descanso de las golondrinas.

»Amame».

Me puse de rodillas en el espacio circular y la Virgen se elevó y vino a sentarse en mi paracaídas.

Me dormí y recité entonces mis más hermosos poemas.

Las llamas de mi poesía secaron los cabellos de la Virgen, que me dijo gracias y se alejó, sentada sobre su rosa blanda.

Y héme aquí solo, como el pequeño huérfano de los naufragios anónimos.

Ah, qué hermoso… qué hermoso.

Veo las montañas, los ríos, las selvas, el mar, los barcos, las flores y los caracoles.

Veo la noche y el día y el eje en que se juntan.

Ah, ah, soy Altazor, el gran poeta, sin caballo que coma alpiste, ni caliente su garganta con claro de luna, sino con mi pequeño paracaídas como un quitasol sobre los planetas.

De cada gota del sudor de mi frente hice nacer astros, que os dejo la tarea de bautizar como a botellas de vino.

Lo veo todo, tengo mi cerebro forjado en lenguas de profeta.

La montaña es el suspiro de Dios, ascendiendo en termómetro hinchado hasta tocar los pies de la amada.

I meet the Virgin, seated on the rose, who says:

"Look at my hands, as transparent as lightbulbs. Do you see the filaments where the blood of my pure light flows?

"Look at my halo. It has a few cracks in it, a proof of my antiquity.

"I am the Virgin, the Virgin without human stain, there's nothing halfway about me, and I am the captain of the other eleven thousand—who were, in fact, excessively restored.

"I speak in a language that fills the heart according to the laws of the communicant clouds.

"I always say good-bye, and stay.

"Love me, my child, for I adore your poetry and I will teach you aerial prowess.

"I have a need for tenderness, kiss my hair, I washed it this morning in clouds of dawn, and now I want to sleep on the mattress of occasional drizzle.

"My glances are a wire on the horizon where swallows rest.

"Love me."

I got down on my knees in that circular space and the Virgin rose and sat on my parachute.

I slept, and then recited my most beautiful poems.

The flames of my poetry dried the Virgin's hair. She thanked me and went off, seated on her soft rose.

And here I am, alone, like the little orphan of anonymous shipwrecks.

Oh how beautiful…how beautiful.

I can see mountains, rivers, forests, the sea, boats, flowers, seashells.

I can see night and day and the axis where they meet.

Oh yes I am Altazor, the great poet, without a horse that eats birdseed or warms its throat with moonbeams, with only my little parachute like a parasol over the planets.

From each bead of sweat on my forehead I give birth to stars, which I leave you the task of baptizing like a watered-down bottle of wine.

I can see it all, my mind is forged in the tongues of prophets.

The mountain is the sigh of God, rising in its swelling thermometer till it touches the feet of the beloved.

Aquél que todo lo ha visto, que conoce todos los secretos sin ser Walt Whitman, pues jamás he tenido una barba blanca como las bellas enfermeras y los arroyos helados.

Aquél que oye durante la noche los martillos de los monederos falsos, que son solamente astrónomos activos.

Aquél que bebe el vaso caliente de la sabiduría después del diluvio obedeciendo a las palomas y que conoce la ruta de la fatiga, la estela hirviente que dejan los barcos.

Aquél que conoce los almacenes de recuerdos y de bellas estaciones olvidadas.

El, el pastor de aeroplanos, el conductor de las noches extraviadas y de los ponientes amaestrados hacia los polos únicos.

Su queja es semejante a una red parpadeante de aerolitos sin testigo.

El día se levanta en su corazón y él baja los párpados para hacer la noche del reposo agrícola.

Lava sus manos en la mirada de Dios, y peina su cabellera como la luz y la cosecha de esas flacas espigas de la lluvia satisfecha.

Los gritos se alejan como un rebaño sobre las lomas cuando las estrellas duermen después de una noche de trabajo continuo.

El hermoso cazador frente al bebedero celeste para los pájaros sin corazón.

Sé triste tal cual las gacelas ante el infinito y los meteoros, tal cual los desiertos sin mirajes.

Hasta la llegada de una boca hinchada de besos para la vendimia del destierro.

Sé triste, pues ella te espera en un rincón de este año que pasa.

Está quizá al extremo de tu canción próxima y será bella como la cascada en libertad y rica como la línea ecuatorial.

Sé triste, más triste que la rosa, la bella jaula de nuestras miradas y de las abejas sin experiencia.

La vida es un viaje en paracaídas y no lo que tú quieres creer.

Vamos cayendo, cayendo de nuestro zenit a nuestro nadir y dejamos el aire manchado de sangre para que se envenenen los que vengan mañana a respirarlo.

Adentro de ti mismo, fuera de ti mismo, caerás del zenit al nadir porque ese es tu destino, tu miserable destino. Y mientras de más alto caigas, más alto será el rebote, más larga tu duración en la memoria de la piedra.

He who has seen it all, who knows all the secrets without being Walt Whitman, for I've never had a beard as white as beautiful nurses and frozen streams.

He who hears in the night the hammers of the counterfeiters of coins, who are only diligent astronomers.

He who drinks the warm glass of knowledge after the flood, obedient to the doves, and who knows the way of weariness, the boiling wake the ships leave behind.

He who knows the storehouses of memories, of beautiful forgotten seasons.

He, shepherd of aeroplanes, guide to the unmatched poles for mislaid nights and experienced west winds.

His whimpering is a blinking net of unwitnessed aerolites.

The day rises in his heart and he lowers his eyelids to create the night of agricultural rest.

He washes his hands in the glances of God, and combs his hair like the light, like the harvest of those thin grains of satisfied rain.

Shouts wander off like a flock over the hills when the stars sleep after a night of continual labor.

The beautiful hunter faces the cosmic waterhole for heartless birds.

Be sad, like gazelles before the infinite and the meteors, like deserts without mirages.

Until the appearance of a mouth swollen with kisses for the vintage of exile.

Be sad, for she awaits you in a corner of this passing year.

Perhaps she's at the end of your next song, and she'll be as beautiful as a free-falling waterfall and rich as the equatorial line.

Be sad, sadder than the rose, that beautiful cage for glances and inexperienced bees.

Life is a parachute voyage and not what you'd like to think it is.

So let's fall, falling from our heights to our depths, let's leave the air stained with blood, so that those who breathe it tomorrow will be poisoned.

Inside yourself, outside yourself, you'll fall from high to low, for that is your fate, your miserable fate. And the greater the height from which you fall, the higher you'll rebound, the longer you'll remain in the memory of stone.

Hemos saltado del vientre de nuestra madre o del borde de una estrella y vamos cayendo.

Ah mi paracaídas, la única rosa perfumada de la atmósfera, la rosa de la muerte, despeñada entre los astros de la muerte.

¿Habéis oído? Ese es el ruido siniestro de los pechos cerrados.

Abre la puerta de tu alma y sal a respirar al lado afuera. Puedes abrir con un suspiro la puerta que haya cerrado el huracán.

Hombre, he ahí tu paracaídas maravilloso como el vértigo.

Poeta, he ahí tu paracaídas, maravilloso como el imán del abismo.

Mago, he ahí tu paracaídas que una palabra tuya puede convertir en un parasubidas maravilloso como el relámpago que quisiera cegar al creador.

¿Qué esperas?

Mas he ahí el secreto del Tenebroso que olvidó sonreír.

Y el paracaídas aguarda amarrado a la puerta como el caballo de la fuga interminable.

We have leapt from the belly of our mother, or from the edge of a star, and we're falling.

Oh my parachute, the only perfumed rose of the stratosphere, the rose of death, cascading through the stars of death.

Have you heard it? The sinister sound of closed chests.

Open the gate of your soul and get out and breathe. With a sigh you can open the gate it took a hurricane to close.

Here's your parachute, Man, wonderful as vertigo.

Here's your parachute, Poet, wonderful as the charms of the chasm.

Here's your parachute, Magician, which one word of yours can transform into a parashoot, wonderful as the lightning bolt that tries to blind the creator.

What are you waiting for?

But here is the secret of the Gloom that forgot how to smile.

The parachute waits tied to the gate like the endlessly runaway horse.

Canto IV

No hay tiempo que perder
Enfermera de sombras y distancias
Yo vuelvo a ti huyendo del reino incalculable
De ángeles prohibidos por el amanecer

Detrás de tu secreto te escondías
En sonrisa de párpados y de aire
Yo levanté la capa de tu risa
Y corté las sombras que tenían
Tus signos de distancia señalados

Tu sueño se dormirá en mis manos
Marcado de las líneas de mi destino inseparable
En el pecho de un mismo pájaro
Que se consume en el fuego de su canto
De su canto llorando al tiempo
Porque se escurre entre los dedos

Sabes que tu mirada adorna los veleros
De las noches mecidas en la pesca
Sabes que tu mirada forma el nudo de las estrellas
Y el nudo del canto que saldrá del pecho
Tu mirada que lleva la palabra al corazón
Y a la boca embrujada del ruiseñor

No hay tiempo que perder
A la hora del cuerpo en el naufragio ambiguo
Yo mido paso a paso el infinito

El mar quiere vencer
Y por lo tanto no hay tiempo que perder
Entonces
    Ah entonces

Canto IV

There's no time to lose
Nurse of the shadows nurse of distance
I'm coming back to you escaping the immeasurable kingdom
Of angels prohibited by dawn

You used to hide behind your secrets
With a smile of eyelids and air
And I lifted the cape of your laughter
And I cut through the shadows
That cast the signs of distance over you

Your dream will sleep in my hands
Marked with the lines of my inseparable fate
In the breast of the same bird
That consumes itself in the fire of its song
Of its song that weeps for time
For time slips through fingers

You know your glance bedecks the sailboats
In the rocking nights of the catch
You know your glance ties the knot of stars
And the knot of song that will come from this chest
Your glance carries the word to the heart
And the enchanted mouth of a nightingale

There's no time to lose
At the hour of the body in the dubious shipwreck
I measure the infinite step by step

The sea waits to conquer
So there's no time to lose
Then
    Ah then

Más allá del último horizonte
Se verá lo que hay que ver

Por eso hay que cuidar el ojo precioso regalo del cerebro
El ojo anclado al medio de los mundos
Donde los buques se vienen a varar
¿Mas si se enferma el ojo qué he de hacer?
¿Qué haremos si han hecho mal de ojo al ojo?
Al ojo avizor afiebrado como faro de lince
La geografía del ojo digo es la más complicada
El sondaje es difícil a causa de las olas
Los tumultos que pasan
La apretura continua
Las plazas y avenidas populosas
Las procesiones con sus estandartes
Bajando por el iris hasta perderse
El rajah en su elefante de tapices
La cacería de leones en selvas de pestañas seculares
Las migraciones de pájaros friolentos hacia otras retinas
Yo amo mis ojos y tus ojos y los ojos
Los ojos con su propia combustión
Los ojos que bailan al son de una música interna
Y se abren como puertas sobre el crimen
Y salen de su órbita y se van como cometas sangrientos al azar
Los ojos que se clavan y dejan heridas lentas a cicatrizar
Entonces no se pegan los ojos como cartas
Y son cascadas de amor inagotables
Y se cambian día y noche
Ojo por ojo
Ojo por ojo como hostia por hostia
Ojo árbol
Ojo pájaro
Ojo río
Ojo montaña
Ojo mar
Ojo tierra

Beyond the last horizon
We'll see what there is to see

So take care of the eye precious gift of the brain
The eye anchored in the middle of the worlds
Where the great ships run aground
But what can one do if the eye falls sick?
What will we do when they give the eye the evil eye?
The bright eye feverish as a lynx-eyed lighthouse
The geography of the eye I may state is most complex
Sounding its depths is difficult on account of the waves
The mobs of passers-by
The constant crush
The crowded avenues and squares
The parades with their banners
Marching down through the iris until they are lost
The rajah on his elephant of rugs
The lion hunt in the jungles of secular eyelashes
The migrations of shivering birds to other retinas
I love my eyes and your eyes and eyes
Eyes with their own flash-point
Eyes that dance to the sound of an inner music
And open like a door onto a crime
And abandon their orbits and go off like bloodstained comets into chance
Eyes so sharp they leave wounds that are slow to heal
And can't be closed like an envelope
They are waterfalls of neverending love
And day and night they change
Eye for an eye
Eye for an eye like host for a host
Treeeye
Birdeye
Rivereye
Mountaineye
Seaeye
Eartheye

Ojo luna
Ojo cielo
Ojo silencio
Ojo soledad por ojo ausencia
Ojo dolor por ojo risa

No hay tiempo que perder
Y si viene el instante prosaico
Siga el barco que es acaso el mejor
Ahora que me siento y me pongo a escribir
¿Qué hace la golondrina que vi esta mañana
Firmando cartas en el vacío?
Cuando muevo el pie izquierdo
¿Qué hace con su pie el gran mandarín chino?
Cuando enciendo un cigarro
¿Qué hacen los otros cigarros que vienen en el barco?
En dónde está la planta del fuego futuro?
Y si yo levanto los ojos ahora mismo
¿Qué hace con sus ojos el explorador de pie en el polo?
Yo estoy aquí
En dónde están los otros?
Eco de gesto en gesto
Cadena electrizada o sin correspondencia
Interrumpido el ritmo solitario
¿Quiénes se están muriendo y quiénes nacen
Mientras mi pluma corre en el papel?

No hay tiempo que perder
Levántate alegría
Y pasa de poro en poro la aguja de tus sedas

Darse prisa darse prisa
Vaya por los globos y los cocodrilos mojados
Préstame mujer tus ojos de verano
Yo lamo las nubes salpicadas cuando el otoño sigue la carreta del asno
Un periscopio en ascensión debate el pudor del invierno

Mooneye
Skyeye
Husheye
Onlyeye for a lonelyeye
A misereye for a lullabeye

There's no time to lose
And if the prosaic moment comes
Follow the ship perhaps it's best
Now that I'm sitting and I start to write
What's that swallow doing the one I saw this morning
Signing letters in space?
When I move my left foot
What does the great Chinese mandarin do with his foot?
When I light a cigarette
What happens to the other cigarettes that came on the boat?
Where is the leaf of the future fire?
And if I raise my eyes just now
What's the explorer on foot to the pole doing with his eyes?
I am here
Where are the others?
Act echoes act
A chain electrified or with no connections
A solitary rhythm interrupted
Who's dying and who's been born
While my pen runs across the paper?

There's no time to lose
Joy get up
And run the needle of your silks from pore to pore

Hurry up hurry up
Travel the worlds and the wet crocodiles
Lend me woman your summer eyes
I lap splattered clouds as autumn follows the donkey cart
A rising periscope debates the modesty of winter

Bajo la perspectiva del volantín azulado por el infinito
Color joven de pájaros al ciento por ciento
Tal vez era un amor mirado de palomas desgraciadas
O el guante importuno del atentado que va a nacer de una mujer o una amapola
El florero de mirlos que se besan volando
Bravo pantorrilla de noche de la más novia que se esconde en su piel de flor

Rosa al revés rosa otra vez y rosa y rosa
Aunque no quiera el carcelero
Río revuelto para la pesca milagrosa

Noche préstame tu mujer con pantorrillas de florero de amapolas jóvenes
Mojadas de color como el asno pequeño desgraciado
La novia sin flores ni globos de pájaros
El invierno endurece las palomas presentes
Mira la carreta y el atentado de cocodrilos azulados
Que son periscopios en las nubes del pudor
Novia en ascensión al ciento por ciento celeste
Lame la perspectiva que ha de nacer salpicada de volantines
Y de los guantes agradables del otoño que se debate en la piel del amor

No hay tiempo que perder
La indecisión en barca para los viajes
Es un presente de las crueldades de la noche
Porque el hombre malo o la mujer severa
No pueden nada contra la mortalidad de la casa
Ni la falta de orden
Que sea oro o enfermedad
Noble sorpresa o espión doméstico para victoria extranjera
La disputa intestina produce la justa desconfianza
De los párpados lavados en la prisión
Las penas tendientes a su fin son travesaños antes del matrimonio
Murmuraciones de cascada sin protección
Las disensiones militares y todos los obstáculos
A causa de la declaración de esa mujer rubia
Que critica la pérdida de la expedición
O la utilidad extrema de la justicia

From the perspective of a kite turned blue by the infinite
The young color of birds at 100%
Perhaps it was a romance watched by hapless doves
Or the rude glove of the crime that will be born to a woman or a poppy
The flowerpot of blackbirds that kiss in midair
Brave calves of night of the sweetheart who hides in her flower skin

Rose upturned and rose returned and rose and rose
Though the warden don't want it
Muddy rivers make for clean fishing

Night lend me your woman with calves of a flowerpot of young poppies
Wet with color like the hapless little donkey
The sweetheart with no flowers no worlds of birds
Winter hardens the current doves
Look at the cart and the crimes of crocodiles turning blue
That are periscopes in the clouds of modesty
Sweetheart rising to 100% celestial
Lap the perspective to be born from a splatter of kites
And the agreeable gloves of autumn that debate in the skin of romance

There's no time to lose
The indecision aboard the tour ship
Is a token of the cruelties of night
For the evil man or the austere woman
Is helpless against the mortality rate in the house
And the lack of order
Whether it be gold or illness
A respectable surprise or domestic espionage for foreign victory
Internal dispute produces justified mistrust
Of eyelids washed in prison
Sorrows reaching their end are the foundation stones of marriage
Murmurs of unprotected waterfalls
Dissensions in the military ranks and the obstacles
On account of the statement by that blonde woman
Who criticizes the loss of the expedition
Or the ultimate utility of justice

Como una separación de amor sin porvenir
La prudencia llora los falsos extravíos de la locura naciente
Que ignora completamente las satisfacciones de la moderación

No hay tiempo que perder
Para hablar de la clausura de la tierra y la llegada del día agricultor a la nada
amante de lotería sin proceso ni niño para enfermedad pues el dolor impre-
visto que sale de los cruzamientos de la espera en este campo de la since-
ridad nueva es un poco negro como el eclesiástico de las empresas para la
miseria o el traidor en retardo sobre el agua que busca apoyo en la unión o
la disensión sin reposo de la ignorancia Pero la carta viene sobre la ruta y la
mujer colocada en el incidente del duelo conoce el buen éxito de la preñez
y la inacción del deseo pasado de la ventaja al pueblo que tiene inclinación
por el sacerdote pues él realza de la caída y se hace más íntimo que el extra-
vío de la doncella rubia o la amistad de la locura

No hay tiempo que perder
Todo esto es triste como el niño que está quedándose huérfano
O como la letra que cae al medio del ojo
O como la muerte del perro de un ciego
O como el río que se estira en su lecho de agonizante
Todo esto es hermoso como mirar el amor de los gorriones
Tres horas después del atentado celeste
O como oir dos pájaros anónimos que cantan a la misma azucena
O como la cabeza de la serpiente donde sueña el opio
O como el rubí nacido de los deseos de una mujer
Y como el mar que no se sabe si ríe o llora
Y como los colores que caen del cerebro de las mariposas
Y como la mina de oro de las abejas
Las abejas satélites del nardo como las gaviotas del barco
Las abejas que llevan la semilla en su interior
Y van más perfumadas que pañuelos de narices
Aunque no son pájaros
Pues no dejan sus iniciales en el cielo
En la lejanía del cielo besada por los ojos

Like the legal separation of a love with no future
Prudence weeps for the unfortunate follies of a latent madness
That utterly ignores the pleasures of moderation

There's no time to lose
In order to speak of the hermitage of the earth and the arrival of the agricul-
tural day to nothingness lover of lotteries with neither progress nor a child
for comfort then the unforeseen pain that comes from the crossroads of
hope in this land of a new sincerity is somewhat obscure like the priest in
the business of misery or the traitor stranded on the water who seeks pro-
tection in the unwavering union or strife of ignorance But the letter comes
along its route and the woman placed in the position of pain knows the suc-
cessful results of pregnancy and the inactivity of past desire gives an advan-
tage to people who have an inclination for the priesthood but he gains in
stature from the fall and becomes more intimate than the follies of the fair
maiden or the friendship of madness

There's no time to lose
All this so sad like the child who's left an orphan
Like the letter that falls in the middle of an eye
Like the dog's death of a blind man
Like the river stretching out on its deathbed
All this so lovely like watching sparrow love
Three hours after the celestial crime
Like hearing two anonymous birds singing to the same lily
Like the snake's head where opium dreams
Like the ruby born of a woman's desires
Like the sea that doesn't know if it laughs or cries
Like the colors that fall from the brains of butterflies
Like the gold mine of bees
Bees satellites to spikenard like seagulls to a boat
The bees that carry the seed within
And drift off more perfumed than handkerchiefs
Though they are not birds
And do not leave their monograms on the sky
On the far-off eye-kissed sky

Y al terminar su viaje vomitan el alma de los pétalos
Como las gaviotas vomitan el horizonte
Y las golondrinas el verano

No hay tiempo que perder
Ya viene la golondrina monotémpora
Trae un acento antípoda de lejanías que se acercan
Viene gondoleando la golondrina

Al horitaña de la montazonte
La violondrina y el goloncelo
Descolgada esta mañana de la lunala
Se acerca a todo galope
Ya viene viene la golondrina
Ya viene viene la golonfina
Ya viene la golontrina
Ya viene la goloncima
Viene la golonchina
Viene la golonclima
Ya viene la golonrima
Ya viene la golonrisa
La golonniña
La golongira
La golonlira
La golonbrisa
La golonchilla
Ya viene la golondía
Y la noche encoge sus uñas como el leopardo
Ya viene la golontrina
Que tiene un nido en cada uno de los dos calores
Como yo lo tengo en los cuatro horizontes
Viene la golonrisa
Y las olas se levantan en la punta de los pies
Viene la golonniña
Y siente un vahido la cabeza de la montaña
Viene la golongira
Y el viento se hace parábola de sílfides en orgía

And at journey's end they vomit the soul of the petals
As seagulls vomit the horizon
And swallows the summer

There's no time to lose
Look here swoops the monochronic swallow
With an antipodal tone of approaching distance
Here swoops the swallowing swallow

At the horslope of the hillizon
The violonswallow with a cellotail
Slipped down this morning from a lunawing
And hurries near
Look here swoops the swooping swallow
Here swoops the whooping wallow
Here swoops the weeping wellow
Look here swoops the sweeping shrillow
Swoops the swamping shallow
Swoops the sheeping woolow
Swoops the slooping swellow
Look here swoops the sloping spillow
The scooping spellow
The souping smellow
The seeping swillow
The sleeping shellow
Look here swoops the swooping day
And the night retracts its claws like a leopard
Swoops the swapping swallow
With a nest in each of the torrid zones
As I have on the four horizons
Swoops the snooping smallow
And waves rise on tiptoe
Swoops the whelping whirllow
And the hillslope's head feels dizzy
Swoops the slapping squallow
And the wind's a parabola of orgiastic sylphs

Se llenan de notas los hilos telefónicos
Se duerme el ocaso con la cabeza escondida
Y el árbol con el pulso afiebrado

Pero el cielo prefiere el rodoñol
Su niño querido el rorreñol
Su flor de alegría el romiñol
Su piel de lágrima el rofañol
Su garganta nocturna el rosolñol
El rolañol
El rosiñol

No hay tiempo que perder
El buque tiene los días contados
Por los hoyos peligrosos que abren las estrellas en el mar
Puede caerse al fuego central
El fuego central con sus banderas que estallan de cuando en cuando
Los elfos exacerbados soplan las semillas y me interrogan
Pero yo sólo oigo las notas del alhelí
Cuando alguien aprieta los pedales del viento
Y se presenta el huracán
El río corre como un perro azotado
Corre que corre a esconderse en el mar
Y pasa el rebaño que devasta mis nervios
Entonces yo sólo digo
Que no compro estrellas en la nochería
Y tampoco olas nuevas en la marería
Prefiero escuchar las notas del alhelí
Junto a la cascada que cuenta sus monedas
O el bromceo del aeroplano en la punta del cielo
O mirar el ojo del tigre donde sueña una mujer desnuda
Porque si no la palabra que viene de tan lejos
Se quiebra entre los labios

Yo no tengo orgullos de campanario
Ni tengo ningún odio petrificado

The telephone wires fill with notes
The sunset sleeps head under the sheets
And the tree with a feverish pulse

But the sky prefers the nighdongale
Its favorite son the nighrengale
Its flower of joy the nighmingale
Its skin of tears the nighfangale
Its nocturnal throat the nighsongale
The nighlangale
The nightingale

There's no time to lose
The steamer has its days marked
By the dangerous holes stars open in the sea
It could fall into the central fire
The central fire with its banners that explode from time to time
Irritated elves blow away the seeds and interrogate me
But I hear only the notes of the wallflower
When someone pushes the pedals of the wind
And the hurricane appears
The river runs like a whipped dog
Runs as it runs to hide itself in the sea
And the flock goes by ruining my nerves
Then I can only say
That I don't buy stars at the nightery
Or new waves at the seastore
I'd rather listen to the notes of the wallflower
Next to the waterfall that counts its change
Or the squeal of the aeroplane at the tip of the sky
Or see the tiger's eye where a naked woman dreams
For if not the word that comes from so far
Will shatter between my lips

I have no towering pride
Nor any petrified hates

Ni grito como un sombrero afectuoso que viene saliendo del desierto
Digo solamente
No hay tiempo que perder
El vizir con lenguaje de pájaro
Nos habla largo largo como un sendero
Las caravanas se alejan sobre su voz
Y los barcos hacia horizontes imprecisos
Él devuelve el oriente sobre las almas
Que toman un oriente de perla
Y se llenan de fósforos a cada paso
De su boca brota una selva
De su selva brota un astro
Del astro cae una montaña sobre la noche
De la noche cae otra noche
Sobre la noche del vacío
La noche lejos tan lejos que parece una muerta que se llevan
Adiós hay que decir adiós
Adiós hay que decir a Dios
Entonces el huracán destruido por la luz de la lengua
Se deshace en arpegios circulares
Y aparece la luna seguida de algunas gaviotas
Y sobre el camino
Un caballo que se va agrandando a medida que se aleja

Darse prisa darse prisa
Están prontas las semillas
Esperando una orden para florecer
Paciencia ya luego crecerán
Y se irán por los senderos de la savia
Por su escalera personal
Un momento de descanso
Antes del viaje al cielo del árbol
El árbol tiene miedo de alejarse demasiado
Tiene miedo y vuelve los ojos angustiados
La noche lo hace temblar
La noche y su licantropía

I don't shout like a friendly hat that comes out of the desert
I only say
There's no time to lose
The vizier speaks to us in bird-language
Long long as a path
Caravans move off over his voice
And ships toward blurred horizons
He restores the orient to souls
That eat orient of pearl
And stuff themselves with matches at every step
A forest sprouts from his mouth
A star sprouts from his forest
From the star a mountain falls on the night
From the night another night falls
On the night of space
The far-off night so far off it seems like a woman's corpse they carry
Good-bye one must say good-bye
Good-bye one must say to God
Then the hurricane wrecked by the tongue's light
Unravels in circular arpeggios
And the moon appears followed by some gulls
And on the road
A horse goes off growing larger as it goes

Hurry up hurry up
The seeds are ready
Waiting for the order to flower
Be patient soon they'll grow
And travel along the paths of sap
Up their private stairway
A minute of rest
Before the tree's voyage to the sky
The tree is afraid of going too far
It's afraid and looks back in anguish
Night makes it tremble
The lycanthropic night

La noche que afila sus garras en el viento
Y aguza los oídos de la selva
Tiene miedo digo el árbol tiene miedo
De alejarse de la tierra

No hay tiempo que perder
Los iceberg que flotan en los ojos de los muertos
Conocen su camino
Ciego sería el que llorara
Las tinieblas del féretro sin límites
Las esperanzas abolidas
Los tormentos cambiados en inscripción de cementerio
Aquí yace Carlota ojos marítimos
Se le rompió un satélite
Aquí yace Matías en su corazón dos escualos se batían
Aquí yace Marcelo mar y cielo en el mismo violoncelo
Aquí yace Susana cansada de pelear contra el olvido
Aquí yace Teresa esa es la tierra que araron sus ojos hoy ocupada por
    su cuerpo
Aquí yace Angélica anclada en el puerto de sus brazos
Aquí yace Rosario río de rosas hasta el infinito
Aquí yace Raimundo raíces del mundo son sus venas
Aquí yace Clarisa clara risa enclaustrado en la luz
Aquí yace Alejandro antro alejado ala adentro
Aquí yace Gabriela rotos los diques sube en las savias hasta el sueño
    esperando la resurrección
Aquí yace Altazor azor fulminado por la altura
Aquí yace Vicente antipoeta y mago

Ciego sería el que llorara
Ciego como el cometa que va con su bastón
Y su neblina de ánimas que lo siguen
Obediente al instinto de sus sentidos
Sin hacer caso de los meteoros que apedrean desde lejos
Y viven en colonias según la temporada
El meteoro insolente cruza por el cielo
El meteplata el metecobre

The night that files its claws on the wind
And sharpens the sounds of the forest
It's afraid I say the tree is afraid
Of going too far from the earth

There's no time to lose
The icebergs that float in the eyes of the dead
Know the way
He who weeps will be blind
Darkness of the endless crypt
Abandoned hopes
Torments turned into cemetery script
Here lies Carlotta seagoing eyes
Crushed by a satellite
Here lies Matías two sharks battled in his heart
Here lies Marcello heaven and hello in the same violoncello
Here lies Susannah drained from straining against the void
Here lies Teresa placed in the terrain her eyes once plowed
Here lies Angelica anchored in the inlet of her arms
Here lies Rosemary rose carried to the infinite
Here lies Raymond rays of mud his veins
Here lies Clarissa clear is her smile encloistered in the light
Here lies Alexander alas under all is yonder
Here lies Gabriela breakwaters broken she rises in sap to the dream that
    awaits resurrection
Here lies Altazor hawk exploded by the altitude
Here lies Vicente antipoet and magician

He who weeps will be blind
Blind as the comet that travels with its staff
And its mist of souls that follow it
Instinctively obedient to its wishes
Never minding the meteoroids that pelt from afar
And live in colonies according to the seasons
The insolent meteoroid crosses the sky
The meteojoid the meteotoid

El metepiedras en el infinito
Meteópalos en la mirada
Cuidado aviador con las estrellas
Cuidado con la aurora
Que el aeronauta no sea el auricida
Nunca un cielo tuvo tantos caminos como éste
Ni fué tan peligroso
La estrella errante me trae el saludo de un amigo muerto hace diez años
Darse prisa darse prisa
Los planetas maduran en el planetal
Mis ojos han visto la raíz de los pájaros
El más allá de los nenúfares
Y el ante acá de las mariposas
¿Oyes el ruido que hacen las mandolinas al morir?
Estoy perdido
No hay más que capitular
Ante la guerra sin cuartel
Y la emboscada nocturna de estos astros

La eternidad quiere vencer
Y por lo tanto no hay tiempo que perder
Entonces
       Ah entonces
Más allá del último horizonte
Se verá lo que hay que ver
La ciudad
Debajo de las luces y las ropas colgadas
El jugador aéreo
Desnudo
Frágil
La noche al fondo del océano
Tierna ahogada
La muerte ciega
       Y su esplendor
Y el sonido y el sonido

The meteovoids in the infinite
The meteonoid in a glance
Aviator be careful with the stars
Careful with the dawn
Lest the aeronaut become a sunicide
The sky has never had as many roads as this
Never has it been so treacherous
An errant star brings me greetings from a friend ten years dead
Hurry up hurry up
Planets are ripening in the planetary
My eyes have seen the root of all birds
Beyond the beyond of waterlilies
And before the before of butterflies
Do you hear the sound that mandolins make when dying?
I am lost
There's nothing left but capitulation
To the war without quarter
And the nightly ambush of these stars

Eternity waits to conquer
And for that reason there's no time to lose
Then
    Ah then
Beyond the last horizon
We'll see what there is to see
The city
Beneath the lights and the hanging wash
The aerial trickster
Naked
Fragile
The night at the bottom of the sea
Tender drowned
Blind death
            And its splendor
And the sound and the sound

Espacio la lumbrera
                    A estribor
                    Adormecido
En cruz
          en luz
La tierra y su cielo
El cielo y su tierra
Selva noche
Y río día por el universo
El pájaro tralalí canta en las ramas de mi cerebro
Porque encontró la clave del eterfinifrete
Rotundo como el unipacio y el espaverso
Uiu uiui
Tralalí tralalá
Aia ai ai aaia i i

Space the light-shaft
                    Drowsy
                    At the starboard
In height
                    in light
Earth and its sky
Sky and its earth
Forest night
And river day through the universe
The bird tralalee sings in the branches of my brain
For I've found the key to the infiniternity
Round as the unimos and the cosverse
Oooheeoo ooheeoohee
Tralalee tralala
Aheeaah ahee ahee aaheeah ee ee

                                        (1931)

Canto VI

Alhaja apoteosis y molusco
Anudado
      noche
          nudo
El corazón
Esa entonces dirección
              nudo temblando
Flexible corazón la apoteosis
Un dos tres
       cuatro
Lágrima
      mi lámpara
          y molusco
El pecho al melodioso
Anudado la joya
Con que temblando angustia
Normal tedio
        Sería pasión
        Muerte el violoncelo
Una bujía el ojo
        Otro otra
Cristal si cristal era
Cristaleza
Magnetismo
        sabéis la seda
Viento flor
      lento nube lento
Seda cristal lento seda
El magnetismo
       seda aliento cristal seda
Así viajando en postura de ondulación
Cristal nube
Molusco sí por violoncelo y joya
Muerte de joya y violoncelo

Canto VI

Trinket apotheosis and mollusk
Knotted
             nude
                    night
The heart
The way that then
                    quivering knot
Apotheosis flexible heart
A two three
             four
Teardrop
         my lamplight
                      and mollusk
Chest to the melody
Knotted jewel
There then the quivering affliction
Normal boredom
                    Could be passion
                    Cello death
The eye a candle
                    Either other
Crystal if crystal it were
Crystalinity
Magnetism
             silk you know
Wind flower
             slow cloud slow
Silk slow crystal silk
Magnetism
             breath silk silk crystal
Thus traveling in the manner of waves
Cloud crystal
Mollusk yes from cello and jewel
Jewel death and cello death

Así sed por hambre o hambre y sed
Y nube y joya
Lento
      nube
      Ala ola ole ala Aladino
El ladino Aladino Ah ladino dino la
Cristal nube
Adónde
        en dónde
Lento lenta
          ala ola
Ola ola el ladino si ladino
Pide ojos
        Tengo nácar
En la seda cristal nube
Cristal ojos
         y perfumes
Bella tienda
Cristal nube
         muerte joya o en ceniza
Porque eterno porque eterna
              lento lento
Al azar del cristal ojos
Gracia tanta
        y entre mares
Miramares
Nombres daba
         por los ojos hojas mago
Alto alto
Y el clarín de la Babel
Pida nácar
        tenga muerte
Una dos y cuatro muerte
Para el ojo y entre mares
Para el barco en los perfumes
Por la joya al infinito

Thus thirst from hunger or hunger and thirst
And cloud and jewel
Slow
  cloud
   A wave a slave a lad in a cave
All add in a wave slave Aladdin's cave all a din
Cloud crystal
Where
   in where
Slowly slow
     a wave a cave
Wave a wave slave if a slave
Begs for eyes
     I have the nacre
In cloud crystal silk Eyes crystal
       and perfumes
The lovely shop
Cloud crystal
    jewel death or in ashes
For heternity for sheternity
      slowly slow
By chance the eyes crystal
Such grace
    between the seas
Sea views
Names given
    for magician leaf eyes
High high
And the bugle of Babel
Beg for nacre
    have death
A two and four death
For the eye between the seas
For the ship on the perfume
For the jewel to infinity
To dress the sky without dismay

Vestir cielo sin desmayo
Se deshoja tan prodigio
El cristal ojo
Y la visita
       flor y rama
Al gloria trino
       apoteosis
Va viajando Nudo Noche
Me daría
       cristaleras
            tanto azar
                  y noche y noche
Que tenía la borrasca
Noche y noche
       Apoteosis
Que tenía cristal ojo cristal seda cristal nube
La escultura seda o noche
Lluvia
   Lana flor por ojo
       Flor por nube
       Flor por noche
Señor horizonte viene viene
Puerta
Iluminando Negro
Puerta hacia ideas estatuarias
Estatuas de aquella ternura
A dónde va
De dónde viene
       el paisaje viento seda
El paisaje
       señor verde
Quién diría
Que se iba
Quién diría cristal noche
Tanta tarde
Tanto cielo que levanta

Such wonder unveiling
The eye crystal
And the journey
                    flower and branch
To glory trilling
                    apotheosis
Goes traveling Knot Night
Would give me
                    crystal pieces
                                    such chance
                                                    and night and night

The storm's
Night and night
                    Apotheosis
Eye crystal silk crystal cloud crystal
Sculpture of silk or night
Rain
     Wool flower by eye
                    Flower by cloud
                    Flower by night
Look here swoops the lord horizon
The door
Shining Black
The door to statuary travels
Statues of that tenderness
Where is it going
Where does it come from
                              silk wind land
The land
          lord green
Who can say
It's leaving
Who can say night crystal
Such evening
Such sky rising

Señor cielo
               cristal cielo
Y las llamas
               y en mi reino
Ancla noche apoteosis
Anudado
               la tormenta
Ancla cielo
               sus raíces
El destino tanto azar
Se desliza deslizaba
Apagándose pradera
Por quien sueña
Lunancero cristal luna
El que sueña
El que reino
               de sus hierros
Ancla mía golondrina
Sus resortes en el mar
Angel mío
               tan obscuro
                              tan color
Tan estatua y tan aliento
Tierra y mano
La marina tan armada
Armaduras los cabellos
Ojos templo
               y el mendigo
Estallado corazón
Montanario
Campañoso
Suenan perlas
Llaman perlas
El honor de los adioses
                              Cristal nube
El rumor y la lazada

Lord sky
        sky crystal
And the flames
           in my kingdom
Night anchors knotted
Apotheosis
        the storm
Sky anchors
        its roots
Fate such chance
Slips slipping off
Dimming the meadow
For whoever dreams
Serelunade moon crystal
In which it dreams
In which I reign
          from its irons
My swallow anchors
Its sources in the sea
My angel
      such darkness
           such color
Such statue and such breath
Earth and hand
Sailors well-armed
Armored hair
Sanctuary eyes
      and the beggar
Heart exploded
Mountain tower
Bell sierra
Pearls ring
Pearls invoke
The honor of good-bye
         Cloud crystal
The whisper and the knotted bow

Nadadora
　　　　Cristal noche
La medusa irreparable
Dirá espectro
　　　　　Cristal seda
Olvidando la serpiente
Olvidando sus dos piernas
Sus dos ojos
Sus dos manos
Sus orejas
Aeronauta
　　　　　en mi terror
Viento aparte
Mandodrina y golonlina
Mandolera y ventolina
Enterradas
Las campanas
Enterrados los olvidos
En su oreja
　　　　　viento norte
Cristal mío
Baño eterno
　　　　　el nudo noche
El gloria trino
　　　　　sin desmayo
Al tan prodigio
Con su estatua
Noche y rama
　　　　　Cristal sueño
　　　　　Cristal viaje
Flor y noche
Con su estatua
　　　　　Cristal muerte

Swimmer
            Night crystal
Ruined Medusa
Will say a ghost
                Silk crystal
Forgetting the serpent
Forgetting its two legs
Its two eyes
Its two hands
Its ears
Aeronaut
            in my terror
Wind aside
Swallowlin and mandotail
Mandowind and gust of linn
Buried
Bells
The forgotten buried
In its ear
            north wind
My crystal
Bath eternal
                night knot
Glory trilling
                without dismay
At such wonder
And its statue
Night and branch
                    Crystal dream
                    Crystal voyage
Flower and night
With their statue
                    Crystal death

Canto VII

Ai aia aia
ia ia ia aia ui
Tralalí
Lali lalá
Aruaru
       urulario
Lalilá
Rimbibolam lam lam
Uiaya zollonario
            lalilá
Monlutrella monluztrella
                lalolú
Montresol y mandotrina
Ai ai
     Montesur en lasurido
     Montesol
Lusponsedo solinario
Aururaro ulisamento lalilá
Ylarca murllonía
Hormajauma marijauda
Mitradente
Mitrapausa
Mitralonga
Matrisola
         matriola
Olamina olasica lalilá
Isonauta
Olandera uruaro
Ia ia campanuso compasedo
Tralalá
Ai ai mareciente y eternauta
Redontella tallerendo lucenario
Ia ia
Laribamba

Canto VII

Ahee aheeah aheeah
eeah eeah eeah aheeah oohee
Tralalee
Lalee lala
Ahruahru
       Urulinary
Laleela
Ecocokoo coo ecku
Ooheeahyah zobbinary
          laleela
Sierrastraluna sierrastralux
           laloloo
Trierrasun and trillolin
Ahee ahee
      Sierrasouth in shoutseairr
      Sierrasun
Luxponsive solinary
Raraurora ecoplaining laleela
Ndanark harmurmony
Antiquash matriquage
Miterdent
Miterlipsis
Miterslonga
Matrilonial
      matrimocean
Roceaning tradocean laleela
Equinaut
Bannocean raruckoo
Eeah eeah campanily acompassee
Tralala
Ahee ahee renaissea and eterninaut
Lucinary shooping astrasphere
Eeah eeah
Larymbimlam

Larimbambamplanerella
Laribambamositerella
Leiramombaririlanla
                    lirilam
Ai i a
Temporía
Ai ai aia
Ululayu
        lulayu
                layu yu
Ululayu
        ulayu
                ayu yu
Lunatando
Sensorida e infimento
Ululayo ululamento
Plegasuena
Cantasorio ululaciente
Oraneva yu yu yo
Tempovío
Infilero e infinauta zurrosía
Jaurinario ururayú
Montañendo oraranía
Arorasía ululacente
Semperiva
            ivarisa tarirá
Campanudio lalalí
                Auriciento auronida
Lalalí
    Io ia
i i i o
Ai a i ai a i i i i o ia

Larymbimbamastraplan
Larymbimbamastramur
Lyralibrarcrystramour
                    Larylyra nx
Ahee ee ah
Temporarr
Ahee ahee aheeah
Ululayou
            lullayou
                        layou you
Ulalayou
            ulayou
                        ahyou you
Moonaluning
Sensiwooned infirmament
Ululayo ululament
Pliasounding
Chanteloping ululaissance
Hallenujah you you yo
Tempolary
Infilite and infinaut buziety
Quaginary uruahyou
Sierratuning faraprair
Ululascent aurorarary
Livfrever
            Lefdalafda dadeedah
Campellationed lalalee
                        Auricental centauroral
Lalalee
        Eeoh eeah
ee ee ee oh
Ahee ah ee ahee ah ee ee ee ee oh eeah

De ESPAÑA, APARTA DE MÍ ESTE CÁLIZ

III

Solía escribir con su dedo grande en el aire:
"¡Viban los compañeros! Pedro Rojas",
de Miranda de Ebro, padre y hombre,
marido y hombre, ferroviario y hombre,
padre y más hombre, Pedro y sus dos muertes.

Papel de viento, lo han matado: ¡pasa!
Pluma de carne, lo han matado: ¡pasa!
¡Abisa a todos compañeros pronto!

Palo en el que han colgado su madero,
lo han matado;
¡lo han matado al pie de su dedo grande!
¡Han matado, a la vez, a Pedro, a Rojas!

¡Viban los compañeros
a la cabecera de su aire escrito!
¡Viban con esta b del buitre en las entrañas
de Pedro
y de Rojas, del héroe y del mártir!

Registrándole, muerto, sorprendiéronle
en su cuerpo un gran cuerpo, para
el alma del mundo,
y en la chaqueta una cuchara muerta.

Pedro también solía comer
entre las criaturas de su carne, asear, pintar

César Vallejo   (Peru, 1892–1938)

From SPAIN, TAKE THIS CUP FROM ME

III

He used to write with his big finger in the air:
"Long live all combanions! Pedro Rojas,"
from Miranda de Ebro, father and man,
husband and man, railroad-worker and man,
father and more man, Pedro and his two deaths.

Wind paper, he was killed: pass on!
Flesh pen, he was killed: pass on!
Advise all combanions quick!

Stick on which they have hanged his log,
he was killed;
he was killed at the base of his big finger!
They have killed, in one blow, Pedro, Rojas!

Long live all combanions
written at the head of his air!
Let them live with this buzzard b in Pedro's
and in Rojas's
and in the hero's and in the martyr's guts!

Searching him, dead, they surprised
in his body a great body, for
the soul of the world,
and in his jacket a dead spoon.

Pedro too used to eat
among the creatures of his flesh, to clean up, to paint

la mesa y vivir dulcemente
en representación de todo el mundo.
Y esta cuchara anduvo en su chaqueta,
despierto o bien cuando dormía, siempre,
cuchara muerta viva, ella y sus símbolos.
¡Abisa a todos compañeros pronto!
¡Viban los compañeros al pie de esta cuchara para siempre!

Lo han matado, obligándole a morir
a Pedro, a Rojas, al obrero, al hombre, a aquél
que nació muy niñín, mirando al cielo,
y que luego creció, se puso rojo
y luchó con sus células, sus nos, sus todavías, sus hambres, sus pedazos.

Lo han matado suavemente
entre el cabello de su mujer, la Juana Vásquez,
a la hora del fuego, al año del balazo
y cuando andaba cerca ya de todo.

Pedro Rojas, así, después de muerto,
se levantó, besó su catafalco ensangrentado,
lloró por España
y volvió a escribir con el dedo en el aire:
"¡Viban los compañeros! Pedro Rojas."
Su cadáver estaba lleno de mundo.

the table and to live sweetly
as a representative of everyone.
And this spoon was in his jacket,
awake or else when he slept, always,
dead alive spoon, this one and its symbols.
Advise all combanions quick!
Long live all combanions at the base of this spoon forever!

He was killed, they forced him to die,
Pedro, Rojas, the worker, the man, the one
who was born a wee baby, looking at the sky,
and who afterward grew up, blushed
and fought with his cells, his nos, his yets, his hungers, his pieces.

He was killed softly
in his wife's hair, Juana Vásquez by name,
at the hour of fire, in the year of the gunshot,
and when he was already close to everything.

Pedro Rojas, thus, after being dead,
got up, kissed his blood-smeared casket,
wept for Spain
and again wrote with his finger in the air:
"Long live all combanions! Pedro Rojas."
His corpse was full of world.

V

¡Ahí pasa! ¡Llamadla! ¡Es su costado!
¡Ahí pasa la muerte por Irún:
sus pasos de acordeón, su palabrota,
su metro del tejido que te dije,
su gramo de aquel peso que he callado… ¡si son ellos!

¡Llamadla! Daos prisa! Va buscándome en los rifles,
como que sabe bien dónde la venzo,
cuál es mi maña grande, mis leyes especiosas, mis códigos terribles.
¡Llamadla! Ella camina exactamente como un hombre, entre las fieras,
se apoya de aquel brazo que se enlaza a nuestros pies
cuando dormimos en los parapetos
y se para a las puertas elásticas del sueño.

¡Gritó! ¡Gritó! ¡Gritó su grito nato, sensorial!
Gritara de vergüenza, de ver cómo ha caído entre las plantas,
de ver cómo se aleja de las bestias,
de oír cómo decimos: ¡Es la muerte!
¡De herir nuestros más grandes intereses!

(Porque elabora su hígado la gota que te dije, camarada;
porque se come el alma del vecino)

¡Llamadla! Hay que seguirla
hasta el pie de los tanques enemigos,
que la muerte es un ser sido a la fuerza,
cuyo principio y fin llevo grabados
a la cabeza de mis ilusiones,
por mucho que ella corra el peligro corriente
que tú sabes
y que haga como que hace que me ignora.

V

There she goes! Call her! It's her side!
There goes Death through Irún:
her accordion steps, her curse word,
her meter of cloth that I've mentioned to you,
her gram of that weight I've kept to myself…they're the ones!

Call her! Hurry! She's searching for me among the rifles,
since she well knows where I defeat her,
what my great cunning is, my deceptive laws, my terrible codes.
Call her! She walks exactly like a man, among wild beasts,
she leans on that arm which entwines our feet
when we sleep on the parapets
and she stops at the elastic gates of dream.

She shouted! She shouted! Shouted her born, sensorial shout!
Would that she shouted from shame, from seeing how she's fallen among
    the plants,
from seeing how she withdraws from the beasts,
from hearing how we say: It's Death!
From wounding our greatest interests!

(Because her liver produces the drop that I told you about, comrade;
because she eats the soul of our neighbor)

Call her! We must follow her
to the foot of the enemy tanks,
for Death is a being been by force,
whose beginning and end I carry engraved
at the head of my illusions,
however much she would run the normal risk
that you know
and though she would pretend to pretend to ignore me.

¡Llamadla! No es un ser, muerte violenta,
sino, apenas, lacónico suceso;
más bien su modo tira, cuando ataca,
tira a tumulto simple, sin órbitas ni cánticos de dicha;
más bien tira su tiempo audaz, a céntimo impreciso
y sus sordos quilates, a déspotas aplausos.
Llamadla, que en llamándola con saña, con figuras,
se la ayuda a arrastrar sus tres rodillas,
como, a veces,
a veces duelen, punzan fracciones enigmáticas, globales,
como, a veces, me palpo y no me siento.

¡Llamadla! ¡Daos prisa! Va buscándome,
con su coñac, su pómulo moral,
sus pasos de acordeón, su palabrota.
¡Llamadla! No hay que perderle el hilo en que la lloro.
De su olor para arriba, ¡ay de mi polvo, camarada!
De su pus para arriba, ¡ay de mi férula, teniente!
De su imán para abajo, ¡ay de mi tumba!

IMAGEN ESPAÑOLA DE LA MUERTE

Call her! Violent Death is not a being,
but, barely, a laconic event;
instead her way aims, when she attacks,
aims at a simple tumult, without orbits or joyous canticles;
instead her audacious moment aims, at an imprecise centime
and her deaf carats, at despotic applause.
Call her, for by calling her with fury, with figures,
you help her drag her three knees,
as, at times,
at times global, enigmatic fractions hurt, pierce,
as, at times, I touch myself and don't feel myself.

Call her! Hurry! She is searching for me,
with her cognac, her moral cheekbone,
her accordion steps, her curse word.
Call her! The thread of my tears for her must not be lost.
From her smell up, woe is my dust, comrade!
From her pus up, woe is my ferule, lieutenant!
From her magnet down, woe is my tomb!

SPANISH IMAGE OF DEATH

VI
Cortejo tras la toma de Bilbao

Herido y muerto, hermano,
criatura veraz, republicana, están andando en tu trono,
desde que tu espinazo cayó famosamente;
están andando, pálido, en tu edad flaca y anual,
laboriosamente absorta ante los vientos.

Guerrero en ambos dolores,
siéntate a oír, acuéstate al pie del palo súbito,
inmediato de tu trono;
voltea;
están las nuevas sábanas, extrañas;
están andando, hermano, están andando.

Han dicho: "¡Cómo! ¡Dónde!…", expresándose
en trozos de paloma,
y en los niños suben sin llorar a tu polvo.
Ernesto Zúñiga, duerme con la mano puesta,
con el concepto puesto,
en descanso tu paz, en paz tu guerra.

Herido mortalmente de vida, camarada,
camarada jinete,
camarada caballo entre hombre y fierra,
tus huesecillos de alto y melancólico dibujo
forman pompa española, pompa
laureada de finísimos andrajos!

Siéntate, pues, Ernesto,
oye que están andando, aquí, en tu trono,
desde que tu tobillo tiene canas.
¿Qué trono?
¡Tu zapato derecho! ¡Tu zapato!

13 Set. 1937

VI
Cortege after the Capture of Bilbao

Wounded and dead, brother,
truthful creature, Loyalist, they are walking on your throne,
ever since your backbone fell famously;
they are walking, pale, on your lean and yearly age,
laboriously entranced before the winds.

Warrior in both sorrows,
sit down and listen, lie down at the foot of the sudden stick,
next to your throne;
turn around;
the new bedsheets are strange;
they are walking, brother, they are walking.

They've said: "How! Where!…" expressing it
in shreds of dove,
and the children go up to your dust without crying.
Ernesto Zúñiga, sleep with your hand placed,
with your concept placed,
your peace at rest, your war at peace.

Mortally wounded by life, comrade,
comrade rider,
comrade horse between man and wild beast,
your delicate bones of high and melancholy design
form Spanish pomp, pomp
laurelled with the finest rags!

Sit up, then, Ernesto,
listen how they are walking, here, on your throne,
ever since your ankle grew gray hair.
What throne?
Your right shoe! Your shoe!

13 September 1937

VII

Varios días el aire, compañeros,
muchos días el viento cambia de aire,
el terreno, de filo,
de nivel el fusil republicano.
Varios días España está española.

Varios días el mal
mobiliza sus órbitas, se abstiene,
paraliza sus ojos escuchándolos.
Varios días orando con sudor desnudo,
los milicianos cuélganse del hombre.
Varios días, el mundo, camaradas,
el mundo está español hasta la muerte.

Varios días ha muerto aquí el disparo
y ha muerto el cuerpo en su papel de espíritu
y el alma es ya nuestra alma, compañeros.
Varios días el cielo,
éste, el del día, el de la pata enorme.

Varios días, Gijón;
muchos días, Gijón;
mucho tiempo, Gijón;
mucha tierra, Gijón;
mucho hombre, Gijón;
y mucho dios, Gijón,
muchísimas Españas ¡ay! Gijón.

Camaradas,
varios días el viento cambia de aire.

5 Nov. 1937

VII

      For several days the air, companions,
for many days the wind changes air,
the terrain, its edge,
its level the Loyalist rifle.
For several days Spain looks Spanish.

      For several days evil
mobilizes its orbits, abstains,
paralyzes its eyes listening to them.
For several days praying with naked sweat,
the civilian-fighters hang from man.
For several days, the world, comrades,
the world looks Spanish unto death.

      For several days here the firing has died
and the body has died in its spiritual role
and the soul, companions, has become our soul.
For several days the sky,
this one, the one with a day, the one with an enormous paw.

      For several days, Gijón;
for many days, Gijón;
for much time, Gijón;
for much land, Gijón;
for much man, Gijón;
and for much god, Gijón,
for very many Spains ay! Gijón.

    Comrades,
for several days the wind changes air.

5 November 1937

IX
Pequeño responso a un héroe de la república

Un libro quedó al borde de su cintura muerta,
un libro retoñaba de su cadáver muerto.
Se llevaron al héroe,
y corpórea y aciaga entró su boca en nuestro aliento;
sudamos todos, el hombligo a cuestas;
caminantes las lunas nos seguían;
también sudaba de tristeza el muerto.

Y un libro, en la batalla de Toledo,
un libro, atrás un libro, arriba un libro, retoñaba del cadáver.

Poesía del pómulo morado, entre el decirlo
y el callarlo,
poesía en la carta moral que acompañara
a su corazón.
Quedóse el libro y nada más, que no hay
insectos en la tumba,
y quedó al borde de su manga el aire remojándose
y haciéndose gaseoso, infinito.

Todos sudamos, el hombligo a cuestas,
también sudaba de tristeza el muerto
y un libro, yo lo vi sentidamente,
un libro, atrás un libro, arriba un libro
retoño del cadáver ex abrupto.

10 Set. 1937

IX
Short Prayer for a Loyalist Hero

A book remained edging his dead waist,
a book was sprouting from his dead corpse.
The hero was carried off,
and corporeal and ominous his mouth entered our breath;
we all sweated, under the load of our navehalls;
moons were following us on foot;
the dead man was also sweating from sadness.

And a book, during the battle for Toledo,
a book, behind a book, above a book, was sprouting from the corpse.

Poetry of the royal purple cheekbone, between saying it
and keeping quiet about it,
poetry in the moral map that had accompanied
his heart.
The book remained and nothing else, for there are no
insects in the tomb,
and at the edge of his sleeve the air remained soaking,
becoming gaseous, infinite.

All of us sweated, under the load of our navehalls,
the dead man was also sweating from sadness
and a book, I saw it feelingly,
a book, behind a book, above a book
sprouted from the corpse abruptly.

10 September 1937

XII
Masa

Al fin de la batalla,
y muerto el combatiente, vino hacia él un hombre
y le dijo: "No mueras, te amo tánto!"
Pero el cadáver ¡ay! siguió muriendo.

Se le acercaron dos y repitiéronle:
"No nos dejes! ¡Valor! ¡Vuelve a la vida!"
Pero el cadáver ¡ay! siguió muriendo.

Acudieron a él veinte, cien, mil, quinientos mil,
clamando: "Tánto amor, y no poder nada contra la muerte!"
Pero el cadáver ¡ay! siguió muriendo.

Le rodearon millones de individuos,
con un ruego común: "¡Quédate hermano!"
Pero el cadáver ¡ay! siguió muriendo.

Entonces, todos los hombres de la tierra
le rodearon; les vio el cadáver triste, emocionado;
incorporóse lentamente,
abrazó al primer hombre; echóse a andar...

10 Nov. 1937

XII
Mass

At the end of the battle,
the combatant dead, a man approached him
and said to him: "Don't die; I love you so much!"
But the corpse, alas! kept on dying.

Two more came up to him and repeated:
"Don't leave us! Be brave! Come back to life!"
But the corpse, alas! kept on dying.

Twenty, a hundred, a thousand, five hundred thousand appeared,
crying out: "So much love, and no power against death!"
But the corpse, alas! kept on dying.

Millions of individuals surrounded him,
with a common plea: "Don't leave us, brother!"
But the corpse, alas! kept on dying.

Then, all the inhabitants of the earth
surrounded him; the corpse looked at them sadly, deeply moved;
he got up slowly,
embraced the first man; started to walk...

10 November 1937

XV
España, aparta de mí este cáliz

Niños del mundo,
si cae España—digo, es un decir—
si cae
del cielo abajo su antebrazo que asen,
en cabestro, dos láminas terrestres;
niños, ¡qué edad la de las sienes cóncavas!
¡qué temprano en el sol lo que os decía!
¡qué pronto en vuestro pecho el ruido anciano!
¡qué viejo vuestro 2 en el cuaderno!

¡Niños del mundo, está
la madre España con su vientre a cuestas;
está nuestra maestra con sus férulas,
está madre y maestra,
cruz y madera, porque os dio la altura,
vértigo y división y suma, niños;
está con ella, padres procesales!

Si cae—digo, es un decir—si cae
España, de la tierra para abajo,
niños ¡cómo vais a cesar de crecer!
¡cómo va a castigar el año al mes!
¡cómo van a quedarse en diez los dientes,
en palote el diptongo, la medalla en llanto!
¡Cómo va el corderillo a continuar
atado por la pata al gran tintero!
¡Cómo vais a bajar las gradas del alfabeto
hasta la letra en que nació la pena!

Niños,
hijos de los guerreros, entre tanto,
bajad la voz que España está ahora mismo repartiendo
la energía entre el reino animal,
las florecillas, los cometas y los hombres.

XV
Spain, Take This Cup from Me

Children of the world,
if Spain falls—I mean, it's just a thought—
if her forearm
falls downward from the sky seized,
in a halter, by two terrestrial plates;
children, what an age of concave temples!
how early in the sun what I was telling you!
how quickly in your chest the ancient noise!
how old your 2 in the notebook!

Children of the world, mother
Spain is with her belly on her back;
our teacher is with her ferules,
she appears as mother and teacher,
cross and wood, because she gave you height,
vertigo and division and addition, children;
she is with herself, legal parents!

If she falls—I mean, it's just a thought—if Spain
falls, from the earth downward,
children, how you will stop growing!
how the year will punish the month!
how you will never have more than ten teeth,
how the diphthong will remain in downstroke, the gold star in tears!
How the little lamb will stay
tied by its leg to the great inkwell!
How you'll descend the steps of the alphabet
to the letter in which pain was born!

Children,
sons of fighters, meanwhile,
lower your voice, for right at this moment Spain is distributing
her energy among the animal kingdom,
little flowers, comets, and men.

¡Bajad la voz, que está
con su rigor, que es grande, sin saber
qué hacer, y está en su mano
la calvera hablando y habla y habla,
la calavera, aquélla de la trenza,
la calavera, aquélla de la vida!

     ¡Bajad la voz, os digo;
bajad la voz, el canto de las sílabas, el llanto
de la materia y el rumor menor de las pirámides, y aún
el de las sienes que andan con dos piedras!
¡Bajad el aliento, y si
el antebrazo baja,
si las férulas suenan, si es la noche,
si el cielo cabe en dos limbos terrestres,
si hay ruido en el sonido de las puertas,
si tardo,
si no veis a nadie, si os asustan
los lápices sin punta, si la madre
España cae—digo, es un decir—
salid, niños del mundo; id a buscarla!…

Lower your voice, for she
sudders convulsively, not knowing
what to do, and she has in her hand
the talking skull, chattering away,
the skull, the one with a braid,
the skull, the one with life!

Lower your voice, I tell you;
lower your voice, the song of the syllables, the wail
of matter and the faint murmur of the pyramids, and even
that of your temples which walk with two stones!
Lower your breathing, and if
the forearm comes down,
if the ferules sound, if it is night,
if the sky fits between two terrestrial limbos,
if there is noise in the creaking of doors,
if I am late,
if you do not see anyone, if the blunt pencils
frighten you, if mother
Spain falls—I mean, it's just a thought—
go out, children of the world, go look for her!...

CANTO DEL MACHO ANCIANO

Sentado a la sombra inmortal de un sepulcro,
o enarbolando el gran anillo matrimonial herido a la manera de palomas que
    se deshojan como congojas,
escarbo los últimos atardeceres.

Como quien arroja un libro de botellas tristes a la Mar-Océano
o una enorme piedra de humo echando sin embargo espanto a los
    acantilados de la historia
o acaso un pájaro muerto que gotea llanto,
voy lanzando los peñascos inexorables del pretérito
contra la muralla negra.

Y como ya todo es inútil,
como los candados del infinito crujen en goznes mohosos,
su actitud llena la tierra de lamentos.

Escucho el regimiento de esqueletos del gran crepúsculo,
del gran crepúsculo cardíaco o demoníaco, maníaco de los enfurecidos
    ancianos,
la trompeta acusatoria de la desgracia acumulada,
el arriarse descomunal de todas las banderas, el ámbito terriblemente pálido
de los fusilamientos, la angustia
del soldado que agoniza entre tizanas y frazadas, a quinientas leguas abiertas
del campo de batalla, y sollozo como un pabellón antiguo.

Hay lágrimas de hierro amontonadas,
pero por adentro del invierno se levanta el hongo infernal del cataclismo
    personal, y catástrofes de ciudades
que murieron y son polvo remoto, aúllan.

Pablo de Rokha

(Chile, 1894–1968)

THE OLD MAN'S SONG

Sitting in the immortal shadow of a tomb,
or raising the great wedding band, wounded like doves who shed feathers
 for tears,
I peck at my final evenings.

Like one who casts a book of sad bottles on the Ocean-Sea
or a giant phantom stone that still strikes terror into the cliffs of history
or perhaps a dead bird dripping tears,
I'm launching the inexorable boulders of the past
against the black rampart.

And since everything is already useless,
since infinity's locks creak on rusty hinges,
my mood fills the earth with laments.

I hear the skeleton regiment of the great twilight,
the great twilight of furious old men, cardiac, demonic, manic,
the trumpet sounding collective disgrace,
the spectacular striking of all the flags, the terribly pale field
of executions, the heartache
of the soldier who agonizes between tinctures and blankets, five hundred
 leagues away
from the battlefield, and I break down like an old pavilion.

There are tears of iron piling up, but
from within winter, personal cataclysm's vicious mushroom rises, and
 those catastrophes of cities
that died and are distant dust, still howl.

Ha llegado la hora vestida de pánico
en la cual todas las vidas carecen de sentido, carecen de destino, carecen
    de estilo y de espada,
carecen de dirección, de voz, carecen
de todo lo rojo y terrible de las empresas o las epopeyas o las vivencias
    ecuménicas,
que justificarán la existencia como peligro y como suicidio; un mito
    enorme,
equivocado, rupestre, de rumiante
fue el existir; y restan las chaquetas solas del ágape inexorable, las risas
    caídas y el arrepentimiento invernal de los excesos,
en aquel entonces antiquísimo con rasgos de santo y de demonio,
cuando yo era hermoso como un toro negro y tenía las mujeres que quería
y un revólver de hombre a la cintura.

    Fallan las glándulas
y el varón genital intimidado por el yo rabioso, se recoge a la medida del
    abatimiento o atardeciendo
araña la perdida felicidad en los escombros;
el amor nos agarró y nos estrujó como a limones desesperados,
yo ando lamiendo su ternura,
pero ella se diluye en la eternidad, se confunde en la eternidad, se destruye
    en la eternidad y aunque existo porque batallo y "mi poesía es
    mi militancia",
todo lo eterno me rodea amenazándome y gritando desde la otra orilla.

    Busco los musgos, las cosas usadas y estupefactas,
lo postpretérito y difícil, arado de pasado e infinitamente de olvido,
    polvoso y mohoso como las panoplias de antaño, como las familias de
    antaño, como las monedas de antaño,
con el resplandor de los ataúdes enfurecidos,
el gigante relincho de los sombreros muertos, o aquello únicamente aquello
que se está cayendo en las formas,
el yo público, la figura atronadora del ser
que se ahoga contradiciéndose.

Clad in panic, the hour has arrived
in which all lives lack significance, lack destiny, lack style and character,
    lack direction and voice, lack
everything that's red and awful in symbols and epics and everyday
    experience,
lives that will excuse existence as risk and as suicide—an enormous myth,
mistaken, thought up
in caves—and the mere sketches of implacable agape, the fading laughter,
    and the icy regret of excesses
are all that remain of those old days with flashes of the saint and the devil,
back when I was handsome as a black bull, when I had any woman I wanted
and a man's pistol at my waist.

    Glands fail
and the biological male in me, threatened by my rage, shrinks to the point
    of humiliation, or,
as evening falls, scrapes together bits of lost happiness in the rubble;
love grabbed us and squeezed us like helpless lemons;
I'm always lapping at her tenderness,
but she gets dissolved in eternity, jumbled in eternity, destroyed in
    eternity, and although I exist because I fight on and "my poetry is
    my militancy,"
all of eternity surrounds me, menacing me, clamoring from the other side.

    I seek out the mossy things, the time-worn and petrified things,
the conditional and the difficult, dug up from the past, from total oblivion,
    rusty and dusty like antique suits of armor, like antique families, like
    antique coins,
with the brilliance of furious coffins,
the monstrous neighing of dead hats, or only those things
that have fallen out of favor,
the public self, the thunderous figure
who drowns in self-contradiction.

Ahora la hembra domina, envenenada,
y el vino se burla de nosotros como un cómplice de nosotros,
    emborrachándonos, cuando nos llevamos la copa a la boca dolorosa,
acorralándonos y aculatándonos contra nosotros mismos como mitos.

Estamos muy cansados de escribir universos sobre universos
y la inmortalidad que otrora tanto amaba el corazón adolescente, se arrastra
como una pobre puta envejeciendo;
sabemos que podemos escalar todas las montañas de la literatura como en
    la juventud heroica, que nos aguanta el ánimo
el coraje suicida de los temerarios, y sin embargo yo,
definitivamente viudo, definitivamente solo, definitivamente viejo, y
    apuñalado de padecimientos,
ejecutando la hazaña desesperada de sobrepujarme,
el autorretrato de todo lo heroico de la sociedad y la naturaleza me abruma;
¿qué les sucede a los ancianos con su propia ex-combatiente sombra?
se confunden con ella ardiendo y son fuego rugiendo sueño de sombra
    hecho de sombra,
lo sombrío definitivo y un ataúd que anda llorando sombra sobre sombra.

Viviendo del recuerdo, amamantándome del recuerdo, el recuerdo
    me envuelve y al retornar a la gran soledad de la adolescencia,
padre y abuelo, padre de innumerables familias,
rasguño los rescoldos, y la ceniza helada agranda la desesperación
en la que todos están muertos entre muertos,
y la más amada de las mujeres, retumba en la tumba de truenos y héroes
labrada con palancas universales o como bramando.

¿En qué bosques de fusiles nos esconderemos de aquestos pellejos
    ardiendo?
porque es terrible el seguirse a sí mismo cuando lo hicimos todo, lo
    quisimos todo, lo pudimos todo y se nos quebraron las manos,
las manos y los dientes mordiendo hierro con fuego;
y ahora como se desciende terriblemente de lo cuotidiano a lo infinito,
    ataúd por ataúd,
desbarrancándonos como peñascos o como caballos mundo abajo,

Now the female is in control, embittered,
and when we raise the cup to our afflicted mouths, the wine taunts us as if
    it were our partner in crime, getting us drunk,
coralling us and cornering us into the myths of our very selves.

    We're so tired of writing universe after universe
and the immortality once so cherished by the adolescent heart now drags
    itself along
like a wretched, aging whore;
we know we can scale every summit of literature that we could in our
    heroic youth, that the daredevils' suicidal nerve
preserves our spirit, and yet I,
widowed forever, alone forever, old forever, and pierced by suffering,
am carrying out the desperate feat of surpassing myself,
am the self-portrait of everything heroic about society, but nature gets in
    the way...
What happens to old men with their own ex-combatant shadows?
They're confounded by her burning and they're fires roaring a dream of
    shadow made from shadow,
eternal gloom and a coffin that goes around crying shadow after shadow.

    Subsisting on memory, suckling on memory, memory surrounds
        me, and on returning to the great solitude of adolescence,
father and grandfather, father of countless families,
I stamp out the embers, and the cold ashes heighten the despair
in which all are dead among the dead,
and the most beloved of women booms in the tomb of thunder and heroes
raised up by the levers of the world, as if she's bellowing.

    In what forest of rifles will we hide from these burning skins?
for it's terrible to go it alone when we did it all together, we wanted it all,
    we could do it all, and we broke our hands,
hands and teeth clenching iron with fire;
and now, as things descend terribly from the quotidian to the infinite,
    coffin by coffin,
tumbling from the cliff like boulders or hell's horses,

vamos con extraños, paso a paso y tranco a tranco midiendo el
    derrumbamiento general,
calculándolo, a la sordina,
y de ahí entonces la prudencia que es la derrota de la ancianidad;
vacías restan las botellas,
gastados los zapatos y desaparecidos los amigos más queridos, nuestro
    viejo tiempo, la época
y tú, Winétt, colosal e inexorable.

Todas las cosas van siguiendo mis pisadas, ladrando
        desesperadamente,
como un acompañamiento fúnebre, mordiendo el siniestro funeral del
    mundo, como el entierro nacional
de las edades, y yo voy muerto andando.

Infinitamente cansado, desengañado, errado,
con la sensación categórica de haberme equivocado en lo ejecutado o
    desperdiciado o abandonado o atropellado al avatar del destino
en la inutilidad de existir y su gran carrera despedazada;
comprendo y admiro a los líderes,
pero soy el coordinador de la angustia del universo, el suicida que apostó
    su destino a la baraja
de la expresionalidad y lo ganó perdiendo el derecho a perderlo,
el hombre que rompe su época y arrasándola, le da categoría y régimen,
pero queda hecho pedazos y a la expectativa;
rompiente de jubilaciones, ariete y símbolo de piedra,
anhelo ya la antigua plaza de provincia
y la discusión con los pájaros, el vagabundaje y la retreta apolillada en los
    extramuros.

Está lloviendo, está lloviendo, está lloviendo,
¡ojalá siempre esté lloviendo, esté lloviendo siempre y el vendaval
    desenfrenado que yo soy íntegro, se asocie
a la personalidad popular del huracán!

we go with strangers, step by step and stride by stride measuring the
    general decline,
working it out, on the quiet,
and from there to the prudence which is the defeat of old age;
the bottles remain empty,
shoes worn out and best friends gone, our old time, our era,
and you, Winétt, colossal and inexorable.

All these things follow in my footsteps, barking desperately,
like a funeral procession, biting at the world's hopeless depravity, like a
    national burial
for the ages, and I walk as if dead.

Infinitely tired, disillusioned, mistaken,
with the categorical sensation of having been wrong about all that was
    done or squandered or abandoned or trampled by the vagaries
    of destiny
in the futility of existence and its great disjointed course;
I understand and admire our leaders,
but I am the coordinator of the universe's anguish, the suicide that
    wagered his destiny on a card game
of expression and won it losing the right to lose it,
the man who cracks open his era and by destroying it affords it character
    and conduct,
but who's left in tatters, waiting around;
reef of retirement, battering ram and symbol of stability,
I already long for the old provincial plaza
and the conversation with the birds, the loafing, and the moth-eaten
    retreat in the suburbs.

It's raining, it's raining, it's raining…
I always hope it's raining, I hope that it rains always and that the wild winds
    I create will be associated with the hurricane's widespread charm.

A la manera de la estación de ferrocarriles,
mi situación está poblada de adioses y de ausencia, una gran lágrima
    enfurecida
derrama tiempo con sueños y águilas tristes;
cae la tarde en la literatura y no hicimos lo que pudimos,
cuando hicimos lo que quisimos con nuestro pellejo.

El aventurero de los océanos deshabitados,
el descubridor, el conquistador, el gobernador de naciones y el fundador de
    ciudades tentaculares,
como un gran capitán frustrado,
rememorando lo soñado como errado y vil o trocando en el escarnio
    celestial del vocabulario
espadas por poemas, entregó la cuchilla rota del canto
al soñador que arrastraría adentro del pecho universal muerto, el cadáver de
    un conductor de pueblos,
con su bastón de mariscal tronchado y echando llamas.

El "borracho, bestial, lascivo e iconoclasta" como el cíclope
        de Eurípides,
queriendo y muriendo de amor, arrasándola
a la amada en temporal de besos, es ya nada ahora más que un león herido y
    mordido de cóndores.

Caduco en "la República asesinada"
y como el dolor nacional es mío, el dolor popular me horada la palabra,
    desgarrándome,
como si todos los niños hambrientos de Chile fueran mis parientes;
el trágico y el dionisíaco naufragan en este enorme atado de lujuria en
    angustia, y la acometida agonal
se estrella la cabeza en las murallas enarboladas de sol caído,
trompetas botadas, botellas quebradas, banderas ajadas, ensangrentadas por
    el martirio del trabajo mal pagado;
escucho la muerte roncando por debajo del mundo
a la manera de las culebras, a la manera de las escopetas apuntándonos a la
    cabeza, a la manera de Dios, que no existió nunca.

Like a railway station,
my condition is populated by good-byes and absence, a great furious tear
that sheds time with sleep and sad eagles;
evening falls on literature and we didn't do what we could
back when we were doing whatever we wanted with ourselves.

The adventurer of uninhabited oceans,
the discoverer, the conqueror, the ruler of nations, and the founder of
    sprawling cities,
a great, frustrated captain,
recalling his dreams as vile and mistaken or bartering swords for poems in
    vocabulary's celestial scorn,
he handed his song's broken knife
to the dreamer who would drag the corpse of a village conductor, his little
    wand
casting flames inside the universal bosom of death.

The "drunk, bestial, lewd and iconoclastic," like Euripides's cyclops,
wanting and dying of love, destroying
his beloved in a storm of kisses, is now nothing more than a lion bitten and
    wounded by condors.

I am obsolete in "the assassinated Republic,"
and since the national pain is mine, the people's pain bores into my
    speech, tearing me apart,
as if all the starving children of Chile were my kin;
a tragic, Dionysian wreck in this vast assemblage of anguished lust, and the
    battle charge
crashes against sunset's raised ramparts,
discarded trumpets, broken bottles, tattered flags, bloodied by the
    martyrdom of minimum wage;
I hear death's rattle beneath the world
in snakes, in shotguns aimed at heads, in God, who never existed.

Hueso de estatua gritando en antiguos panteones, amarillo
y aterido como crucifijo de prostituta,
llorando estoy, botado, con el badajo de la campana del corazón hecho
    pedazos,
entre cabezas destronadas, trompetas enlutadas y cataclismos,
como carreta de ajusticiamiento, como espada de batallas perdidas en
    montañas, desiertos y desfiladeros, como zapato loco.

Anduve todos los caminos preguntando por el camino,
e intuyó mi estupor que una sola ruta, la muerte adentro de la muerte
    edificaba su ámbito adentro de la muerte,
reintegrándose en oleaje oscuro a su epicentro;
he llegado adonde partiera, cansado y sudando sangre como el Jesucristo
    de los olivos, yo que soy su enemigo;
y sé perfectamente que no va a retornar ninguno
de los actos pasados o antepasados, que son el recuerdo de un recuerdo
    como lloviendo años difuntos del agonizante ciclópeo,
porque yo siendo el mismo soy distinto, soy lo distinto mismo y lo mismo
    distinto;
todo lo mío ya es irreparable;
y la gran euforia alcohólica en la cual naufragaría el varón conyugal de
    entonces,
conmemorando los desbordamientos felices,
es hoy por hoy un vino terrible despedazando las vasijas o clavo ardiendo.

Tal como esos molos muertos del atardecer, los deseos y la
    ambición catastrófica,
están rumiando verdad deshecha y humo en los sepulcros de los
    estupendos panteones extranjeros, que son ríos malditos
a la orilla del mar de ceniza que llora abriendo su boca de tromba.

El garañón desenfrenado y atrabiliario, cuyos altos y anchos veinte
    años meaban las plazas públicas del mundo,
dueño del sexo de las doncellas más hermosas y de los lazos trenzados de
    doce corriones,

Like a headstone clamoring in old cemeteries, yellow
and numb as a prostitute's cross,
I'm crying and cast off with the broken heart's bell clapper,
among dethroned kings, mourning trumpets, and cataclysms;
like an execution cart, like the sword of battles lost in mountains, deserts,
and canyons, like a senseless old shoe.

I wandered all the roads asking about the road,
and they sensed my astonishment that a single route, death inside of death,
marked out its territory inside of death,
reintegrating itself into the dark waves of its epicenter;
weary and sweating blood like Jesus Christ of the olive trees, I, his enemy,
have come to where it would split;
and I know perfectly well that it will not restore any
past events or ancestors, that they are the memory of a memory,
encumbering the great dying man's final days,
for I, being similar, am distinct, I am similarly distinct and distinctly similar;
all that is mine is already irreparable;
and the great alcoholic euphoria in which the conjugal male would
once drown,
commemorating happy excesses,
is now a bad wine ruining the barrels, or a thorn in my side.

Like those ruined levees of dusk, wishes, and tragic ambition
dwell on repudiated truth and smoke in the tombs of those grand foreign
cemeteries, which are accursed rivers
at the edge of the ash sea that weeps by opening the mouth of its
whirlwind.

The wild and irascible stallion who for twenty long and drawn-out
years pissed on the world's public squares,
owner of the most beautiful maidens' sex and of whips braided from
twelve ropes,

da la lástima humillatoria del cazador de leones decrépito y dramático, al
cual la tormenta de las pasiones acumuladas como culebras en un torreón
hundido, lo azota;
me repugna la sexualidad pornográfica, y el cadáver de Pan enamorado de la
niña morena;
pero el viejo es de intuición y ensoñación e imaginación cínica como el niño
o el gran poeta a caballo en el espanto,
tremendamente amoral y desesperado, y como es todo un hombre a esas
alturas, anda
levantándoles las polleras a las hembras chilenas e internacionales y cayendo
de derrota en derrota en la batalla entre los hechos y los sueños;
es mentira la ancianidad agropecuaria y de égloga, porque el anciano se está
vengando, cuando el anciano se está creando su pirámide;
como aquellos vinos añejos, con alcohol reconcentrado en sus errores y ecos
de esos que rugen como sables o como calles llenas de suburbio,
desgarraríamos los toneles si pudiese la dinamita adolorida del espíritu
arrasar su condensación épica, y sol caído, su concentración trágica,
pero los abuelos sonríen en equivalente frustrados, no porque son
gangochos enmohecidos, sino rol marchito, pero con fuego adentro del
ánimo.

Sabemos que tenemos el coraje de los asesinados y los crucificados
por ideas,
la dignidad antigua y categórica de los guerreros de religión,
pero los huesos síquicos flaquean, el espanto cruje de doliente y se caen de
bruces los ríñones, los pulmones, los cojones de las médulas categóricas.

Agarrándonos a la tabla de salvación de la poesía, que es una gran
máquina negra,
somos los santos carajos y desocupados de aquella irreligiosidad horrenda
que da vergüenza porque desapareció cuando desapareció el último
"dios" de la tierra,
y la nacionalidad de la personalidad ilustre, se pudre de eminente y de
formidable como divino oro judío;
todo lo miramos en pasado, y el pasado, el pasado, el pasado es el porvenir
de los desengañados y los túmulos;
yo, en este instante, soy como un navío

deals out the humiliating shame that plagues the decrepit and dramatic
    lion hunter, whose tormented passions accumulate like snakes in a
    sunken tower;
I'm disgusted by pornographic sexuality, Pan's corpse enamored with the
    little brunette girl;
but the old man has intuition and fantasy and a skeptical imagination, like
    a child or a great poet on a frightened horse,
extremely amoral and desperate, and since he's all man at that age, he
    goes around
peeking under Chilean and foreign girls' skirts and suffering defeat after
    defeat in the battle between fact and fantasy;
the pastoral old age of eclogues is a lie, for the old man is seeking
    vengeance when he constructs his pyramid;
like those aged wines, with alcohol concentrated in its errors, with hints of
    warmongers or suburbia's busy streets,
we would crack open the barrels if the soul's tormented dynamite
    could obliterate his epic condensation, and at sunset, his tragic
    concentration,
but the grandparents smile in frustration, not because they're moldy old
    potato sacks, but because of their diminished role, with fire still inside
    their spirit.

    We know that we possess the courage of those murdered and
        crucified for ideas,
and the old, absolute dignity of religious warriors,
but our mental strength declines, our ghost creaks with suffering, and the
    kidneys, the lungs, and the heart and soul's balls fall to the ground.

    Clutching at the life preserver of poetry, the huge black machine,
we're the screwed saints dispossessed of that horrendous irreligiosity,
    shameful because it disappeared when the last "gods" on earth
    disappeared,
and the nationalism of the VIP reeks of power and privilege, like hallowed
    Jewish gold;
we look at everything in past tense, and the past, the past, the past is the
    future of the disillusioned and the burial mounds;
at this moment, I'm like a ship

que avanza mar afuera con todo lo remoto en las bodegas
y acordeones de navegaciones;
querríamos arañar la eternidad y a patadas, abofeteándola, agujerear su
    acerbo y colosal acero;
olorosos a tinajas y a tonelería o a la esposa fiel, a lágrima deshabitada,
a lo chileno postpretérito o como ruinoso y relampagueante, nuestros
    viejos sueños de antaño ya hogaño son delirio, nuestros viejos sueños
    de antaño,
son llanto usado y candelabros de espantajos, valores de orden y
    categorías sin vivencias.

        Envejeciendo con nosotros, la época en desintegración entra en
            coma, entra en sombra, entra toda
la gran tiniebla de quien rodase periclitando, pero por adentro le sacamos
    los nuevos estilos contra los viejos estilos arrastrándolos del infierno
    de los cabellos
restableciendo lo inaudito de la juventud, el ser rebelde, insurgente,
    silvestre e iconoclasta.

        La idolatrábamos, e idolatrándola, nos revolcábamos
en la clandestinidad de la mujer ajena y retornábamos como sudando lo
    humano, chorreando lo humano, llorando lo humano, o despavoridos
o acaso más humanos que lo más humano entre lo más humano, más
    bestias humanas, más error, más dolor, más terror,
porque el hombre es precisamente aquello, lo que deviene sublimidad en
    la gran caída, flor de victorias-derrotas llamando, gritando, llorando
    por lo desaparecido, como grandes, tremendos mares-océanos
    degollándose en oleajes,
criatura de aventura contra el destino, voz de los naufragios en los
    naufragios resplandeciendo, estrella de tinieblas,
ahora no caemos porque no podemos y como no caemos, a la misma
    altura, morimos, porque el cuero del cuerpo, como los viejos veleros,
    se prueba en la tormenta;
del dolor del error salió la poesía, del dolor del error
y el hombre enorme, contradictorio, aforme, acumulado, el hombre es el
    eslabón perdido de una gran cadena de miserias, el hombre expoliado
    y azotado por el hombre,

that goes out to sea with every fleeting memory in the hold and
accordions for navigation;
we wanted to round up eternity and beat it senseless, to pierce its bitter,
    colossal steel;
as if scented of jugs and water casks, or of the faithful wife, of the
    deserted tear,
of the Chilean post-preterite, or as if ruinous and glinting, our old dreams
    of yesteryear are now a delirium, our old dreams of yesteryear
are exhausted bouts of tears and phantoms' candelabras, just empty
    concepts and sequences.

      Aging with us, the disintegrating era enters a coma, enters a
          shadow, fully enters
the vast, sprawling darkness of deterioration, but from within it we bring
    out its new styles against the old styles, dragging them from hell by
    the hair,
restoring what's most extraordinary about youth: being rebellious,
    insurgent, wild, and iconoclastic.

      We idolized her, and idolizing her, we fell head over heels
into the conspiracy of foreign women, and we returned as if sweating the
    human, dripping the human, weeping the human, crying the human,
    the terror-stricken,
or possibly more human than the most human among the most human,
    more human beasts, more error, more pain, more terror,
for man is precisely all those things, those that become sublime in the
    great fall, the flower of victory—the defeats calling, screaming, crying
    for what's been lost, like great, tremendous seas—oceans annihilating
    themselves in surges,
a creature of adventure pitted against fate, the voice of shipwrecks among
    shining shipwrecks, a star in the darkness,
and now we don't fall because we can't, and since we can't fall to the
    same level, we die, for the body's hide, like old sailboats, is tested in
    the storm;
poetry came from the pain of failure, from the pain of failure
and from man, heinous, contradictory, formless, impugned, man is the link
    missing from a great chain of miseries, man robbed and beaten by man,

y hoy devuelvo a la especie la angustia individual;
adentro del corazón ardiendo nosotros la amamantamos con fracasos que
 son batallas completamente ganadas en literatura, contra la literatura;
la amamos y la amábamos con todo lo hondo del espíritu,
furiosos con nosotros, hipnotizados, horrorizados, idiotizados, con el ser
 montañés que eramos,
agrario-oceánicos de Chile, ahora es ceniza,
ceniza y convicción materialista, ceniza y desesperación helada, lo trágico
 enigmático, paloma del mundo e historia del mundo, y aquella belleza
 inmensa e idolatrada, Luisa Anabalón,
como un gran águila negra, nos está mordiendo las entrañas.

 Ruge la muerte con la cabeza ensangrentada y sonríe pateándonos,
y yo estoy solo, terriblemente solo, medio a medio de la multitud que amo
 y canto, solo y funeral como en la adolescencia, solo, solo entre los
 grandes murallones de las provincias despavoridas,
solo y vacío, solo y oscuro, solo y remoto, solo y extraño, solo y tremendo,
enfrentándome a la certidumbre de hundirme para siempre en las tinieblas
 sin haberla inmortalizado con barro llorado,
y extraño como un lobo de mar en las lagunas.

 Los años náufragos escarban, arañan, espantan
son demoníacos y ardientes como serpientes de azufre, porque son besos
 rugiendo, pueblos blandiendo la contradicción, gestos mordiendo,
el pan candeal quemado del presente, esta cosa hueca y siniestra de
 saberse derrumbándose,
cayendo al abismo abierto por nosotros mismos, adentro de nosotros
 mismos, con nosotros mismos
que nos fuimos cavando y alimentando de vísceras.

 Así se está rígido, en círculo, como en un ataúd redondo y como
 de ida y vuelta, aserruchando sombra, hachando sombra,
 apuñalando sombra,
viajando en un tren desorbitado y amargo que anda tronchado en tres
 mitades y llora inmóvil,

and today I return personal anguish to the species;
inside our impassioned heart we nurse her with our failures, battles fought
    entirely in literature, against literature;
we love her and we loved her from the depths of our soul,
furious with ourselves, hypnotized, horrified, stupefied, with the
    backwoods conviction that we were
agrarian-oceanic citizens of Chile, but now she's ash,
ash and materialistic conviction, ash and cold desperation, the enigmatic
    tragedy, the world's dove and the world's story...that immense and
    idolized beauty, Luisa Anabalón,
like a great black eagle, she snatches up our entrails as a memento.

    Death roars with a bloody head and smiles while abusing us,
and I'm alone, terribly alone, in the middle of the crowd that I love, and
    I sing, alone and depressed as in adolescence, alone, alone among the
    great ramparts of the terrified provinces,
alone and empty, alone and dark, alone and distant, alone and strange,
    alone and tremendous,
facing the certainty of always sinking in the darkness without having
    immortalized it in doleful clay,
out of place like a sea lion in the lagoons.

    The shipwreck years poke, claw, terrify,
they're demonic and ardent as the devils of hell, for they're raucous kisses,
    people brandishing the contradiction, snapping faces,
the burnt loaf of the present, this hollow and sinister affair of knowing how
    to self-destruct,
falling into the abyss opened by ourselves, within ourselves, the very selves
whose entrails we were digging out and eating.

    And so one becomes fixed, going around in circles, as if in a
        revolving coffin, on a round trip,
sawing the shadow, chopping the shadow, stabbing the shadow,
traveling on a derailed train, bitter to be cut in three halves and weeping
    silently,

sin itinerario ni línea, ni conductor, ni brújula,
y es como si todo se hubiese cortado la lengua entera con un pedazo de
andrajo.

Muertas las personas, las costumbres, las palabras, las ciudades en las
que todas las murallas están caídas, como guitarras de desolación, y
las hojas profundas, yertas,
yo ando tronando, desorientado, y en gran cantidad
melancólicamente uncido a antiguas cosas arcaicas que periclitaron, a maneras
de ser que son yerbajos o lagartos de ruinas,
y me parece que las vías públicas son versos añejos y traicionados o cirios
llovidos;
la emotividad épica se desgarra universalmente
en el asesinato general del mundo, planificado por los verdugos de los
pueblos, a la espalda de los pueblos entre las grandes alcantarillas de
dólares,
o cuando miramos al mistificador, ahíto de banquetes episcopales
hartarse de condecoraciones y dinero con pelos, hincharse y doparse
enmascarándose en una gran causa humana y refocilándose como un gran
demonio y un gran podrido y un gran engendro de Judas condecorado
de bienestar burgués sobre el hambre gigante de las masas, relajándolas y
humillándolas.

Encima de bancos de palo que resuenan como tabernas, como mítines,
como iglesias
o como sepulcros, como acordeones de ladrones de mar en las oceanías de las
cárceles o como átomos en desintegración,
sentados los ancianos me aguardan desde cinco siglos hace con los brazos
cruzados a la espalda,
a la espalda de las montañas huracanadas que les golpean los testículos,
arrojándolos a la sensualidad de la ancianidad, que es terrible, arrojándolos
a patadas de los hogares y de las ciudades, porque estos viejos lesos son todos
trágicos,
arrojándolos, como guiñapos o pingajos, a la nada quebrada de los apátridas a
los que nadie quiere porque nadie teme.

with neither itinerary, nor line, nor conductor, nor compass,
and it's as if everything's tongue had been cut out with a piece of rag.

    The people, the customs, the words, the cities in which all walls
        have fallen like guitars of desolation, they are dead, and the
        boundless leaves are motionless,
as I wander thundering, disoriented, and ever so melancholically yoked to
    old, archaic things that have fallen out of style, to manners
that are weeds or lizards in the ruins,
and it seems to me that public ways are stale and betrayed verses, or
    melted candles;
epic emotivity universally breaks down
in the general murder of the world, planned by the people's executioners,
    behind the people's backs, in the great sewers of dollars,
or while we're busy watching the bamboozler, glutted on Episcopal
    banquets,
satiated on decorations and minutiae, aggrandizing and drugging himself
    by touting a great human cause and reinventing himself as a great
    demon and a great crook and the great spawn of Judas, all dressed up
in bourgeois concern over the tremendous hunger of the masses, placating
    and humiliating them.

    Upon the woody banks that echo like taverns, like rallies, like
        churches
or like tombs, like pirates' accordions in the Oceania of prisons, or like
    atoms in disintegration,
the elders from five centuries ago sit and wait for me with their arms
    crossed behind their backs,
behind the mountains of hurricanes that pound their testicles, hurling
    them to old age's terrible embrace, throwing them
out of their homes and cities, for these wounded old men are all tragic,
sending them to the broken nothingness of exile like rag dolls or tatters,
    the things that no one wants, that no one fears.

Entiendo el infierno universal, y como no estoy viviendo en el techo
del cielo, me ofende personalmente la agresión arcangélica de la
Iglesia y del Estado,
el "nido de ratas", y la cínica metafísica de "el arte por el arte",
la puñalada oscuramente aceitada de flor y la cuchillada con serrucho
de los contemporáneos, que son panteón de arañas,
el ojo de lobo del culebrón literario, todo amarillo,
elaborando con desacatos la bomba cargada de versiones horizontales, la
manzana y la naranja envenenadas;
contemplo los incendios lamiendo los penachos muertos,
apuñalada la montaña en el estómago y el torreón de los extranjeros
derrumbándose,
veo como fuegos de gas formeno, veo como vientos huracanados los
fenómenos,
y desde adentro de las tinieblas a las que voy entrando por un portalón
con intuición de desesperación y costillares de ataúdes,
la antigua vida se me revuelve en las entrañas.

La miseria social me ofende personalmente,
y al resonar en mi corazón las altas y anchas masas humanas, las altas y
anchas masas de hoy,
como una gran tormenta me va cruzando, apenas
soy yo mismo íntegro porque soy mundo humano, soy el retrato bestial de
la sociedad partida en clases,
y hoy por hoy trabajo mi estilo arando los descalabros.

Las batallas ganadas son heridas marchitas, pétalos
de una gran rosa sangrienta,
por lo tanto combato de acuerdo con mi condición de insurgente, dando
al pueblo voz y estilo,
sabiendo que perderé la guerra eterna,
que como el todo me acosa y soy uno entero, mientras más persona
delcosmos asuma,
será más integral la última ruina;
parece que encienden lámparas en otro siglo del siglo, en otro
mundo del mundo ya caído, el olvido

I understand universal hell, and since I'm not living high in the sky,
      I am personally offended by the Church and State's archangelic
      aggression,
the "rat's nest," and the metaphysical clinic of "art for art's sake,"
the darkly flower-oiled knife wound and the handsaw gash of my
contemporaries, with their ghastly spider den,
the wolf's eye of the literary soap opera, pure yellow,
contemptuously building a bomb out of parallel texts, apples, and
      poisoned oranges;
I contemplate the flames licking the dead plumes,
the mountain stabbed in the stomach and the foreigners' turret
      self-destructing,
I see how fires of gas form, I see how winds ravage phenomena,
and from inside the darkness that I'm entering via a gateway of desperate
      intuition and coffin frames,
the old life stirs in my bowels.

      Social misery personally offends me,
and upon the ringing in my heart of the far and wide masses of humans,
      the far and wide masses of today,
like a great storm passing over me, soon
I myself am whole, for I am the human world, I am the brutal portrait of
      society split into classes,
and nowadays I work my style cultivating disasters.

      The victorious battles are withered wounds, petals
of a great bloody rose,
so I fight according to my insurgent condition, giving voice and style to
      the people,
knowing that I will lose the eternal war,
that as the totality menaces me and I am a single being, more human than
      the cosmos assumes,
the final ruin will be all the more thorough;
it seems they light lamps in a different century within the century, in another
world of the already fallen world, oblivion

echa violetas muertas en las tumbas y todo lo oscuro
se reúne en torno a mi sombra,
mi sombra, mi sombra a edad remota comparable o a batea de aldea en
    la montaña,
y el porvenir es un sable de sangre.

No atardeciendo paz, sino el sino furioso de los crepúsculos
    guillotinados,
la batalla campal de los agonizantes,
y la guerra oscura del sol contra sí mismo, la matanza
que ejecuta la naturaleza inmortal
y asesina, como comadrona de fusilamientos.

Esculpí el mito del mundo en las metáforas,
la imagen de los explotados y los azotados de mi época y di vocabulario
al ser corriente sometido al infinito,
multitudes y muchedumbres al reflejar mi voz su poesía, la poesía se
    sublimó en expresión de todos los pueblos,
el anónimo y el decrépito y el expósito hablaron su lengua
y emergió desde las bases la mitología general de Chile y el dolor colonial
    enarbolando su ametralladora;
militante del lenguaje nuevo, contra el lenguaje viejo enfilo mi caballo;
ahora las formas épicas que entraron en conflicto con los monstruos
    usados como zapatos de tiburón muerto,
o dieron batalla a los sirvientes de los verdugos de los sirvientes,
transforman las derrotas en victorias, que son derrotas victoriosas y son
    victorias derrotosas, el palo de llanto del fracaso en una rosa negra,
pero yo estoy ansioso a la ribera del suceder dialéctico, que es
    instantáneamente pretérito,
sollozando entre vinos viejos, otoños viejos, ritos viejos de las viejas
    maletas de la apostasía universal, protestando y pateando,
y el pabellón de la juventud resplandece de huracanes
despedazados, su canción vecinal y trágica como aquella paloma enferma,
    como un puñal de león enfurecido, como una sepultura viuda
o un antiguo difunto herido que se pusiera a llorar a gritos.

tosses dead violets into the tombs and all that is dark
gathers around my shadow,
my shadow, my shadow at a relatively distant age, at the village trough in
    the mountains,
and the future is a bloody sword.

      No peace at twilight, only the furious fate of the guillotined dusk,
the pitched battle of dying men,
and the sun's dark war against itself, the carnage
committed by immortal and murderous Mother Nature,
that midwife of executions.

      I sculpted the myth of the world in metaphors,
the image of my era's exploited and beaten, and I gave voice
to the ordinary being at the mercy of infinity,
crowds and throngs echoing my voice in poetry, poetry sublimated in the
    expression of all people,
the anonymous and the decrepit and the abandoned spoke its language,
and from the grassroots emerged the general mythology of Chile and
    colonial pain, waving its machine gun;
militant of the new language, opposing the old language that guided
    my horse;
the epic forms that engaged in conflict with monsters, out of date like
    sharkskin shoes,
or battled the servants of servants' executioners,
now transform defeats into victories, which are defeated victories and
    victorious defeats, the loser's flood of tears on a black rose,
but I am anxious at the shore of dialectical succession, which is instantly
    antiquated,
sobbing among old wines, autumns, old men, the old rites of old baggage
    of universal apostasy, kicking and screaming,
and the banner of the youth is resplendent with shreds of hurricane,
their song is tragic and close to home like a sick dove's, like the strike of
    enraged lion, like a widowed tomb
or the slain man who has begun to wail in agony.

Ya no se trilla a yegua ni se traduce a Heráclito, y Demócrito es
　　desconocido del gran artista, nadie ahora lee a Teognis de
　　Megara, ni topea en la ramada coral, amamantado con la
　　guañaca rural de la República,
el subterráneo familiar es la sub-conciencia o la in-conciencia que
　　alumbran pálidas o negras lámparas,
y todos los viajeros de la edad estamos como acuchillados y andamos
　　como ensangrentados de fantasmas y catástrofes,
quemados, chorreados, apaleados del barro con llanto de la vida,
con la muleta de la soledad huracanando las veredas y las escuelas.

　　Avanza el temporal de los reumatismos
y las arterias endurecidas son látigos que azotan el musgoso y mohoso y
　　lúgubre
caminar del sesentón, su cara de cadáver apaleado,
porque se van haciendo los viejos piedras de sepulcros,
tumba y respetuosidad, es decir: la hoja caída y la lástima,
el sexo del muerto que está boca-arriba adentro de la tierra,
como vasija definitivamente vacía.

　　Como si fuera otro volveré a las aldeas de la adolescencia,
y besaré la huella difunta de su pie florido y divino como el vuelo de un
　　picaflor o un prendedor de brillantes,
pero su cintura de espiga melancólica ya no estará en mis brazos.

　　No bajando, sino subiendo al final secular, gravita la senectud
　　despavorida,
son los dientes caídos como antiguos acantilados a la orilla del mar
　　innumerable que deviene un panteón ardiendo,
la calavera erosionada y la pelambrera
como de choclo abandonado en las muertas bodegas, esas están heladas y
　　telarañosas
en las que el tiempo aúlla como perro solo, y el velámen
de los barcos sonando a antaño está botado en las alcantarillas del gusano;
es inútil ensillar la cabalgadura
de otrora, y galopar por el camino real llorando y corcoveando con caballo
　　y todo

In a time when nobody thrashes whores or translates Heraclitus,
and Democritus is unknown to the great artist, when no
one reads Theognis of Megara or happens upon branches
of coral, the familiar foundation, suckled by the Republic's
domesticated goat,
is the subconscious or unconscious that lights pale or black lamps,
and all of us aged travelers are like stab victims, we go around like we're
afflicted by ghosts or catastrophes,
burnt, soaked, and battered by the mud, a lifetime of tears,
with solitude's crutch stomping sidewalks and schools like a hurricane.

The days of rheumatism advance
and hardened arteries are whips that lash at the mossy and moldy and
gloomy
path of a man in his sixties, his cadaver face battered,
because old men become signposts for graves, tombs, and solemnity:
the limp leaf and the shame,
the genitalia of the dead man face-up inside the earth,
like a vessel that's decidedly empty.

As if I were another, I'll return to the villages of my adolescence,
and I'll kiss the vanished prints of her foot, florid and divine like the flight
of a hummingbird or a brooch of diamonds,
but my arms will no longer embrace her waist of melancholy herringbone.

Not falling, but rising to the secular end, terrifying old age
encroaches,
with teeth that fall away like old cliffs on the shore of the fathomless sea,
which becomes a burning cemetery,
the eroded skeleton and the shock of hair
like cornsilk left in dead cellars, freezing and covered in cobwebs,
where time howls like a solitary dog, and the boat sails
reminiscent of the past get thrown into sewers of maggots;
it's useless to saddle another's
beast of burden, and to gallop along the main road crying and grumbling,
horse and all,

o disparar un grito de revólver,
los aperos crujen porque sufren como el costillar del jinete
que no es la bestia chilena y desenfrenada
con mujeres sentadas al anca, estremeciendo los potreros de sus capitanías.

La gran quimera de la vida humana
como un lobo crucificado o aquella dulce estrella a la cual mataran todos
    los hijos
yace como yacen yaciendo los muertos adentro del universo.

"Caín, Caín, ¿qué hiciste de tu hermano?",
dice el héroe de la senectud cavando con ensangrentado estupor su sepulcro,
la historia le patea la cabeza como una vaca rubia derrumbándolo barranca
    abajo,
pero es leyenda él, categoría, sueño del viento acariciando los naranjos
    atrabiliarios de su juventud,
don melancólico, y la última cana del alma
se le derrama como la última hoja del álamo o la última gota de luz
    estremeciendo los desiertos.

Parten los trenes del destino, sin sentido, como navíos de fantasmas.

Los victoriosos están muertos, los derrotados están muertos,
cuando la ancianidad apunta la escopeta negra, estupenda, en los órganos
    desesperados como caballo de soldado desertor,
todos, no nosotros en lo agonal agonizantes, todos están agonizando, todos
pero el agonizante soy yo, yo soy el agonizante entre batallas, entre
    congojas, entre banderas y fusiles, solo, completamente solo, y lúgubre,
    sin editor, plagiado y abandonado en el abismo,
peleando con escombros azotados,
peleando con el pretérito, por el pretérito, adentro del pretérito, en
    pretericiones horribles,
peleando con el futuro, completamente desnudo
hasta la cintura, peleando y peleando con todos vosotros,

or to let off a revolver's cry,
the harnesses creaking, suffering like the ribs of the rider
who is not that unbridled Chilean beast
with women at his haunches, working their captain's pastures.

The Great Chimera of human life,
like a crucified wolf or that sweet star under which they'll slaughter all
the children,
lies as the dead lie deep inside the universe.

"Cain, Cain, what did you do with your brother?"
says the hero in his sixties, digging his grave in a blood-soaked stupor,
history
kicks his head like a ruddy cow, sending him down a hill,
but he's a legend, an archetype, a dream of wind caressing the caustic
idiots of his youth,
Mr. Melancholy, and the soul's last gray hair
falls out like the poplar's last leaf or the last drop of light quivering over
the desert.

Destiny's trains depart, senseless as a ship of ghosts.

The victorious are dead, the defeated are dead,
and when old age points a black, stupendous shotgun at organs desperate
as a deserter's horse,
everyone, not just us in the throes of death, everyone is in the throes of
death, everyone,
but I am the one in death throes, I am the one in the throes of death,
among battles, among anguishes, among flags and rifles, alone,
completely alone, and gloomy, without an editor, plagiarized and left in
the abyss,
battling with thrashed debris,
battling with the past, for the past, inside the past, on bad terms,
battling with the future, completely naked
to the waist, battling and battling with all of you

por la grandeza y la certeza de la pelea,
peleando y contra-peleando a la siga maldita de la inmortalidad ajusticiada.

  Entre colchones que ladran y buques náufragos con dentadura de
   prostitutas enfurecidas o sapos borrachos, ladrones y cabrones
   empapelados con pedazos de escarnio,
agarrándose a una muralla por la cual se arrastran enormes arañas con
 ojo viscoso
o hermafroditas con cierto talento de caracol haciendo un arte mínimo con
 pedacitos de atardecer amarillo, nos batimos a espada con el oficio del
 estilo,
cuando en los andamios de los transatlánticos
como pequeños simios con chaleco despavorido, juegan a la ruleta los
 grandes poetas de ahora.

  Cien puñales de mar me apuñalaron
y la patada estrangulada
de lo imponderable, fue la ley provincial del hombre pobre que se opone al
 pobre hombre y es maldito,
vi morir, refluir a la materia enloquecida, llorando
a la más amada de las mujeres, tronchado, funerario, estupefacto, mordido
 de abismos,
baleado y pateado por los fusileros del horror, y en tales instantes espero los
 acerbos días de la calavera que adviene cruzando los relámpagos con la
 cuchilla entre los dientes.

  Voy a estallar adentro del sepulcro suicidándome en cadáver.

  Como si rugiera desde todo lo hondo de los departamentos y las
   provincias
de pétalos y jergones de aldea o mediaguas
descomunales, o por debajo de los barrios sobados como látigos de triste
 jinete, embadurnados con estiércol de ánimas
o siúticos ajusticiados, con sinuosidades y bellaquerías de una gran mala
 persona,
acomodado a las penumbras y las culebras, clínico, el complejo de
 inferioridad y resentimiento

for the greatness and certainty of battle,
battling and retaliating against the damned pursuit of a condemned
  immortality.

Among clamoring mattresses and ships wrecked by the teeth of
  angry prostitutes, drunken gossips, burglars and bastards
  plastered in scraps of ridicule,
clinging to a wall crawling with huge, viscous-eyed spiders
or hermaphrodites with a certain snail-like talent for making minimalist art
  with little dabs of dusky yellow, we bat ourselves with the tastemaker's
  sword
when the great modern poets play roulette
on the gangways of transatlantic ships like miniature apes in straitjackets.

One hundred sea daggers stabbed me
and the poor man's provincial law against the poor man was an accursed,
  asphyxiating blow, unimaginable;
I saw the most beloved of women die,
the crazed substance flow out, flow back, I wept
and was broken, funereal, stunned, bitten by abysses,
shot and beaten by horror's riflemen, and at every moment
I await the cruel days of the skull that arrives across flashes of lightning
  with a knife between its teeth.

I'm going to explode in the grave killing my own corpse.

As if it were rumbling from the deepest depths of the districts and
  provinces
of petals, from the straw pallets of villages, from hideous
shanties, from beneath neighborhoods worn as a sad cowboy's whips and
  smeared with the shit of souls
and executed snobs, as if it possessed the wiles and guile of a very bad man,
as if it were accustomed to snakes and darkness, as if it were clinical, the
  resentment-inferiority complex

se asoma roncando en las amistosidades añejas,
con el gran puñal-amistad chorreado de vino, chorreado de adulaciones,
   chorreado de sebo comunal,
y al agarrar la misericordia, y azotar con afecto al fantasma,
sonríe el diente de oro de la envidia, la joroba social, lo inhibidísimo, la
   discordia total, subterránea, en la problemática del fracasado,
escupiéndonos los zapatos abandonados en las heroicas bravuras antiguas.

   Todos los ofidios hacen los estilos disminuidos de las alcobas e
      invaden la basura de la literatura,
de la literatura universal, que es la pequeña cabeza tremenda del jíbaro de la
   época, agarrándose del cogote del mundo, agarrándose de los calzoncillos
   de "Dios", agarrándose de los estropajos del sol, de la literatura del éxito,
el aguardiente pálido y pornográfico de los académicos o formalistas u
   onanistas o figuristas o asesinos descabezados o pervertidos
sexuales con el vientre rugiente como una catedral o una diagonal entre
   Sodoma y Gomorra, la cama de baba con las orejas negras como un huevo
   de difunto
o un veneno letal administrado por carajos eclesiásticos,
y el Arte Grande y Popular les araña la guata de murciélagos del infierno con
   fierros ardiendo, el abdomen
de rana o de ramera para el día domingo.

   Aquestas personas horrendas, revolcándose
en el pantano de los desclazados del idealismo o masturbándose o
   suicidándose a patadas ellos contra ellos,
mientras el denominador común humano total se muere de hambre
en las cavernas de la civilización, y "la cultura capitalista" desgarra a
   dentelladas
la desgracia de la infancia proletaria con el Imperialismo, o la tuberculosis
es una gran señora que se divierte fotografiando los moribundos
estimulándose las hormonas con la caridad sádico-metafísica, especie de
   brebaje de degolladores,
y la clase rectora, tan idiota como habilísima e imbécil,
nos alarga un litro de vino envenenado o un gobierno de carabinas…

rears its ugly head in old friendships,
with the great friendship dagger dripping with wine, with flattery, dripping
   with communal lard,
and upon seizing mercy and whipping the ghost with affection,
it smiles with the gold teeth of envy, of the social grind, of super-inhibition,
   the total discord deep down within the loser's problems,
spitting on the shoes we abandoned during our old brave heroics.

   All those snakes write bedroom scenes with no style and populate
      the literature of filth,
world literature, the tremendously puny brain of the contemporary
   dimwit, grabbing hold of the world's neck, grabbing hold of the
   underwear of "God," grabbing hold of the sun's castoffs, of best-selling
   literature,
the pale and pornographic booze of academics, formalists, onanists,
   figurists, demented killers, sexual perverts
with bellies that rumble like cathedrals, like a street through Sodom and
   Gomorrah, the drool-stained bed with ears as black as a dead man's
   sperm,
a lethal poison administered by priestly pricks,
and Popular and Great Art scratches the bellies of the bats of hell with hot
   pokers, the stomachs
of frogs or of whores in honor of Sunday.

   These hideous people, wallowing
in the swamp of downwardly mobile idealists, stroking themselves or
   killing themselves by beating the shit out of themselves,
while the total human common denominator starves to death
in civilization's caves, and "capitalist culture" chews apart the children of
   the proletariat through Imperialism or tuberculosis,
a great lady who enjoys photographing the dying,
stimulating her hormones with sado-metaphysical charity, that special
   elixir of executioners
and the ruling class, as idiotic as they are overeducated and imbecilic,
handing us a liter of poisoned wine or a semi-automatic government...

Medio a medio de este billete con heliotropos agusanados
o demagogos de material plástico o borrachos anti-dionisíacos simoníacos
   o demoníacos,
nuestra heroicidad vieja de labriegos
se afirma en los estribos huracanados y afila la cuchilla, pero pelea con la
   propia, terrible sombra
enfrentándose al cosmopolita
desde todo lo hondo de la nacionalidad a la universalidad lanzada
y estrujándose el corazón, se extrae el lenguaje.

La soledad heroica nos confronta con la ametralladora y el ajenjo
      del inadaptado
y nos enfrenta a la bohemia del piojo sublime del romanticismo,
entonces, o ejecutamos como ejecutamos, la faena de la creación oscura y
   definitiva en el anonimato universal arrinconándonos, o caemos
de rodillas en el éxito por el éxito, aclamados y coronados
por picaros y escandalosos, vivientes y sirvientes del banquete civil,
   acomodados a la naipada, comedores en panteones de panoplias y
   botellas metafísicas,
porque el hombre ama la belleza y la mujer retratándolas
y retratándose como proceso y como complejo, en ese vórtice que sublima
   lo cuotidiano en lo infinito.

Completamente ahítos como queridos de antiguos monarcas más o
      menos pelados, desintegrados y rabones,
caminan por encima de la realidad gesticulando,
creyendo que el sueño es el hecho, que disminuyendo se logran síntesis y
   categorías, que la manea es la grandeza
y aplaudidos por enemigos nos insultan,
como cadáveres de certámenes enloquecidos que se pusiesen de pie de
   repente, rajando los pesados gangochos en los que estaban forrados y
   amortajados a la manera de antaño,
llorando y pataleando, gritando y pataleando en mares de sangre
   inexorable,
dopados con salarios robados en expoliaciones milenarias y cavernarias
   ejecuciones de cómplices.

In the center of this bill with its wormy heliotropes
or fake plastic demagogues or anti-Dionysian drunks, simonists or
    satanists,
our old peasant heroism
is affirmed in our tempestuous rages and it sharpens our blade, but the
    fight with one's own formidable shadow,
clashing with the cosmopolitan
from the depths of nationality to presumptuous universality and wringing
its heart, is how language gets made.

    Heroic solitude arms us with a machine gun and the misfit's
        absinthe
and pits us against the Bohemia of romanticism's sublime lice,
and then we create the way we create, our labor of obscure and final
    creation in reclusive, worldwide anonymity, rather than fall to our
knees for success after success, acclaimed and crowned
by charlatans and gossips, servants and patrons of the civil banquet,
    cardsharps, those who dine in the pantheons of metaphysical
    panoplies and bottles,
for man loves beauty and woman, portraying them
and portraying himself as a process and as a complex, in that vortex which
    sublimates the everyday in the infinite.

    Totally fed up like the darlings of old, half-broke monarchs,
        moldering and stubby,
they walk all over reality, gesticulating,
believing that the dream is the deed, that oppression creates synthesis and
    order, that shackles are a blessing,
and, lauded by our enemies, they insult us,
like corpses from mad contests suddenly risen from the dead, tearing away
    the heavy sheets in which they were wrapped and shrouded in the
    old style,
crying and kicking, screaming and kicking in seas of inexorable blood
    tainted
with wages stolen in thousand-year-old pillagings and prehistoric
    executions of conspirators.

El aullido general de la miseria imperialista da la tónica a mi rebelión,
    escribo con cuchillo
y pólvora, a la sombra de las pataguas de Curicó, anchas como vacas,
los padecimientos de mi corazón y del corazón de mi pueblo, adentro del
    pueblo y los pueblos del mundo y el relincho de los caballos desensillados
    o las bestias chúcaras.

    Y como yo ando buscando los pasos perdidos de lo que no existió
        nunca,
o el origen del hombre en el vocabulario, la raíz animal de la Belleza con
    estupor y errores labrada, y la tónica de las altas y anchas muchedumbres
    en las altas y anchas multitudes del país secular de Chile,
el ser heroico está rugiendo en nuestra épica nueva, condicionado por el
    espanto nacional del contenido;
como seguramente lloro durmiendo a lágrimas piramidales que estallan, las
    escrituras que son sueño sujeto a una cadena inexorable e imagen que
    nadie deshace ni comprendió jamás, arrastran las napas de sangre
que corren por debajo de la Humanidad y al autodegollarse en el lenguaje,
    organizándolo, el lenguaje mío
me supera, y mi cabeza es un montón de escombros que se incendian, una
    guitarra muerta, una gran casa de dolor abandonada;
el junio o julio helado me abrigan de sollozos
y aunque estos viejos huesos de acero vegetal se oponen a la invasión de la
    nada que avanza con su matraca espeluznante,
comprendo que transformo fuerzas por aniquilamiento y devengo otro suceso
    en la naturaleza.

    Oh! antiguo esplendor perdido entre monedas y maletas de cementerio,
        oh! pathos clásico,
oh! atrabiliario corazón enamorado de una gran bandera despedazada,
la desgracia total, definitiva está acechándonos con su bandeja de cabezas
    degolladas en el desfiladero.

    Retornan los vacunos del crepúsculo tranco a tranco,
a los establos lugareños, con heno tremendo, porque los asesinarán a la
    madrugada,

The ubiquitous howl of imperialist poverty sets the tone for my
        rebellion,
and in the shadow of Curicó's patagua trees, wide as cows, I write with a
        knife and gunpowder
of my heart's anguish and my village's heart, inside of my village and the
        villages of the world and the grunts of unbridled horses or wild beasts.

        And as I go searching for the lost traces of that which never existed,
or for man's origin in the dictionary, for the animal root of Beauty with
        stupor and error stitched in, and for the tenor of the vast crowds in the
        vast multitudes of Chile's secular country,
the heroic self is roaring in our new epic, conditioned by the national fear
        of content;
as I cry myself to sleep with explosions of pyramidal tears, the writings
        which are sleep linked to an inexorable chain and an image that no one
        ever resolved or understood drag the aquifers of blood
that run from below Humanity up to self-annihilation in language,
        organizing it, and my language
exceeds me, my head is a mound of garbage that catches fire, a dead guitar,
        a mansion of abandoned pain;
icy June and July, they warm me with sobs,
and although these old bones of vegetable steel oppose the invasion of the
        nothingness that approaches with its ghastly rattle,
I'm aware that I trade power for annihilation and become just another
        event in nature.

        Oh! old splendor lost among the cemetery's coins and trunks, oh!
        classical pathos,
oh! ill-tempered heart in love with a great, tattered flag,
total disgrace is stalking us in the canyon with its platter of severed heads.

        Step by step the cattle of twilight return
to the imposing hay bales of the local stables to be killed at dawn,

y rumiando se creen felices al aguardar la caricia de la cuchilla,
el hombre, como el toro o como el lobo se derrumba en su lecho que es acaso
   su sepulcro,
contento como jumento de panadería.

Si todos los muertos se alzasen de adentro de todos los viejos, entre
   matanzas y campanas,
se embanderaría de luz negra la tierra, e iría
como un ataúd cruzando lo oceánico con las alas quebradas de las arboladuras.

A la agonía de la burguesía, le corresponde esta gran protesta social
   de la poesía revolucionaria, y los ímpetus dionisíacos tronchados o
   como bramando
por la victoria universal del comunismo,
o relampagueando a la manera de una gran espada o cantando como el pan
   en la casa modesta
emergen de la sociedad en desintegración que reflejo
en acusaciones públicas, levantadas como barricadas en las encrucijadas
   del arte;
mis poemas son banderas y ametralladoras,
salen del hambre nacional hacia la entraña de la explotación humana,
y como rebota en Latinoamérica
el impacto mundial de la infinita energía socialista que asoma en las auroras
   del proletariado rugiente,
saludo desde adentro del anocheciendo la calandria madrugadora;
y aunque me atore de adioses que son espigas y vendimias de otoños muy
   maduros,
el levantamiento general de las colonias, los azotados y los fusilados de la
   tierra encima del ocaso de los explotadores y la caída de la esclavitud
   contra los propios escombros de sus verdugos,
una gran euforia auroral satura mis padecimientos
y resuena la trompeta de la victoria en los quillayes y los maitenes del sol
   licantenino.

Parezco un general caído en las trincheras,
ajusticiado y sin embargo acometedor en grande coraje: capaz de matar por la
   libertad o la justicia,

and as they chew they believe they're happy awaiting the stroke of the
   blade;
man, like a bull or a wolf, collapses on a bed that may also be his grave,
content as the village idiot.

   If all of the ghosts rose up from within all the old men, halfway
         between massacre and celebration,
the earth would wrap itself in black light, and it would head on
like a coffin crossing the ocean with broken sails.

   This great social protest of revolutionary poetry is due to the agony
         of the bourgeoisie, and the Dionysian impulse, as if crippled,
         bellowing
for communism's worldwide victory,
or as if flashing like a great sword or singing like bread in a modest home,
emerges from the disintegrating society that I address
in public pronouncements set up like barricades at the crossroads of art;
my poems are flags and machine guns,
they exit the national hunger via the bowels of human exploitation,
and, as the global impact of infinite socialist energy that looms in the dawn
   of the roaring proletariat
rebounds in Latin America,
I greet the morning lark from inside of dusk;
and although I'm choked up with good-byes, the final harvests and
   vintages of ripest autumn,
the general revolt of the world's colonies, the beaten and shot atop
   the fall of their exploiters and slavery's collapse upon the rubble of
   slavemasters,
it saturates my suffering with a great dawning euphoria
and the trumpet of victory resounds among the lupine sun's soapbarks
   and evergreens.

   I'm like a general fallen in the trenches,
condemned yet still a courageous aggressor: able to kill for freedom or
   justice,

dolorido y convencido de todo lo heroico del Arte Grande,
bañando de recuerdos tu sepulcro que se parece a una inmensa religión atea,
a plena conciencia de la inutilidad de todos los lamentos,
porque ya queda apenas de la divina, peregrina, grecolatina flor, la voz de las
    generaciones.

Indiscutiblemente soy pueblo ardiendo,
entraña de roto y de huaso, y la masa humana me duele, me arde, me ruge
en la médula envejecida como montura de inquilino del Mataquito,
por eso comprendo al proletariado no como pingajo de oportunidades
    bárbaras,
sino como hijo y padre de esa gran fuerza concreta de todos los pueblos,
que empuja la historia con sudor heroico y terrible
sacando del arcano universal la felicidad del hombre, sacando del andrajo
    espigas y panales.

Los demonios enfurecidos con un pedazo de escopeta en el hocico, o
    el antiguo y eximio
caimán de terror desensillándose, revolcándose, refocilándose,
entre escobas de fuego y muelas de piedra y auroras de hierro gasificado
piden que me fusilen,
y mis plagiarios que me ahorquen con un sapo de santo en el cogote.

Luchando con endriagos y profetas
emboscados en grandes verdades, con mártires de títeres
hechos con zapatos viejos
en material peligrosísimo y de pólvora, usados por debajo del cinturón
    reglamentario,
enfermó mi estupor cordillerano de civilización urbana;
en tristes, terribles sucesos, no siembro trigo como los abuelos, siembro
    gritos de rebelión en los pueblos hambrientos,
la hospitalidad provincial empina la calabaza y nos emborrachamos
como dioses que devienen pobres, se convierten en atardeceres públicos y
    echan la pena afuera
dramáticamente, caballos de antaño,
y emerge el jinete de la épica social americana todo creando solo;

pained by and convinced of everything heroic about Great Art,
turning it into an immense atheistic religion by bathing your grave in
    memories,
fully aware of the futility of all the laments,
because there's hardly anything left of the divine, the pilgrim, the Greco-
    Roman flower, the generational voice.

Without question, I am the burning populace,
the essence of the common man and the peasant, and the human mass
    pains me, inflames me, it roars
in my core that's worn down like a Mataquito tenant farmer's saddle,
that's why I think of the proletariat not as an ill-fated mess, but
as son and father to that great concrete strength of the entire population,
which drives history forward with terrible, heroic labor,
extracting man's happiness through general alchemy, extracting seeds and
    sweets from debris.

The furious devils wearing gun parts on their faces, and the old and
        distinguished
alligator of terror unsaddling himself, reveling, delighting,
among sweeps of fire and mounds of stone and the dawn of iron clouds
they order that I be shot,
that my imitators string me up with a saintly toad around my neck.

Fighting with demons and prophets cloaked in great truths,
with martyrs of puppets made from old shoes in highly dangerous and
    explosive material, not the regulation stuff,
I poisoned my Andean wonder with urban civilization;
during miserable and terrible times I don't plant wheat like my
    grandparents, I plant cries of rebellion in starving people,
provincial hospitality raises the chalice and we get drunk
like gods who've gone broke, yesteryear's horse now plain twilight,
    dramatically casting aside
its sorrow, and the horseman of the American social epic emerges, creating
    everything on his own;

recuerdo al amigo Rabelais y al compadre

Miguel de Cervantes, tomando mi cacho labrado en los mesones de las tabernas
   antiquísimas, las bodegas y las chinganas flor de invierno, y agarro

de la solapa de la chaqueta a la retórico-poética del siútico edificado con
   escupitajos de cadáver,

comparto con proletarios, con marineros, con empleados, con campesinos de
   "3ª clase", mi causeo y mi botella,

bebo con arrieros y desprecio a la intelectualidad podrida.

A la aldea departamental llegaron los desaforados, y un sigilo de
   alpargatas

se agarró del caserón de los tatarabuelos,

entre las monturas y las coyundas sacratísimas del polvoso antepasado remoto,

la culebra en muletas del clandestinaje te habita,

el tinterillo y el asesino legal hacen sonar sus bastones de ladrones y de
   camaleones de la gran chancleta

y la mala persona arrojó a las mandíbulas del can aventurero

la heredad desgarradoramente familiar de las montañas de Licantén y las vegas
   nativas de los costinos en donde impera la lenteja real de Jacob y Esaú y la
   pregunta blanca de la gaviota.

Como billete sucio en los bolsillos del pantalón del alma

el tiempo inútil va dejando su borra de toneles desocupados, y echando
   claveles de acaeceres marchitos a la laguna de la amargura;

buscamos lo rancio en las despensas y en la tristeza: el queso viviendo muerto
   en los múltiplos de las oxidaciones que estallan como palancas, las canciones

arcaicas y la penicilina de los hongos remotos, con sombrero de catástrofes.

El nombre rugiente va botado, encadenado, ardiendo

como revólver rojo a la cintura del olvido, como ramo de llanto, como hueso de
   viento, como saco de cantos o consigna ineluctable,

como biblioteca sin bibliotecario, como gran botella

oceánica, como bandera de quijadas de oro, y dicen las gentes por debajo del
   poncho:

"renovó con *Los Gemidos* la literatura castellana",

como quien hablara de un muerto ilustre a la orilla del mar desaparecido.

I think of my friend Rabelais and my buddy
Miguel de Cervantes drinking from my well-worn cup in the inns of ancient
     taverns, in hole-in-the-wall wineries and dive-bars, and I grab
the poser's corpse spit–enriched rhetorical poetics by the lapels,
share my cause and my bottle with proletarians, with sailors, with clerks,
     with "third-class" farmers,
drink with mule-drivers and spit on the rotten intelligentsia.

          The outlaws came to the main village, and a gang of roughnecks
captured my great-great-grandparents' manor,
now the shady, limping loan shark lives
among my dusty old forebears' saddles and hallowed yokes,
the bureaucrat and the crooked lawyer round up their cadre of slipshod
     flatterers and thieves
and to the jaws of an imperialist cur the villain tossed the plundered family
     estate of the Licantén mountains, of the coast's native plains, where
     Jacob and Esau's real lentils and the seagull's blank question reign.

          Like dirty bills in the soul's pant pockets,
wasted time keeps giving up its hoard of idle vessels and casting
bouquets of dwindling scenes into the lagoon of bitterness;
we look for what's rotten in the pantry and in grief: cheese both alive and
     dead from so many oxidations that erupt like machines, the old
songs and the penicillin of exotic mushrooms with catastrophic caps.

          The roaring name gets cast aside, shackled, burning
like a red gun at the waist of oblivion, like a bouquet of tears, like a bone of
     wind, like a bag of songs, like an urgent command,
like a library without a librarian, like a giant bottle on the ocean,
like the insignia of the golden jaw, and the man on the street says,
"Renew Spanish literature with *The Wailing*,"
like he's talking about an illustrious death on the shore of a lost sea.

Contra la garra bárbara de Yanquilandia
que origina la poesía del colonialismo en los esclavos y los cipayos
    ensangrentados, contra la guerra, contra la bestia imperial, yo levanto
el realismo popular constructivo, la epopeya embanderada de dolor
    insular, heroica y remota en las generaciones,
sirvo al pueblo en poemas y si mis cantos son amargos y acumulados de
    horrores ácidos y trágicos o atrabiliarios como océanos en libertad,
yo doy la forma épica al pantano de sangre caliente clamando por debajo
    en los temarios americanos;
la caída fatal de los imperios económicos refleja en mí su panfleto de
    cuatrero vil, yo lo escupo transformándolo en imprecación y en
    acusación poética, que emplaza las masas en la batalla por la liberación
    humana, y tallando
el escarnio bestial del imperialismo
lo arrojo a la cara de la canalla explotadora, a la cara de la oligarquía
    mundial, a la cara de la aristocracia feudal de la República
y de los poetas encadenados con hocico de rufianes intelectuales;
gente de fuerte envergadura, opongo la bayoneta de la insurgencia colonial
    a la retórica capitalista,
el canto del macho anciano, popular y autocrítico
tanto al masturbador artepurista, como al embaucador populachista, que
    entretiene a las muchedumbres y frena las masas obreras,
y al anunciar la sociedad nueva, al poema enrojecido de dolor nacional, le
    emergen
por adentro de las rojas pólvoras, grandes guitarras dulces, y la sandía
    colosal la alegría

No ingresaremos al huracán de silencio con huesos
de las jubilaciones públicas, a conquistar criadas y a calumniar los
    polvorosos ámbitos
jamás, el corazón sabrá rajarse en el instante preciso y definitivo
como la castaña muy madura haciendo retumbar los extramuros,
haciendo rodar, bramando, llorar la tierra inmensa de las sepulturas

Against the barbaric claw of Yankeeland,
where colonial poetry originates within slaves and blood-soaked Indians,
     against the war, against the imperial beast, I establish
popular constructivist realism, the epic adorned with provincial pain,
     heroic and spanning generations,
I serve the people in poems, and if my songs are bitter and horrific, harsh
     and tragic, ill-tempered as unruly oceans,
that's because I give epic form to the swamp of boiling blood clamoring
     beneath American agendas;
the fatal downfall of economic empires reveals to me its loathsome horse-
     thief propaganda, and I spit it out transforming it into blasphemy
     and poetic indictment, which summons the masses in the struggle for
     human liberation, and incorporating
the brutal ridicule of imperialism,
I throw it in the face of the exploitative swine, in the face of the global
     oligarchy, in the face of the feudal aristocracy of the Republic,
and in the faces of the poets who are chained to the snouts of intellectual
     thugs;
vips, I raise the bayonet of colonial insurgency against your capitalist
     rhetoric,
the song of the old man, vernacular and self-critical,
as much for the writerly masturbator as it is for the populist impostor who
     entertains the throngs and holds back the working masses,
and upon announcing a new society, from inside this poem tinged with
     national pain sprout
red fireworks, large handmade guitars and the humongous watermelon
     of ecstasy.

We won't ever buy into the hurricane of silence with the bones
of public pensions in order to win the affection of maids and to slander
     their dusty ways,
but like an overripe chestnut the heart will know to break open at the very
     last minute,
causing the outskirts to rumble, to
upend, roaring, and the vast tracts of tombs to weep.

Si no fui más que un gran poeta con los brazos quebrados
y el acordeón del Emperador de los aventureros o el espanto del mar me
    llamaban al alma,
soy un guerrero del estilo como destino, apenas,
un soñador acongojado de haber soñado y estar soñando, un "expósito" y un
    "apátrida"
de mi época, y el arrepentimiento
de lo que no hicimos, corazón, nos taladra las entrañas
como polilla del espíritu, aserruchándonos.

    A la luz secular de una niña muerta, madre de hombres y mujeres, voy
        andando y agonizando.

    El cadáver del sol y mi cadáver
con la materia horriblemente eterna, me azotan la cara desde todo, lo hondo
    de los siglos, y escucho
aquí, llorando, así, la espantosa clarinada migratoria.

    No fui dueño de fundo, ni marino, ni atorrante, ni contrabandista o
        arriero cordillerano,
mi voluntad no tuvo caballos ni mujeres en la edad madura
y a mi amor lo arrasó la muerte azotándolo con su aldabón tronchado,
    despedazado e inútil y su huracán oliendo a manzana asesinada.

    Contemplándome o estrellándome
en todos los espejos rotos de la nada, polvoso
y ultrarremoto desde el origen.

    El callejón de los ancianos muere donde mueren las últimas águilas.…

    Soy el abuelo y tú una inmensa sombra,
el gran lenguaje de imágenes inexorables, nacional-internacional, inaudito
y extraído del subterráneo universal, engendra
la calumnia, la difamación, la mentira, rodeándome de chacales
    ensangrentados que me golpean la espalda,
y cuando yo hablo ofendo el rencor anormal del pequeño;

If I was no more than a great poet with broken arms
and the pirate emperor's accordion or the menacing ocean called my soul,
at least I am a warrior of style as destiny,
a dreamer dismayed at having dreamed and at dreaming, a "foundling"
    and a "refugee"
of my era, and regret for
what we did not do, my love, chews up our insides
like moths of the spirit, bringing us down.

      I go walking and dying by the secular light of a dead girl, mother to
    men and women.

      The sun's corpse and my corpse
with their horribly eternal material, they slap my face from the depths of
    centuries, and I listen
here, crying thus, my dreadful migratory call.

      I wasn't the owner of an estate, or a sailor, or a vagabond, or a
        smuggler, or an Andean mule-driver,
I didn't choose horses or women in my old age
or for my love to be destroyed by death, pounding it with his old knocker,
    mangled and useless, his hurricane reeking of a ravaged precinct.

      Gazing into or smashing myself against
all the broken mirrors of oblivion, so distant
and dusty from the beginning.

      The alley of the old men dies where the last eagles die...

      I am a grandfather and you're an immense shadow,
the great language of inexorable images, national-international, inaudible
and extracted from beneath the world, engenders
slander, defamation, falsehood, surrounding me with bloody jackals that
    strike at my back,
and when I speak I incite the odd rancor of the small-minded;

he llegado a esa altura irreparable en la que todos estamos solos,
    Luisa Anabalón,
y como yo emerjo acumulando toda la soledad que me dejaste
    derrumbándote, destrozándote, desgarrándote contra la nada en un
    clamor de horror, me rodea la soledad definitiva;
sé perfectamente que la opinión pública de Chile y todo lo humano están
    conmigo,
que el pulso del mundo es mi pulso y por adentro de mi condición fatal
    galopa el potro del siglo la carretera de la existencia,
que la desgarrada telaraña literaria
está levantando un monumento a nuestra antigua heroicidad,
pero no puedo superar lo insuperable.

    Como los troncos añosos de la vieja alameda muerta, lleno de nidos
        y panales,
voy amontonando inviernos sobre inviernos
en las palabras ya cansadas con el peso tremendo de la eternidad …

    Tranqueo los pueblos rugiendo libros, sudando libros, mordiendo
        libros y terrores
contra un régimen que asesina niños, mujeres, viejos con macabro trabajo
    esclavo, arrinconando en su ataúd
a la pequeña madre obrera en la flor de su ternura,
ando y hablo entre mártires tristes y héroes de la espoliación, sacando mi
    clarinada a la vanguardia de las épocas, oscura e imprecatoria
de adentro del espanto local que levanta su muralla de puñales y de fusiles.

    El Díaz y el Loyola de los arcaicos genes ibero-vascos están
        muriendo en mí como murieron cuando agonizaba tu perfil
        colosal, marino, grecolatino, vikingo,
las antiguas diosas mediterráneas de los Anabalones del Egeo y las
    walkirias de Winétt-hidromiel,
adiós!… cae la noche herida en todo lo eterno por los balazos del sol
    decapitado que se derrumba gritando cielo abajo…

I've reached those hopeless heights where we are all alone, Luisa Anabalón,
and as I emerge gathering all the loneliness that you left me by
demolishing yourself, destroying yourself, clawing at yourself in a horrible
    clamor while opposing the nothing, absolute loneliness surrounds me;
I know perfectly well that public opinion in Chile and everything human
    is with me,
that the pulse of the world is my pulse and from within my fatal condition
    the century's colt gallops along the highway of existence,
that the shameless literary network
is raising a monument to our ancient heroism,
yet I cannot surmount the insurmountable.

       Like the decrepit trunks of the old, dead grove filled with nests and
          honeycombs,
I pile winters upon winters
in words already weary with the burden of eternity...

       By roaring out books, sweating out books, beating up books, I
          barricade the population against the terrors of
a regime that murders women and children and old men through macabre
    slave labor,
that forces the tiny working mother in the prime of her youth to an
    early grave,
I walk and talk among tragic martyrs and heroes of this exploitation,
       drawing out my epic, vanguard clarion call, sinister and blasphemous,
from within the local terror, which raises its wall of daggers and rifles.

       The Diazes and the Loyolas of the ancient Iberian-Basque genes
          are dying in me, just as they died when I agonized over your
          colossal profile, aquiline, Greco-Roman, Viking,
the ancient mediterranean goddesses of the Anabalons of Egeo and the
    Valkyries of Winétt—sweet wine,
good-bye!... night falls, eternally wounded by the rays of a beheaded sun,
    ruined, shouting down the sky...

POEMA CONJETURAL

El doctor Francisco Laprida, asesinado el día 22 de setiembre de
1829 por los montoneros de Aldao, piensa antes de morir:

Zumban las balas en la tarde última.
Hay viento y hay cenizas en el viento,
se dispersan el día y la batalla
deforme, y la victoria es de los otros.
Vencen los bárbaros, los gauchos vencen.
Yo, que estudié las leyes y los cánones,
yo, Francisco Narciso de Laprida,
cuya voz declaró la independencia
de estas crueles provincias, derrotado,
de sangre y de sudor manchado el rostro,
sin esperanza ni temor, perdido,
huyo hacia el Sur por arrabales últimos.
Como aquel capitán del Purgatorio
que, huyendo a pie y ensangrentando el llano,
fue cegado y tumbado por la muerte
donde un oscuro río pierde el nombre,
así habré de caer. Hoy es el término.
La noche lateral de los pantanos
me acecha y me demora. Oigo los cascos
de mi caliente muerte que me busca
con jinetes, con belfos y con lanzas.

Yo que anhelé ser otro, ser un hombre
de sentencias, de libros, de dictámenes,
a cielo abierto yaceré entre ciénagas;
pero me endiosa el pecho inexplicable
un júbilo secreto. Al fin me encuentro

Jorge Luis Borges (Argentina, 1899–1986)

....

CONJECTURAL POEM

Francisco Laprida, assassinated on the 22 of September of 1829
by the revolutionaries from Aldao, reflects before his death:

Bullets whine on that last afternoon.
There is wind; and there is ash on the wind.
Now they subside, the day and the disorder
of battle, victory goes to the others,
to the barbarians. The gauchos win.
I, Francisco Narciso de Laprida,
who studied law and the civil canon,
whose voice proclaimed the independence
of these harsh provinces, am now defeated,
my face smeared with mingled blood and sweat,
lost, feeling neither hope nor fear,
in flight to the last outposts in the South.
Like that captain in the *Purgatorio*
who, fleeing on foot, leaving a bloodstained trail,
where some dark stream obliterates his name,
so must I fall. This day is the end.
The darkness spreading across the marshes
pursues me and pins me down. I hear the hooves
of my hot-breathing death hunting me down
with horsemen, whinnying, and lances.

I who dreamed of being another man,
well-read, a man of judgment and opinion,
will lie in a swamp under an open sky;
but a secret and inexplicable joy
makes my heart leap. At last I come face to face

con mi destino sudamericano.
A esta ruinosa tarde me llevaba
el laberinto múltiple de pasos
que mis días tejieron desde un día
de la niñez. Al fin he descubierto
la recóndita clave de mis años,
la suerte de Francisco de Laprida,
la letra que faltaba, la perfecta
forma que supo Dios desde el principio.
En el espejo de esta noche alcanzo
mi insospechado rostro eterno. El círculo
se va a cerrar. Yo aguardo que así sea.

Pisan mis pies la sombra de las lanzas
que me buscan. Las befas de mi muerte,
los jinetes, las crines, los caballos,
se ciernen sobre mí... Ya el primer golpe,
ya el duro hierro que me raja el pecho,
el íntimo cuchillo en la garganta.

with my destiny as a South American.
The complicated labyrinth of steps
that I have traced since one day in my childhood
led me to this disastrous afternoon.
At last I have discovered
the long-hidden secret of my life,
the destiny of Francisco de Laprida,
the missing letter, the key, the perfect form
known only to God from the beginning.
In the mirror of this night I come across
my eternal face, unknown to me. The circle
is about to close. I wait for it to happen.

My feet tread on the shadows of the lances
that point me out. The jeering at my death,
the riders, the tossing manes, the horses
loom over me… Now comes the first thrust,
now the harsh iron, ravaging my chest,
the knife, so intimate, opening my throat.

De LAS ALTURAS DE MACCHU PICCHU

I

Del aire al aire, como una red vacía,
iba yo entre las calles y la atmósfera, llegando y despidiendo,
en el advenimiento del otoño la moneda extendida
de las hojas, y entre la primavera y las espigas,
lo que el más grande amor, como dentro de un guante
que cae, nos entrega como una larga luna.

(Días de fulgor vivo en la intemperie
de los cuerpos: aceros convertidos
al silencio del ácido:
noches deshilachadas hasta la última harina:
estambres agredidos de la patria nupcial.)

Alguien que me esperó entre los violines
encontró un mundo como una torre enterrada
hundiendo su espiral más abajo de todas
las hojas de color de ronco azufre:
más abajo, en el oro de la geología,
como una espada envuelta en meteoros,
hundí la mano turbulenta y dulce
en lo más genital de lo terrestre.

Puse la frente entre las olas profundas,
descendí como gota entre la paz sulfúrica,
y, como un ciego, regresé al jazmín
de la gastada primavera humana.

Pablo Neruda

(Chile, 1904–1973)

From THE HEIGHTS OF MACCHU PICCHU

I

From air to air, like an empty net,
I went between the streets and atmosphere, arriving and departing,
in the advent of autumn the outstretched coin
of the leaves, and between springtime and the ears of corn,
all that the greatest love, as within a falling
glove, hands us like a long moon.

(Days of vivid splendor in the inclemency
of corpses: steel transformed
into acid silence:
nights frayed to the last flour:
beleaguered stamens of the nuptial land.)

Someone awaiting me among the violins
discovered a world like an entombed tower
spiraling down beneath all
the harsh sulfur-colored leaves:
farther down, in the gold of geology,
like a sword enveloped in meteors,
I plunged my turbulent and tender hand
into the genital matrix of the earth.

I put my brow amid the deep waves,
descended like a drop amid the sulfurous peace,
and, like a blind man, returned to the jasmine
of the spent human springtime.

II

Si la flor a la flor entrega el alto germen
y la roca mantiene su flor diseminada
en su golpeado traje de diamante y arena,
el hombre arruga el pétalo de la luz que recoge
en los determinados manantiales marinos
y taladra el metal palpitante en sus manos.
Y pronto, entre la ropa y el humo, sobre la mesa hundida,
como una barajada cantidad, queda el alma:
cuarzo y desvelo, lágrimas en el océano
como estanques de frío: pero aún
mátala y agonízala con papel y con odio,
sumérgela en la alfombra cotidiana, desgárrala
entre las vestiduras hostiles del alambre.

No: por los corredores, aire, mar o caminos,
quién guarda sin puñal (como las encarnadas
amapolas) su sangre? La cólera ha extenuado
la triste mercancía del vendedor de seres,
y, mientras en la altura del ciruelo, el rocío
desde mil años deja su carta transparente
sobre la misma rama que lo espera, oh corazón, oh frente triturada
entre las cavidades del otoño:

Cuántas veces en las calles del invierno de una ciudad o en
un autobús o un barco en el crepúsculo, o en la soledad
más espesa, la de la noche de fiesta, bajo el sonido
de sombras y campanas, en la misma gruta del placer humano,
me quise detener a buscar la eterna veta insondable
que antes toqué en la piedra o en el relámpago que el beso desprendía.
(Lo que en el cereal como una historia amarilla
de pequeños pechos preñados va repitiendo un número
que sin cesar es ternura en las capas germinales,
y que, idéntica siempre, se desgrana en marfil
y lo que en el agua es patria transparente, campana
desde la nieve aislada hasta las olas sangrientas.)

II

If the lofty germ is carried from flower to flower
and the rock preserves its flower disseminated
in its hammered suit of diamond and sand,
man crumples the petal of light which he gathers
in determinate deep-sea springs
and drills the quivering metal in his hands.
And all along, amid clothing and mist, upon the sunken table,
like a jumbled quantity, lies the soul:
quartz and vigilance, tears in the ocean
like pools of cold: yet he still
torments it under the habitual rug, rips it
in the hostile vestments of wire.

No: in corridors, air, sea or on roads,
who guards (like red poppies) his blood
without a dagger? Rage has extenuated
the sad trade of the merchant of souls,
and, while at the top of the plum tree, the dew
has left for a thousand years its transparent letter
upon the same branch that awaits it, O heart, O brow crushed
between the autumn cavities:

How many times in the wintry streets of a city or in
a bus or a boat at dusk, or in the deepest
loneliness, a night of revelry beneath the sound
of shadows and bells, in the very grotto of human pleasure
I've tried to stop and seek the eternal unfathomable lode
that I touched before on stone or in the lightning unleashed by a kiss.
(Whatever in grain like a yellow tale
of swollen little breasts keeps repeating a number
perpetually tender in the germinal layers,
and which, always identical, is stripped to ivory,
and whatever in water is a transparent land, a bell
from the distant snows down to the bloody waves.)

No pude asir sino un racimo de rostros o de máscaras
precipitadas, como anillos de oro vacío,
como ropas dispersas hijas de un otoño rabioso
que hiciera temblar el miserable árbol de las razas asustadas.

No tuve sitio donde descansar la mano
y que, corriente como agua de manantial encadenado,
o firme como grumo de antracita, o cristal,
hubiera devuelto el calor o el frío de mi mano extendida.

Qué era el hombre? En qué parte de su conversación abierta
entre los almacenes y los silbidos, en cuál de sus movimientos metálicos
vivía lo indestructible, lo imperecedero, la vida?

I could grasp nothing but a clump of faces or precipitous
masks, like rings of empty gold,
like scattered clothes, offspring of an enraged autumn
that would have made the miserable tree of the frightened races shake.

I had no place to rest my hand,
which, fluid like the water of an impounded spring
or firm as a chunk of anthracite or crystal,
would have returned the warmth or cold of my outstretched hand.

What was man? In what part of his conversation begun
amid shops and whistles, in which of his metallic movements
lived the indestructible, the imperishable, life?

III

El ser como el maíz se desgranaba en el inacabable
granero de los hechos perdidos, de los acontecimientos
miserables, del uno al siete, al ocho,
y no una muerte, sino muchas muertes llegaba a cada uno:
cada día una muerte pequeña, polvo, gusano, lámpara
que se apaga en el lodo del suburbio, una pequeña muerte de alas gruesas
entraba en cada hombre como una corta lanza
y era el hombre asediado del pan o del cuchillo,
el ganadero: el hijo de los puertos, o el capitán oscuro del arado,
o el roedor de las calles espesas:

todos desfallecieron esperando su muerte, su corta muerte diaria:
y su quebranto aciago de cada día era
como una copa negra que bebían temblando.

III

Like corn man was husked in the bottomless
granary of forgotten deeds, the miserable course of
events, from one to seven, to eight,
and not one death but many deaths came to each:
every day a little death, dust, maggot, a lamp
quenched in the mire of the slums, a little thick-winged death
entered each man like a short lance,
and man was driven by bread or by knife:
herdsman, child of the seaports, dark captain of the plow,
or rodent of the teeming streets:

all were consumed awaiting their death, their daily ration of death:
and the ominous adversity of each day was like
a black glass from which they drank trembling.

IV

La poderosa muerte me invitó muchas veces:
era como la sal invisible en las olas,
y lo que su invisible sabor diseminaba
era como mitades de hundimientos y altura
o vastas construcciones de viento y ventisquero.
Yo al férreo filo vine, a la angostura
del aire, a la mortaja de agricultura y piedra,
al estelar vacío en los pasos finales
y a la vertiginosa carretera espiral:
pero, ancho mar, oh muerte!, de ola en ola no vienes,
sino como un galope de claridad nocturna
o como los totales números de la noche.
Nunca llegaste a hurgar en el bolsillo, no era
posible tu visita sin vestimenta roja:
sin auroral alfombra de cercado silencio:
sin altos enterrados patrimonios de lágrimas.

No pude amar en cada ser un árbol
con su pequeño otoño a cuestas (la muerte de mil hojas)
todas las falsas muertes y las resurrecciones
sin tierra, sin abismo:
quise nadar en las más anchas vidas,
en las más sueltas desembocaduras,
y cuando poco a poco el hombre fue negándome
y fue cerrando paso y puerta para que no tocaran
mis manos manantiales su inexistencia herida,
entonces fui por calle y calle y río y río,
y ciudad y ciudad y cama y cama,
y atravesó el desierto mi máscara salobre,
y en las últimas casas humilladas, sin lámpara, sin fuego,
sin pan, sin piedra, sin silencio, solo,
rodé muriendo de mi propia muerte.

IV

Mighty death invited me many times:
it was like the invisible salt in the waves,
and what its invisible taste disseminated
was like halves of sinking and rising
or vast structures of wind and glacier.
I came to the cutting edge, to the narrows
of the air, to the shroud of agriculture and stone,
to the stellar void of the final steps
and the vertiginous spiraling road:
but, wide sea, O death! you do not come in waves
but in a galloping nocturnal clarity
or like the total numbers of the night.
You never rummaged around into pockets, your visit
was not possible without red vestments:
without an auroral carpet of enclosed silence:
without towering entombed patrimonies of tears.

I could not love in each being a tree
with a little autumn on its back (the death of a thousand leaves),
all the false deaths and resurrections
without land, without abyss:
I've tried to swim in the most expansive lives,
in the most free-flowing estuaries,
and when man went on denying me
and kept blocking path and door so that
my headspring hands could not touch his wounded inexistence,
then I went from street to street and river to river,
city to city and bed to bed,
my brackish mask traversed the desert,
and in the last humiliated homes, without light or fire,
without bread, without stone, without silence, alone,
I rolled on dying of my own death.

V

No eras tú, muerte grave, ave de plumas férreas,
la que el pobre heredero de las habitaciones
llevaba entre alimentos apresurados, bajo la piel vacía:
era algo, un pobre pétalo de cuerda exterminada:
un átomo del pecho que no vio al combate
o el áspero rocío que no cayó en la frente.
Era lo que no pudo renacer, un pedazo
de la pequeña muerte sin paz ni territorio:
un hueso, una campana que morían en él.
Yo levanté las vendas del yodo, hundí las manos
en los pobres dolores que mataban la muerte,
y no encontré en la herida sino una racha fría
que entraba por los vagos intersticios del alma.

V

It was not you, solemn death, iron-plumed bird,
that the poor heir of these rooms
carried, between rushed meals, under his empty skin:
rather a poor petal with its cord exterminated:
an atom from the breast that did not come to combat
or the harsh dew that did not fall on his brow.
It was what could not be revived, a bit
of the little death without peace or territory:
a bone, a bell that died within him.
I raised the bandages dressed in iodine, sank my hands
into the pitiful sorrows killed by death,
and in the wound I found nothing but a chilling gust
that entered through the vague interstices of the soul.

VI

Entonces en la escala de la tierra he subido
entre la atroz maraña de las selvas perdidas
hasta ti, Macchu Picchu.
Alta ciudad de piedras escalares,
por fin morada del que lo terrestre
no escondió en las dormidas vestiduras.
En ti, como dos líneas paralelas,
la cuna del relámpago y del hombre
se mecían en un viento de espinas.

Madre de piedra, espuma de los cóndores.

Alto arrecife de la aurora humana.

Pala perdida en la primera arena.

Ésta fue la morada, éste es el sitio:
aquí los anchos granos del maíz ascendieron
y bajaron de nuevo como granizo rojo.

Aquí la hebra dorada salió de la vicuña
a vestir los amores, los túmulos, las madres,
el rey, las oraciones, los guerreros.

Aquí los pies del hombre descansaron de noche
junto a los pies del águila, en las altas guaridas
carniceras, y en la aurora
pisaron con los pies del trueno la niebla enrarecida,
y tocaron las tierras y las piedras
hasta reconocerlas en la noche o la muerte.

Miro las vestiduras y las manos,
el vestigio del agua en la oquedad sonora,
la pared suavizada por el tacto de un rostro

VI

And so I scaled the ladder of the earth
amid the atrocious maze of lost jungles
up to you, Macchu Picchu.
High citadel of terraced stones,
at long last the dwelling of him whom the earth
did not conceal in its slumbering vestments.
In you, as in two parallel lines,
the cradle of lightning and man
was rocked in a wind of thorns.

Mother of stone, sea spray of the condors.

Towering reef of the human dawn.

Spade lost in the primal sand.

This was the dwelling, this is the site:
here the full kernels of corn rose
and fell again like red hailstones.

Here the golden fiber emerged from the vicuña
to clothe love, tombs, mothers,
the king, prayers, warriors.

Here man's feet rested at night
beside the eagle's feet, in the high gory
retreats, and at dawn
they trod the rarefied mist with feet of thunder
and touched lands and stones
until they recognized them in the night or in death.

I behold vestments and hands,
the vestige of water in the sonorous void,
the wall tempered by the touch of a face

que miró con mis ojos las lámparas terrestres,
que aceitó con mis manos las desaparecidas
maderas: porque todo, ropaje, piel, vasijas,
palabras, vino, panes,
se fue, cayó a la tierra.

Y el aire entró con dedos
de azahar sobre todos los dormidos:
mil años de aire, meses, semanas de aire,
de viento azul, de cordillera férrea,
que fueron como suaves huracanes de pasos
lustrando el solitario recinto de la piedra.

that beheld with my eyes the earthen lamps,
that oiled with my hands the vanished
wood: because everything—clothing, skin, vessels,
words, wine, bread—
is gone, fallen to earth.

And the air flowed with orange-blossom
fingers over all the sleeping:
a thousand years of air, months, weeks of air,
of blue wind, of iron cordillera,
like gentle hurricanes of footsteps
polishing the solitary precinct of stone.

VIII

Sube conmigo, amor americano.

Besa conmigo las piedras secretas.
La plata torrencial del Urubamba
hace volar el polen a su copa amarilla.
Vuela el vacío de la enredadera,
la planta pétrea, la guirnalda dura
sobre el silencio del cajón serrano.
Ven, minúscula vida, entre las alas
de la tierra, mientras—cristal y frío, aire golpeado—
apartando esmeraldas combatidas,
oh agua salvaje, bajas de la nieve.

Amor, amor, hasta la noche abrupta,
desde el sonoro pedernal andino,
hacia la aurora de rodillas rojas,
contempla el hijo ciego de la nieve.

Oh, Wilkamayu de sonoros hilos,
cuando rompes tus truenos lineales
en blanca espuma, como herida nieve,
cuando tu vendaval acantilado
canta y castiga despertando al cielo,
qué idioma traes a la oreja apenas
desarraigada de tu espuma andina?

Quién apresó el relámpago del frío
y lo dejó en la altura encadenado,
repartido en sus lágrimas glaciales,
sacudido en sus rápidas espadas,
golpeando sus estambres aguerridos,
conducido en su cama de guerrero,
sobresaltado en su final de roca?

VIII

Rise up with me, American love.

Kiss the secret stones with me.
The torrential silver of the Urubamba
makes the pollen fly to its yellow cup.
It spans the void of the grapevine,
the petrous plant, the hard wreath
upon the silence of the highland casket.
Come, minuscule life, between the wings
of the earth, while—crystal and cold, pounded air
extracting assailed emeralds—
O, wild water, you run down from the snow.

Love, love, even the abrupt night,
from the sonorous Andean flint
to the dawn's red knees,
contemplates the snow's blind child.

O, sonorous threaded Wilkamayu,
when you beat your lineal thunder
to a white froth, like wounded snow,
when your precipitous storm
sings and batters, awakening the sky,
what language do you bring to the ear recently
wrenched from your Andean froth?

Who seized the cold's lightning
and left it shackled in the heights,
dispersed in its glacial tears,
smitten in its swift swords,
hammering its embattled stamens,
borne on its warrior's bed,
startled in its rocky end?

Qué dicen tus destellos acosados?
Tu secreto relámpago rebelde
antes viajó poblado de palabras?
Quién va rompiendo sílabas heladas,
idiomas negros, estandartes de oro,
bocas profundas, gritos sometidos,
en tus delgadas aguas arteriales?

Quién va cortando párpados florales
que vienen a mirar desde la tierra?
Quién precipita los racimos muertos
que bajan en tus manos de cascada
a desgranar su noche desgranada
en el carbón de la geología?

Quién despeña la rama de los vínculos?
Quién otra vez sepulta los adioses?

Amor, amor, no toques la frontera,
ni adores la cabeza sumergida:
deja que el tiempo cumpla su estatura
en su salón de manantiales rotos,
y, entre el agua veloz y las murallas,
recoge el aire del desfiladero,
las paralelas láminas del viento,
el canal ciego de las cordilleras,
el áspero saludo del rocío,
y sube, flor a flor, por la espesura,
pisando la serpiente despeñada.

En la escarpada zona, piedra y bosque,
polvo de estrellas verdes, selva clara,
Mantur estalla como un lago vivo
o como un nuevo piso del silencio.

What are your tormented sparks saying?
Did your secret insurgent lightning
once journey charged with words?
Who keeps on shattering frozen syllables,
black languages, golden banners,
deep mouths, muffled cries,
in your slender arterial waters?

Who keeps on cutting floral eyelids
that come to gaze from the earth?
Who hurls down the dead clusters
that fell in your cascade hands
to strip the night stripped
in the coal of geology?

Who flings the branch down from its bonds?
Who once again entombs farewells?

Love, love, never touch the brink
or worship the sunken head:
let time attain its stature
in its salon of shattered headsprings,
and, between the swift water and the walls,
gather the air from the gorge,
the parallel sheets of the wind,
the cordilleras' blind canal,
the harsh greeting of the dew,
and, rise up, flower by flower, through the dense growth,
treading the hurtling serpent.

In the steep zone—forest and stone,
mist of green stars, radiant jungle—
Mantur explodes like a blinding lake
or a new layer of silence.

Ven a mi propio ser, al alba mía,
hasta las soledades coronadas.
El reino muerto vive todavía.

Y en el Reloj la sombra sanguinaria
del cóndor cruza como una nave negra.

Come to my very heart, to my dawn,
up to the crowned solitudes.
The dead kingdom is still alive.

And over the Sundial the sanguinary shadow
of the condor crosses like a black ship.

IX

Águila sideral, viña de bruma.
Bastión perdido, cimitarra ciega.
Cinturón estrellado, pan solemne.
Escala torrencial, párpado inmenso.
Túnica triangular, polen de piedra.
Lámpara de granito, pan de piedra.
Serpiente mineral, rosa de piedra.
Nave enterrada, manantial de piedra.
Caballo de la luna, luz de piedra.
Escuadra equinoccial, vapor de piedra.
Geometría final, libro de piedra.
Témpano entre las ráfagas labrado.
Madrépora del tiempo sumergido.
Muralla por los dedos suavizada.
Techumbre por las plumas combatida.
Ramos de espejo, bases de tormenta.
Tronos volcados por la enredadera.
Régimen de la garra encarnizada.
Vendaval sostenido en la vertiente.
Inmóvil catarata de turquesa.
Campana patriarcal de los dormidos.
Argolla de las nieves dominadas.
Hierro acostado sobre sus estatuas.
Inaccesible temporal cerrado.
Manos de puma, roca sanguinaria.
Torre sombrera, discusión de nieve.
Noche elevada en dedos y raíces.
Ventana de las nieblas, paloma endurecida.
Planta nocturna, estatua dc los truenos.
Cordillera esencial, techo marino.
Arquitectura de águilas perdidas.
Cuerda del cielo, abeja de la altura.
Nivel sangriento, estrella construida.
Burbuja mineral, luna de cuarzo.

IX

Sidereal eagle, vineyard of mist.
Lost bastion, blind scimitar.
Spangled waistband, solemn bread.
Torrential stairway, immense eyelid.
Triangular tunic, stone pollen.
Granite lamp, stone bread.
Mineral serpent, stone rose.
Entombed ship, stone headspring.
Moonhorse, stone light.
Equinoctial square, stone vapor.
Ultimate geometry, stone book.
Tympanum fashioned amid the squalls.
Madrepore of sunken time.
Rampart tempered by fingers.
Ceiling assailed by feathers.
Mirror bouquets, stormy foundations.
Thrones toppled by the vine.
Regime of the enraged claw.
Hurricane sustained on the slopes.
Immobile cataract of turquoise.
Patriarchal bell of the sleeping.
Hitching ring of the tamed snows.
Iron recumbent upon its statues.
Inaccessible dark tempest.
Puma hands, bloodstained rock.
Towering sombrero, snowy dispute.
Night raised on fingers and roots.
Window of the mists, hardened dove.
Nocturnal plant, statue of thunder.
Essential cordillera, searoof.
Architecture of lost eagles.
Skyrope, heavenly bee.
Bloody level, man-made star.
Mineral bubble, quartz moon.

Serpiente andina, frente de amaranto.
Cúpula del silencio, patria pura.
Novia del mar, árbol de catedrales.
Ramo de sal, cerezo de alas negras.
Dentadura nevada, trueno frío.
Luna arañada, piedra amenazante.
Cabellera del frío, acción del aire.
Volcán de manos, catarata oscura.
Ola de plata, dirección del tiempo.

Andean serpent, brow of amaranth.
Cupola of silence, pure land.
Seabride, tree of cathedrals.
Cluster of salt, black-winged cherry tree.
Snow-capped teeth, cold thunderbolt.
Scored moon, menacing stone.
Headdresses of the cold, action of the air.
Volcano of hands, obscure cataract.
Silver wave, pointer of time.

XII

Sube a nacer conmigo, hermano.

Dame la mano desde la profunda
zona de tu dolor diseminado.
No volverás del fondo de las rocas.
No volverás del tiempo subterráneo.
No volverá tu voz endurecida.
No volverán tus ojos taladrados.
Mírame desde el fondo de la tierra,
labrador, tejedor, pastor callado:
domador de guanacos tutelares:
albañil del andamio desafiado:
aguador de las lágrimas andinas:
joyero de los dedos machacados:
agricultor temblando en la semilla:
alfarero en tu greda derramado:
traed a la copa de esta nueva vida
vuestros viejos dolores enterrados.
Mostradme vuestra sangre y vuestro surco,
decidme: aquí fui castigado,
porque la joya no brilló o la tierra
no entregó a tiempo la piedra o el grano:
señaladme la piedra en que caísteis
y la madera en que os crucificaron,
encendedme los viejos pedernales,
las viejas lámparas, los látigos pegados
a través de los siglos en las llagas
y las hachas de brillo ensangrentado.
Yo vengo a hablar por vuestra boca muerta.
A través de la tierra juntad todos
los silenciosos labios derramados
y desde el fondo habladme toda esta larga noche
como si yo estuviera con vosotros anclado,
contadme todo, cadena a cadena,

XII

Rise up to be born with me, my brother.

Give me your hand from the deep
zone of your disseminated sorrow.
You'll not return from the bottom of the rocks.
You'll not return from subterranean time.
Your stiff voice will not return.
Your drilled eyes will not return.
Behold me from the depths of the earth,
laborer, weaver, silent herdsman:
tamer of the tutelary guanacos:
mason of the defied scaffold:
bearer of the Andean tears:
jeweler with your fingers crushed:
tiller trembling in the seed:
potter spilt in your clay:
bring to the cup of this new life, brothers,
all your timeless buried sorrows.
Show me your blood and your furrow,
tell me: I was punished here,
because the jewel did not shine or the earth
did not surrender the gemstone or kernel on time:
show me the stone on which you fell
and the wood on which you were crucified,
strike the old flintstones,
the old lamps, the whips sticking
throughout the centuries to your wounds
and the war clubs glistening red.
I've come to speak through your dead mouths.
Throughout the earth join all
the silent scattered lips
and from the depths speak to me all night long,
as if I were anchored with you,
tell me everything, chain by chain,

eslabón a eslabón, y paso a paso,
afilad los cuchillos que guardasteis,
ponedlos en mi pecho y en mi mano,
como un río de rayos amarillos,
como un río de tigres enterrados,
y dejadme llorar, horas, días, años,
edades ciegas, siglos estelares.

Dadme el silencio, el agua, la esperanza.

Dadme la lucha, el hierro, los volcanes.

Apegadme los cuerpos como imanes.

Acudid a mis venas y a mi boca.

Hablad por mis palabras y mi sangre.

link by link, and step by step,
sharpen the knives that you've kept,
put them in my breast and in my hand,
like a river of yellow lightning,
like a river of buried jaguars,
and let me weep hours, days, years,
blind ages, stellar centuries.

Give me silence, water, hope.

Give me struggle, iron, volcanoes.

Cling to my body like magnets.

Hasten to my veins and to my mouth.

Speak through my words and my blood.

EL SOLILOQUIO DEL INDIVIDUO

Yo soy el Individuo.
Primero viví en una roca
(Allí grabé algunas figuras).
Luego busqué un lugar más apropiado.
Yo soy el Individuo.
Primero tuve que procurarme alimentos,
Buscar peces, pájaros, buscar leña,
(Ya me preocuparía de los demás asuntos).
Hacer una fogata,
Leña, leña, dónde encontrar un poco de leña,
Algo de leña para hacer una fogata,
Yo soy el Individuo.
Al mismo tiempo me pregunté,
Fui a un abismo lleno de aire;
Me respondió una voz:
Yo soy el Individuo.
Después traté de cambiarme a otra roca,
Allí también grabé figuras,
Grabé un río, búfalos,
Grabé una serpiente.
Yo soy el Individuo.
Pero no. Me aburrí de las cosas que hacía,
El fuego me molestaba,
Quería ver más,
Yo soy el Individuo.
Bajé a un valle regado por un río,
Allí encontré lo que necesitaba,
Encontré un pueblo salvaje,
Una tribu,

Nicanor Parra

(Chile, 1914–)

SOLILOQUY OF THE INDIVIDUAL

I am the Individual.
The first thing I saw was a rock
(And there I etched some figures).
Then I searched for a more suitable spot.
I am the Individual.
The first thing I needed was to find myself something to eat,
To search for fish, for birds, to search for firewood,
(Soon enough I'd be concerned with other matters).
To make a fire,
Firewood, firewood, where to find a bit of firewood,
Some scrap of firewood to make a fire,
I am the Individual.
At the same time I wondered,
I entered an abyss full of air;
A voice answered me back:
I am the Individual.
Later I tried to move to another rock,
And there too I etched figures,
I etched a river, some buffalo,
I etched a snake
I am the Individual.
But no. I grew bored of the things I was doing,
The fire irritated me,
I wanted to see more,
I am the Individual.
I went down into a valley irrigated by a river,
And there I found what I needed,
I found a primitive people,
A tribe,

Yo soy el Individuo.
Vi que allí se hacían algunas cosas,
Figuras grababan en las rocas,
Hacían fuego, ¡también hacían fuego!
Yo soy el Individuo.
Me preguntaron que de dónde venía.
Contesté que sí, que no tenía planes determinados,
Contesté que no, que de ahí en adelante.
Bien.
Tomé entonces un trozo de piedra que encontré en un río
Y empecé a trabajar con ella,
Empecé a pulirla,
De ella hice una parte de mi propia vida.
Pero esto es demasiado largo.
Corté unos árboles para navegar,
Buscaba peces,
Buscaba diferentes cosas,
(Yo soy el Individuo).
Hasta que me empecé a aburrir nuevamente.
Las tempestades aburren,
Los truenos, los relámpagos,
Yo soy el Individuo.
Bien. Me puse a pensar un poco,
Preguntas estúpidas se me venían a la cabeza,
Falsos problemas.
Entonces empecé a vagar por unos bosques.
Llegué a un árbol y a otro árbol,
Llegué a una fuente,
A una fosa en que se veían algunas ratas:
Aquí vengo yo, dije entonces,
¿Habéis visto por aquí una tribu,
Un pueblo salvaje que hace fuego?
De este modo me desplacé hacia el oeste
Acompañado por otros seres,
O más bien solo.
Para ver hay que creer, me decían,

I am the Individual.
I saw that some things were being done there,
They were etching figures in the rocks,
They were making fire—they were also making fire!
I am the Individual.
They asked me where I'd come from.
I answered yes, that I had no fixed plans,
I answered no, that from that time forward.
Fine.
Then I grabbed a chunk of stone I found in a river
And I began to work with it,
I began to polish it,
I made it into a part of my very own life.
But this is going on too long.
I cut down some trees to set sail,
I searched for fish,
I searched for different things,
(I am the Individual).
Until I began to grow bored once again.
Storms are boring,
Thunder, lightning,
I am the Individual.
Fine. I started to think a bit,
Stupid questions came into my head.
False challenges.
So I began to wander through some woods.
I reached a tree and then another tree;
I reached a fountain,
A pit in which I could make out some rats:
Here I come, I said then,
Has any of you seen a tribe around here,
A primitive people that can make fire?
In this way I set off toward the west
Accompanied by other beings,
Or actually, rather, alone.
You have to believe in order to see, they told me,

Yo soy el Individuo.
Formas veía en la obscuridad,
Nubes tal vez,
Tal vez veía nubes, veía relámpagos,
A todo esto habían pasado ya varios días,
Yo me sentía morir;
Inventé unas máquinas,
Construí relojes,
Armas, vehículos,
Yo soy el Individuo.
Apenas tenía tiempo para enterrar a mis muertos,
Apenas tenía tiempo para sembrar,
Yo soy el Individuo.
Años más tarde concebí unas cosas,
Unas formas,
Crucé las fronteras
Y permanecí fijo en una especie de nicho,
En una barca que navegó cuarenta días,
Cuarenta noches,
Yo soy el Individuo.
Luego vinieron unas sequías,
Vinieron unas guerras,
Tipos de color entraron al valle,
Pero yo debía seguir adelante,
Debía producir.
Produje ciencia, verdades inmutables,
Produje tanagras,
Di a luz libros de miles de páginas,
Se me hinchó la cara,
Construí un fonógrafo,
La máquina de coser,
Empezaron a aparecer los primeros automóviles,
Yo soy el Individuo.
Alguien segregaba planetas,
¡Árboles segregaba!
Pero yo segregaba herramientas,

I am the Individual.
I glimpsed shapes in the darkness,
Clouds perhaps,
Perhaps I glimpsed clouds, I glimpsed lightning,
With all that, several days had passed,
I felt myself dying;
I invented some machines,
I built clocks,
Weapons, vehicles,
I am the Individual.
I barely had time to bury my dead,
I barely had time to sow,
I am the Individual.
Years later I conceived a few things,
A few shapes,
I crossed the borders
And remained immobile in a sort of niche,
On a boat that sailed forty days,
Forty nights,
I am the Individual.
Later a series of droughts occurred,
A series of wars occurred,
Black guys entered the valley,
But I had to keep moving forward,
I had to produce.
I produced science, immutable truths,
I produced Tanagras,
I birthed books with thousands of pages,
My face swelled up,
I built a phonograph,
The sewing machine,
The first automobiles began to make an appearance,
I am the Individual.
Someone was setting aside planets,
setting aside trees!
But I was setting aside tools,

Muebles, útiles de escritorio,
Yo soy el Individuo.
Se construyeron también ciudades,
Rutas,
Instituciones religiosas pasaron de moda,
Buscaban dicha, buscaban felicidad,
Yo soy el Individuo.
Después me dediqué mejor a viajar,
A practicar, a practicar idiomas,
Idiomas,
Yo soy el Individuo.
Miré por una cerradura,
Sí, miré, qué digo, miré,
Para salir de la duda miré,
Detrás de unas cortinas,
Yo soy el Individuo.
Bien.
Mejor es tal vez que vuelva a ese valle,
A esa roca que me sirvió de hogar,
Y empiece a grabar de nuevo,
De atrás para adelante grabar
El mundo al revés.
Pero no: la vida no tiene sentido.

Furniture, office supplies,
I am the Individual.
Cities too were built,
Roads
Religious institutions went out of style,
They were seeking good fortune, they were seeking happiness,
I am the Individual.
Then I decided, better to devote my time to traveling,
To practicing, to practicing languages,
Languages,
I am the Individual.
I looked through a keyhole,
Yes, I looked, what can I say, I looked,
To free myself of doubt I looked,
Behind a set of curtains,
I am the Individual.
Fine.
Better perhaps that I return to that valley,
To that rock that served as my home,
And begin to etch anew,
From backward to forward to etch
The world in reverse.
But no: life has no meaning.

¿QUÉ SE AMA CUANDO SE AMA?

¿Qué se ama cuando se ama, mi Dios: la luz terrible de la vida
o la luz de la muerte? ¿Qué se busca, qué se halla, qué
es eso: amor? ¿Quién es? ¿La mujer con su hondura, sus rosas, sus volcanes,
o este sol colorado que es mi sangre furiosa
cuando entro en ella hasta las últimas raíces?

¿O todo es un gran juego, Dios mío, y no hay mujer
ni hay hombre sino un solo cuerpo: el tuyo,
repartido en estrellas de hermosura, en partículas fugaces
de eternidad visible?

Me muero en esto, oh Dios, en esta guerra
de ir y venir entre ellas por las calles, de no poder amar
trescientas a la vez, porque estoy condenado siempre a una,
a esa una, a esa única que me diste en el viejo paraíso.

Gonzalo Rojas

(Chile, 1917–2011)

WHEN YOU LOVE WHAT DO YOU LOVE?

When you love what do you love, my God: terrible light of life
or death's light? What do you look for, what uncover, what
is it: love? And who? Woman with her depths, her roses, her volcanoes,
or this flushed sun, my furious blood
as I enter to her final roots?

Or is it all a great game, God, with no woman
or man but just one body: yours,
shared out in beauty-stars, in brief grains
of visible eternity?

It kills me, oh God, this war
of going and coming among them in the streets, unable to love
three hundred at a time, condemned as I am to one,
this one, this one alone, you gave me in that old paradise.

NO OYES LADRAR A LOS PERROS

—Tú que vas allá arriba, Ignacio, dime si no oyes alguna señal de algo o si ves alguna luz en alguna parte.

—No se ve nada.

—Ya debemos estar cerca.

—Sí, pero no se oye nada.

—Mira bien.

—No se ve nada.

—Pobre de ti, Ignacio.

La sombra larga y negra de los hombres siguió moviéndose de arriba abajo, trepándose a las piedras, disminuyendo y creciendo según avanzaba por la orilla del arroyo. Era una sola sombra, tambaleante.

La luna venía saliendo de la tierra, como una llamarada redonda.

—Ya debemos estar llegando a ese pueblo, Ignacio. Tú que llevas las orejas de fuera, fíjate a ver si no oyes ladrar los perros. Acuérdate que nos dijeron que Tonaya estaba detrasito del monte. Y desde qué horas que hemos dejado el monte. Acuérdate, Ignacio.

—Sí, pero no veo rastro de nada.

—Me estoy cansando.

—Bájame.

El viejo se fue reculando hasta encontrarse con el paredón y se recargó allí, sin soltar la carga de sus hombros. Aunque se le doblaban las piernas, no quería sentarse, porque después no hubiera podido levantar el cuerpo de su hijo, al que allá atrás, horas antes, le habían ayudado a echárselo a la espalda. Y así lo había traído desde entonces.

—¿Cómo te sientes?

—Mal.

Hablaba poco. Cada vez menos. En ratos parecía dormir. En ratos parecía tener frío. Temblaba. Sabía cuándo le agarraba a su hijo el temblor por las sacudidas que le daba, y porque los pies se le encajaban en los ijares

Juan Rulfo (Mexico, 1918–1986)

YOU DON'T HEAR DOGS BARKING

"You up there, Ignacio, tell me if you hear some sign or see some light somewhere."

"I don't see anything."

"We must be close."

"Yes, but I can't hear a thing."

"Look hard."

"I don't see anything."

"So much the worse for you, Ignacio."

The men's long, dark shadow continued moving up and down, climbing over the rocks, getting smaller and larger as it went along the edge of the arroyo. It was a single shadow, reeling.

The moon was emerging from the earth, like a round flare.

"We must be close to that village, Ignacio. Your ears aren't covered, so try to see if you don't hear dogs barking. Remember, they told us Tonaya was just on the other side of the hills. And we left the hills hours ago."

"Yes, but I don't see a sign of anything."

"I'm getting tired."

"Put me down."

The old man backed up to a thick wall and bent over without letting his load down from his shoulders. Though his legs were buckling, he didn't want to sit because then he wouldn't have been able to lift his son's body again. They had helped him put him on his back a while ago, hours before. And he'd been carrying him all the way since then.

"How do you feel?"

"Bad."

He said little. Less and less. At times he looked asleep. At times he looked to be cold. He trembled. He knew when the tremors were taking over his son because of his shaking and because his feet would dig into his father's flanks like spurs. Later his son's hands, clapped around his neck,

como espuelas. Luego las manos del hijo, que traía trabadas en su pescuezo, le zarandeaban la cabeza como si fuera una sonaja. Él apretaba los dientes para no morderse la lengua y cuando acababa aquello le preguntaba:

—¿Te duele mucho?

—Algo—contestaba él.

Primero le había dicho: "Apéame aquí… Déjame aquí… Vete tú solo. Yo te alcanzaré mañana o en cuanto me reponga un poco." Se lo había dicho como cincuenta veces. Ahora ni siquiera eso decía.

Allí estaba la luna. Enfrente de ellos. Una luna grande y colorada que les llenaba de luz los ojos y que estiraba y oscurecía más su sombra sobre la tierra.

—No veo ya por dónde voy—decía él.

Pero nadie le contestaba.

El otro iba allá arriba, todo iluminado por la luna, con su cara descolorida, sin sangre, reflejando una luz opaca. Y él acá abajo.

—¿Me oíste, Ignacio? Te digo que no veo bien.

Y el otro se quedaba callado.

Siguió caminando, a tropezones. Encogía el cuerpo y luego se enderezaba para volver a tropezar de nuevo.

—Este no es ningún camino. Nos dijeron que detrás del cerro estaba Tonaya. Ya hemos pasado el cerro. Y Tonaya no se ve, ni se oye ningún ruido que nos diga que está cerca. ¿Por qué no quieres decirme qué ves, tú que vas allá arriba, Ignacio?

—Bájame, padre.

—¿Te sientes mal?

—Sí.

—Te llevaré a Tonaya a como dé lugar. Allí encontraré quien te cuide. Dicen que allí hay un doctor. Yo te llevaré con él. Te he traído cargando desde hace horas y no te dejaré tirado aquí para que acaben contigo quienes sean.

Se tambaleó un poco. Dio dos o tres pasos de lado y volvió a enderezarse.

—Te llevaré a Tonaya.

—Bájame.

Su voz se hizo quedita, apenas murmurada:

—Quiero acostarme un rato.

would clutch at his head and shake him as if he were a rattle.

He grit his teeth so he wouldn't bite his tongue and when he had finished he asked:

"Does it hurt a lot?"

"Some," Ignacio answered.

First he had said: "Put me down here... Leave me here... Go on without me. I'll catch up with you tomorrow or when I'm a bit better." Ignacio had said it about fifty times. Now he didn't even say that.

The moon was there. In front of them. A large reddish moon that filled his eyes with light and lengthened and darkened their shadow on the earth even more.

"I no longer see where I'm going," the father said.

But no one answered.

The son was up there, all lit up by the moon, with his pale face, bloodless, reflecting an opaque light. And he was underneath.

"Did you hear me, Ignacio? I'm telling you I can't see well."

The other one remained silent.

He continued walking, faltering. He would bend his body and straighten himself up only to falter again.

"This isn't a road. They told us Tonaya was on the other side of the ridge. We've already left the ridge behind. And Tonaya is nowhere to be seen, nor is there any sound that could tell us it's nearby. Why don't you want to tell me what you see, since you're up there, Ignacio?"

"Put me down, Father."

"Do you feel bad?"

"Yes."

"I'll get you to Tonaya no matter what. I'll find someone to take care of you over there. They say there's a doctor in the town. I'll take you to him. I've carried you for hours and won't drop you here so whoever is after you can finish you off."

He staggered a little. He took two or three steps to the side and straightened himself up again.

"I'll take you to Tonaya."

"Put me down."

His voice was faint, almost a whisper:

"I want to lie down for a while."

—Duérmete allí arriba. Al cabo te llevo bien agarrado.

La luna iba subiendo, casi azul, sobre un cielo claro. La cara del viejo, mojada en sudor, se llenó de luz. Escondió los ojos para no mirar de frente, ya que no podía agachar la cabeza agarrotada entre las manos de su hijo.

—Todo esto que hago, no lo hago por usted. Lo hago por su difunta madre. Porque usted fue su hijo. Por eso lo hago. Ella me reconvendría si yo lo hubiera dejado tirado allí, donde lo encontré, y no lo hubiera recogido para llevarlo a que lo curen, como estoy haciéndolo. Es ella la que me da ánimos, no usted. Comenzando porque a usted no le debo más que puras dificultades, puras mortificaciones, puras vergüenzas.

Sudaba al hablar. Pero el viento de la noche le secaba el sudor. Y sobre el sudor seco, volvía a sudar.

—Me derrengaré, pero llegaré con usted a Tonaya, para que le alivien esas heridas que le han hecho. Y estoy seguro de que, en cuanto se sienta usted bien, volverá a sus malos pasos. Eso ya no me importa. Con tal que se vaya lejos, donde yo no vuelva a saber de usted. Con tal de eso… Porque para mí usted ya no es mi hijo. He maldecido la sangre que usted tiene de mí. La parte que a mí me tocaba la he maldecido. He dicho: "¡Que se le pudra en los riñones la sangre que yo le di!" Lo dije desde que supe que usted andaba trajinando por los caminos, viviendo del robo y matando gente… Y gente buena. Y si no, allí esta mi compadre Tranquilino. El que lo bautizó a usted. El que le dio su nombre. A él también le tocó la mala suerte de encontrarse con usted. Desde entonces dije: "Ese no puede ser mi hijo."

—Mira a ver si ya ves algo. O si oyes algo. Tú que puedes hacerlo desde allá arriba, porque yo me siento sordo.

—No veo nada.

—Peor para ti, Ignacio.

—Tengo sed.

—¡Aguántate! Ya debemos estar cerca. Lo que pasa es que ya es muy noche y han de haber apagado la luz en el pueblo. Pero al menos debías de oír si ladran los perros. Haz por oír.

—Dame agua.

—Aquí no hay agua. No hay más que piedras. Aguántate. Y aunque la hubiera, no te bajaría a tomar agua. Nadie me ayudaría a subirte otra vez y yo solo no puedo.

"Sleep up there. After all, I've got a good hold on you."

The moon was ascending, almost blue, into a clear sky. The old man's face, drenched with sweat, filled with light. He hid his eyes so as not to look directly at it, since he could no longer hold his head straight, as it was gripped tightly between his son's hands.

"Everything I'm doing, I'm not doing for you. I'm doing it for your late mother. Because you were her son. That's why I'm doing it. She would reproach me if I had left you lying there, where I found you, and had not picked you up and carried you to where they can take care of you, like I'm doing. It's she who gives me courage, not you. Starting with the fact that I owe you nothing but difficulty, nothing but humiliation, nothing but shame."

He sweated as he spoke. But the night wind dried the sweat. And he sweated again over the dried sweat.

"I'll break my back, but I'll get to Tonaya with you, so the injuries they've inflicted on you can be healed. Although I'm sure that, once you're well, you will return to your evil ways. That doesn't matter to me anymore. As long as you go far away, where I no longer hear anything about you. As long as that happens... Because to me you're no longer my son. I've cursed the blood you have from me. The part you got from me I've cursed. I've said: 'Let the blood I gave him rot in his kidneys!' I said it from the moment I knew you had taken to the road, robbing to make a living and killing people... and good people. And not only that, there's my compadre Tranquilino. The man who baptized you. Who gave you your name. He had the ill luck to run into you, too. From that time on I said: 'This can't be my son.'"

"Look and see if you can see anything. Or if you hear anything. You can do it from up there, because I'm feeling deaf."

"I can't see anything."

"So much the worse for you, Ignacio."

"I'm thirsty."

"Live with it! We must be close. It's because it's already very late and they must have turned the lights off in the village. But at least you should hear if the dogs are barking. Try to hear."

"Give me water."

"There's no water here. There's nothing but rocks. Hang in there. And even if there were, I wouldn't put you down for a drink of water. No one would help me put you back up there and I can't do it by myself."

—Tengo mucha sed y mucho sueño.

—Me acuerdo cuando naciste. Así eras entonces.

Despertabas con hambre y comías para volver a dormirte. Y tu madre te daba agua, porque ya te habías acabado la leche de ella. No tenías llenadero. Y eras muy rabioso. Nunca pensé que con el tiempo se te fuera a subir aquella rabia a la cabeza... Pero así fue. Tu madre, que descanse en paz, quería que te criaras fuerte. Creía que cuando tú crecieras irías a ser su sostén. No te tuvo más que a ti. El otro hijo que iba a tener la mató. Y tú la hubieras matado otra vez si ella estuviera viva a estas alturas.

Sintió que el hombre aquel que llevaba sobre sus hombros dejó de apretar las rodillas y comenzó a soltar los pies, balanceándolos de un lado para otro. Y le pareció que la cabeza; allá arriba, se sacudía como si sollozara.

Sobre su cabello sintió que caían gruesas gotas, como de lágrimas.

—¿Lloras, Ignacio? Lo hace llorar a usted el recuerdo de su madre, ¿verdad? Pero nunca hizo usted nada por ella. Nos pagó siempre mal. Parece que, en lugar de cariño, le hubiéramos retacado el cuerpo de maldad. ¿Y ya ve? Ahora lo han herido. ¿Qué pasó con sus amigos? Los mataron a todos. Pero ellos no tenían a nadie. Ellos bien hubieran podido decir: "No tenemos a quién darle nuestra lástima." ¿Pero usted, Ignacio?

Allí estaba ya el pueblo. Vio brillar los tejados bajo la luz de la luna. Tuvo la impresión de que lo aplastaba el peso de su hijo al sentir que las corvas se le doblaban en el último esfuerzo. Al llegar al primer tejaván, se recostó sobre el pretil de la acera y soltó el cuerpo, flojo, como si lo hubieran descoyuntado.

Destrabó difícilmente los dedos con que su hijo había venido sosteniéndose de su cuello y, al quedar libre, oyó cómo por todas partes ladraban los perros.

—¿Y tú no los oías, Ignacio? —dijo—. No me ayudaste ni siquiera con esta esperanza.

"I'm very thirsty and very sleepy."

"I remember when you were born. That's how you were then. You would wake up hungry and would eat before you went back to sleep. And your mother would give you water, because you had already gone through her milk. You wouldn't be full. And you would get mad. I never thought that as time went by, that madness would go to your head… But that's what happened. Your mother, may she rest in peace, wanted you to grow up strong. She thought that when you'd grown up you would look after her. You were all she had. The other child she was going to have killed her. And you would have killed her again if she were alive at this point."

He felt the man he was carrying on his shoulders stop pressing inward with his knees and let his feet go, they were swinging from one side to the other. And he felt the head, up above, shake as if it were sobbing.

He felt thick drops fall on his head, like tears.

"Are you crying, Ignacio? The memory of your mother is making you cry, right? But you never did anything for her. You always repaid us badly. It seems as if, instead of affection, we had filled your body with malice. And now you see? They've wounded you. What happened to your friends? Did they kill them all? But they had no one. They might have been able to say: 'We have no one to give our sorrows to.' But you, Ignacio?"

At last the village was there. He saw the roofs shining under the moonlight. He had the impression his son's weight was crushing him when he felt the back of his knees bend in their final effort. When he reached the first dwelling, he leaned against a wall next to the sidewalk and let go of the body, limp, as if its joints had been removed.

With difficulty, he unclenched the fingers with which his son had been clinging to his neck, and, once free, he heard the dogs barking everywhere.

"And you didn't hear them, Ignacio?" he said. "You didn't help me even with that hope."

YA NO

Ya no será
ya no
no viviremos juntos
no criaré a tu hijo
no coseré tu ropa
no te tendré de noche
no te besaré al irme
nunca sabrás quién fui
por qué me amaron otros.
No llegaré a saber
por qué ni cómo nunca
ni si era verdad
lo que dijiste que era
ni quién fuiste
ni quién fui para ti
ni cómo hubiera sido
vivir juntos
querernos
esperarnos
estar.
Ya no soy más que yo
para siempre y tú
ya
no serás para mí
más que tú. Ya no estás
en un día futuro
no sabré dónde vives
con quién
ni si te acuerdas.

Idea Vilariño (Montevideo, 1920–2009)

NOT ANYMORE

This won't be
not anymore
we won't live together
I won't raise your son
I won't sew your clothes
I won't have you at night
I won't kiss you as I leave
you'll never know who I was
why others loved me.
I will never know
why or how ever
or if it was even true
what you said it was
or who you were
or who I was for you
or how it might have been
to live together
to love one another
to wait for each other
to be.
I'm no longer more than I
forever and you
won't be
any more than you
for me. You're no longer
in a future day
I won't know where you live
with who
or if you even remember.

No me abrazarás nunca
como esa noche
nunca.
No volveré a tocarte.
No te veré morir.

You'll never hold me
like that night
never.
I won't ever touch you again.
I won't see you die.

ORACIÓN POR MARILYN MONROE

Señor
recibe a esta muchacha conocida en toda la tierra con el nombre de
   Marilyn Monroe,
aunque ese no era su verdadero nombre
(pero Tú conoces su verdadero nombre, el de la huerfanita violada a los
   9 años
y la empleadita de tienda que a los 16 se había querido matar)
y que ahora se presenta ante Ti sin ningún maquillaje
sin su Agente de Prensa
sin fotógrafos y sin firmar autógrafos
sola como un astronauta frente a la noche espacial.

Ella soñó cuando niña que estaba desnuda en una iglesia (según cuenta
   el *Time*)
ante una multitud postrada, con las cabezas en el suelo
y tenía que caminar en puntillas para no pisar las cabezas.
Tú conoces nuestros sueños mejor que los psiquiatras.
Iglesia, casa, cueva, son la seguridad del seno materno
pero también algo más que eso...
Las cabezas son los admiradores, es claro
(la masa de cabezas en la oscuridad bajo el chorro de luz).
Pero el templo no son los estudios de la 20th Century-Fox.
El templo—de mármol y oro—es el templo de su cuerpo
en el que está el Hijo del Hombre con un látigo en la mano
expulsando a los mercaderes de la 20th Century-Fox
que hicieron de Tu casa de oración una cueva de ladrones.

Señor
en este mundo contaminado de pecados y de radiactividad,
Tú no culparás tan sólo a una empleadita de tienda

Ernesto Cardenal

(Nicaragua, 1925–)

PRAYER FOR MARILYN MONROE

Lord
embrace this muchacha known everywhere on Earth by the name
    Marilyn Monroe,
though that was not her real name
(but You know her real name, given to the orphan girl raped at 9
and the little shopgirl who at 16 had wanted to kill herself)
and who now presents herself before You without any makeup
without her Press Agent
without photographers and without signing autographs
alone like an astronaut facing the galactic night.

When she was a girl she dreamed she was naked in a church (according
    to *Time*)
before a prostrate crowd with their heads to the floor
and she had to tiptoe through to avoid stepping on the heads.
You know our dreams better than any psychiatrist.
Church, house, cave: havens of the maternal breast
but also something more than that...
The heads are her admirers, that's clear
(the mass of heads in the darkness beneath the stream of light).
But the temple is not the studios of 20th Century Fox.
The temple—made of marble and gold—is the temple of her body
in which the son of Man lodges with a whip in his hand
casting out the merchants of 20th Century Fox
who made Your house of prayer into a den of thieves.

Lord
in this world polluted with sin and radioactivity,
You would not blame someone who's just a little shopgirl

Que como toda empleadita de tienda soñó con ser estrella de cine.
Y su sueño fue realidad (pero como la realidad del tecnicolor).
Ella no hizo sino actuar según el script que le dimos
—El de nuestras propias vidas—Y era un script absurdo.
Perdónala, Señor, y perdónanos a nosotros
por nuestra 20th Century
por esa Colosal Super-Producción en la que todos hemos trabajado.

Ella tenía hambre de amor y le ofrecimos tranquilizantes.
Para la tristeza de no ser santos
      se le recomendó el Pscioanálisis.
Recuerda Señor su creciente pavor a la cámara
y el odio al maquillaje—insistiendo en maquillarse en cada escena—
y cómo se fue haciendo mayor el horror
y mayor la impuntualidad a los estudios.

Como toda empleadita de tienda
soñó ser estrella de cine.
Y su vida fue irreal como un sueño que un psiquiatra interpreta y archiva.

Sus romances fueron un beso con los ojos cerrados
que cuando se abren los ojos
se descubre que fue bajo reflectores
      ¡y apagan los reflectores!
y desmontan las dos paredes del aposento (era un set cinematográfico)
mientras el Director se aleja con su libreta
      porque la escena ya fue tomada.
O como un viaje en yate, un beso en Singapur, un baile en Río
la recepción en la mansión del Duque y la Duquesa de Windsor
      vistos en la salita del apartamento miserable.

La película terminó sin el beso final.
La hallaron muerta en su cama con la mano en el teléfono.
Y los detectives no supieron a quién iba a llamar.
Fue
como alguien que ha marcado el número de la única voz amiga

who like any little shopgirl dreamed of being a movie star.
And her dream became a reality (but like technicolor reality).
She did nothing more than act according to the script we gave her,
the script of our own lives, and it was absurd.
Forgive her, Lord, and forgive us
for our 20th Century
for that Colossal Super-Production we've all helped to create.

She was hungry for love and we offered her tranquilizers.
For her sadness that we are not saints
        she was prescribed Psychoanalysis.
Remember Lord her growing terror of the camera
and her hatred of makeup insisting on making herself up for each scene
and how her horror grew ever greater
and ever greater her lack of punctuality at the studios.

Like any little shopgirl
she dreamed of being a movie star.
And her life was unreal like a dream a psychiatrist interprets and files away.

Her romances were a kiss with eyes closed
and when the eyes open
they discover it occurred under spotlights
        and the spotlights have gone dark!
And they take down the two walls of the chamber (it was a movie set)
while the Director wanders away with his notebook
        because the scene was already shot.
Or like a journey by yacht, a kiss in Singapore, a dance in Río
    a reception at the mansion of the Duke and Duchess of Windsor
        glimpsed from the foyer of the miserable apartment.

The movie ended without the final kiss.
They found her dead in her bed with her hand on the telephone.
And the detectives did not know who she was going to call.
It was like someone who has dialed the number of the one single
    friendly voice

y oye tan sólo la voz de un disco que le dice: WRONG NUMBER
o como alguien que herido por los gangsters
alarga la mano a un teléfono desconectado.

Señor:
quienquiera que haya sido el que ella iba a llamar
y no llamó (y tal vez no era nadie
o era Alguien cuyo número no está en el Directorio de los Angeles)
   ¡contesta Tú al teléfono!

and hears only a voice on vinyl that says: WRONG NUMBER
Or like someone wounded by gangsters
reaching a hand toward a disconnected telephone.

Lord:
whoever she might have been going to call
and did not call (and perhaps it was no one
or it was Someone whose number is not in the Directory of Angels)
    You should answer the phone!

ALGO SOBRE LA MUERTE DE MAYOR SABINES

Primera Parte

I

Déjame reposar,
aflojar los músculos del corazón
y poner a dormitar el alma
para poder hablar,
para poder recordar estos días,
los más largos del tiempo.

Convalecemos de la angustia apenas
y estamos débiles, asustadizos,
despertando dos o tres veces de nuestro escaso sueño
para verte en la noche y saber que respiras.
Necesitamos despertar para estar más despiertos
en esta pesadilla llena de gentes y de ruidos.

Tú eres el tronco invulnerable y nosotros las ramas,
por eso es que este hachazo nos sacude.
Nunca frente a tu muerte nos paramos
a pensar en la muerte,
ni te hemos visto nunca sino como la fuerza y la alegría.
No lo sabemos bien, pero de pronto llega
un incesante aviso,
una escapada espada de la boca de Dios
que cae y cae y cae lentamente.
y he aquí que temblamos de miedo,
que nos ahoga el llanto contenido,
que nos aprieta la garganta el miedo.
Nos echamos a andar y no paramos

Jaime Sabines (Mexico, 1926–1999)

A FEW WORDS ON THE DEATH OF MAJOR SABINES

First Part

I

Let me rest,
loosen the muscles of my heart
and let my soul doze off
so I can speak,
so I can remember those days,
the longest days ever.

We're just recovering from our distress,
are weak and jumpy,
waking two or three times from poor sleep
to watch you at night and see that you're breathing.
We need to wake up to be more awake than we are
in this nightmare teeming with people and noises.

You're the invincible trunk and we're your branches,
which is why this ax blow shakes us.
Faced with your death we never stop
to think about death,
nor have we seen you as anything but strength and joy.
We don't know why, but suddenly
an incessant alarm is ringing,
a dislodged sword from the mouth of God
slowly falls and falls and falls.
Here we are, trembling in fear,
choking on our bottled-up cries,
fear clamping our throats.
We start to walk and never stop,

de andar jamás, después de medianoche,
en ese pasillo del sanatorio silencioso
donde hay una enfermera despierta de ángel.
Esperar que murieras era morir despacio,
estar goteando del tubo de la muerte,
morir poco, a pedazos.

No ha habido hora más larga que cuando no dormías,
ni túnel más espeso de horror y de miseria
que el que llenaban tus lamentos,
tu pobre cuerpo herido.

II

Del mar, también del mar,
de la tela del mar que nos envuelve,
de los golpes del mar y de su boca,
de su vagina oscura,
de su vómito,
de su pureza tétrica y profunda,
vienen la muerte, Dios, el aguacero
golpeando las persianas,
la noche, el viento.

De la tierra también,
de las raíces agudas de las casas,
del pie desnudo y sangrante de los árboles,
de algunas rocas viejas que no pueden moverse,
de lamentables charcos, ataúdes del agua,
de troncos derribados en que ahora duerme el rayo,
y de la yerba, que es la sombra de las ramas del cielo,
viene Dios, el manco de cien manos,
ciego de tantos ojos,
dulcísimo, impotente.
(Omniausente, lleno de amor,
el viejo sordo, sin hijos,
derrama su corazón en la copa de su vientre.)

pacing, after midnight,
the hallway of that silent clinic
where a nurse sits, an angel on call.
Waiting for you to die was to die slowly,
was to drip from death's tube,
was to die a little, a piece at a time.

An hour has never lasted longer than when you weren't sleeping,
nor has there been a tunnel thicker with terror and disgrace
than the tunnel filled with your groans,
your poor, wounded body.

   II

From the sea, from the sea as well,
from the enveloping fabric of the sea,
from the pounding of the sea and from its mouth,
from its dark vagina,
from its vomit,
from its deep and dismal purity,
come death, God, the heavy rain
pounding on the blinds,
the night, the wind.

From the earth as well,
from the houses' sharp roots,
from the bleeding, naked base of the trees,
from certain old, unmovable rocks,
from grievous pools, coffins of water,
from felled trunks where the lightning bolt now sleeps,
and from the grass, the shadow cast by branches of the sky,
comes God, armless one with a hundred hands,
blind one with myriad eyes,
exceedingly kind, impotent.
(All-departed, full of love,
the old, deaf, childless man
pours his heart into the cup of his belly.)

De los huesos también,
de la sal más entera de la sangre,
del ácido más fiel,
del alma más profunda y verdadera,
del alimento más entusiasmado,
del hígado y del llanto,
viene el oleaje tenso de la muerte,
el frío sudor de la esperanza,
y viene Dios riendo.

Caminan los libros a la hoguera.
Se levanta el telón: aparece el mar.

(Yo no soy el autor del mar.)

III

Siete caídas sufrió el elote de mi mano
antes de que mi hambre lo encontrara,
siete veces mil veces he muerto
y estoy risueño como en el primer día.
Nadie dirá: no supo de la vida
más que los bueyes, ni menos que las golondrinas.
Yo siempre he sido el hombre, amigo fiel del perro,
hijo de Dios desmemoriado,
hermano del viento.
¡A la chingada las lágrimas!, dije,
y me puse a llorar
como se ponen a parir.

Estoy descalzo, me gusta pisar el agua y las piedras,
las mujeres, el tiempo,
me gusta pisar la yerba que crecerá sobre mi tumba
(si es que tengo una tumba algún día).
Me gusta mi rosal de cera
en el jardín que la noche visita.

From the sea as well,
from the purest salt of the blood,
from the most faithful acid,
from the deepest and truest soul,
from the most elated food,
from the liver and the cry,
come the tense swell of death
and the cold sweat of hope,
comes God, laughing.

The books walk to the bonfire.
The curtain rises: there is the sea.

(I'm not the one who wrote the sea.)

III

The cob of my fist fell seven times
before my hunger found it;
seven times a thousand times I've died,
and I'm as cheerful as I was on the first day.
No one shall say: he knew no more of life
than the oxen, nor any less than the swallows.
I've always been man, dog's best friend,
absentminded son of God,
brother of the wind.
Tears, go fuck yourselves, I said
and I began to cry,
like someone giving birth.

I'm barefoot, I like to walk on water and rocks,
women, time,
I like to walk on the grass that will grow on my grave
(that is, if I have a grave someday).
I like my wax rosebush
in the garden where night comes to visit.

Me gustan mis abuelos de totomoste
y me gustan mis zapatos vacíos
esperándome como el día de mañana.
¡A la chingada la muerte!, dije,
sombra de mi sueño,
perversión de los ángeles,
y me entregué a morir
como una piedra al río,
como un disparo al vuelo de los pájaros.

IV

Vamos a hablar del Príncipe Cáncer,
Señor de los Pulmones, Varón de la Próstata,
que se divierte arrojando dardos
a los ovarios tersos, a las vaginas mustias,
a las ingles multitudinarias.

Mi padre tiene el ganglio más hermoso del cáncer
en la raíz del cuello, sobre la subclavia,
tubérculo del bueno de Dios,
ampolleta de la buena muerte,
y yo mando a la chingada a todos los soles del mundo.
El Señor Cáncer, El Señor Pendejo,
es sólo un instrumento en las manos obscuras
de los dulces personajes que hacen la vida.

En las cuatro gavetas del archivero de madera
guardo los nombres queridos,
la ropa de los fantasmas familiares,
las palabras que rondan
y mis pieles sucesivas.

También están los rostros de algunas mujeres,
los ojos amados y solos
y el beso casto del coito.

I like my corn-husk grandparents
and I like my empty shoes,
waiting for me like tomorrow.
Death, go fuck yourself, I said,
shadow of my sleep,
perversion of the angels;
and I prepared to die
like a stone tossed into the river,
like a shot fired at birds in flight.

IV

Let's talk about Prince Cancer,
Lord of the Lungs, Liege of the Prostate,
who amuses himself throwing darts
at silky ovaries, withered vaginas,
myriad groins.

My father has the loveliest ganglion of cancer
at the base of his neck, under his clavicle,
a tubercle sent by good old God,
a blister sent by good old death,
and I tell every sun on earth to go fuck itself.
Lord Cancer, Lord Asshole,
he's just a tool in the dark hands
of those sweet characters who create life.

I store the cherished names,
the clothes of family ghosts,
the words hanging in the air,
and my successive skins
in the four drawers of the wooden filing cabinet.

They also hold certain women's faces,
eyes, beloved and alone,
and the chaste kiss of intercourse.

Y de las gavetas salen mis hijos.
¡Bien haya la sombra del árbol
llegando a la tierra,
porque es la luz que llega!

V

De las nueve de la noche en adelante
viendo la televisión y conversando
estoy esperando la muerte de mi padre.
Desde hace tres meses, esperando.
En el trabajo y en la borrachera,
en la cama sin nadie y en el cuarto de niños,
en su dolor tan lleno y derramado,
su no dormir, su queja y su protesta,
en el tanque de oxígeno y las muelas
del día que amanece, buscando la esperanza.

Mirando su cadáver en los huesos
que es ahora mi padre,
e introduciendo agujas en las escasas venas,
tratando de meterle la vida, de soplarle
en la boca el aire…

(Me avergüenzo de mí hasta los pelos
por tratar de escribir estas cosas.
¡Maldito el que crea que esto es un poema!)

Quiero decir que no soy enfermero,
padrote de la muerte,
orador de panteones, alcahuete,
pinche de Dios, sacerdote de las penas.
Quiero decir que a mí me sobra el aire…

And from these drawers my children spring.
Blessed be the tree's shadow
falling on the earth,
for it is the falling light!

     v

From nine in the evening on,
watching television and talking,
I wait for my father to die.
Waiting, for the last three months.
At work and in a drunken stupor,
in bed by myself and in the children's room,
in his pain, replete and spilling over,
his sleeplessness, his complaints and protests,
in the oxygen tank and the teeth
of the dawning day, in search of hope.

Seeing my father's corpse
in the bones he has become
and sticking needles into his meager veins,
trying to inject him with life, to blow
air into his mouth…

(Trying to write these things down
fills me with shame from head to toe.
Goddamn anyone who thinks this is a poem!)

What I mean is, I'm not a nurse,
death's pimp,
a graveside orator, a panderer,
God's errand boy, a priest of sorrows.
What I mean is, I have more than enough…

VI

Te enterramos ayer.
Ayer te enterramos.
Te echamos tierra ayer.
Quedaste en la tierra ayer.
Estás rodeado de tierra
desde ayer.
Arriba y abajo y a los lados
por tus pies y por tu cabeza
está la tierra desde ayer.
Te metimos en la tierra,
te tapamos con tierra ayer.
Perteneces a la tierra
desde ayer.
Ayer te enterramos
en la tierra, ayer.

VII

Madre generosa
de todos los muertos,
madre tierra, madre,
vagina del frío,
brazos de intemperie,
regazo del viento,
nido de la noche,
madre de la muerte,
recógelo, abrígalo,
desnúdalo, tómalo,
guárdalo, acábalo.

VIII

No podrás morir.
Debajo de la tierra
no podrás morir.

VI

Yesterday we buried you.
We buried you yesterday.
Yesterday we covered you in dirt.
We left you in the dirt.
You're surrounded by dirt
since yesterday.
Since yesterday there's dirt
above and below you, to either side,
by your feet and by your head.
We stuck you in the dirt,
covered you with dirt yesterday.
You belong to the dirt
since yesterday.
Yesterday we buried you
in the dirt, yesterday.

VII

Bountiful mother
of all the dead,
mother earth, mother,
vagina of the cold,
embrace of the elements,
lap of the wind,
nest of the night,
mother of death,
gather him, wrap him,
undress him, take him,
keep him, finish him.

VIII

You cannot die.
Under the ground
you cannot die.

Sin agua y sin aire
no podrás morir.
Sin azúcar, sin leche,
sin frijoles, sin carne,
sin harina, sin higos,
no podrás morir.
Sin mujer y sin hijos
no podrás morir.
Debajo de la vida
no podrás morir.
En tu tanque de tierra
no podrás morir.
En tu caja de muerto
no podrás morir.
En tus venas sin sangre
no podrás morir.
En tu pecho vacío
no podrás morir.
En tu boca sin fuego
no podrás morir.
En tus ojos sin nadie
no podrás morir.
En tu carne sin llanto
no podrás morir.
No podrás morir.
No podrás morir.
No podrás morir.
Enterramos tu traje,
tus zapatos, el cáncer;
no podrás morir.
Tu silencio enterramos.
Tu cuerpo con candados.
Tus canas finas,
tu dolor clausurado.
No podrás morir.

Without water or air
you cannot die.
Without sugar, without milk,
without beans, without meat,
without flour, without figs,
you cannot die.
Without your wife or children
you cannot die.
Under life
you cannot die.
In your tank of dirt
you cannot die.
In your box of death
you cannot die.
In your bloodless veins
you cannot die.
In your empty chest
you cannot die.
In your fireless mouth
you cannot die.
In your peopleless eyes
you cannot die.
In your weepless flesh
you cannot die.
You cannot die.
You cannot die.
You cannot die.
We buried your suit,
your shoes, the cancer;
you cannot die.
We buried your silence.
Your padlocked body.
Your fine gray hair,
your closed-up pain.
You cannot die.

IX

Te fuiste no sé a dónde.
Te espera tu cuarto.
Mi mamá, Juan y Jorge
te estamos esperando.
Nos han dado abrazos
de condolencia, y recibimos
cartas, telegramas, noticias
de que te enterramos,
pero tu nieta más pequeña
te busca en el cuarto,
y todos, sin decirlo,
te estamos esperando.

X

Es un mal sueño largo,
una tonta película de espanto,
un túnel que no acaba
lleno de piedras y de charcos.
¡Qué tiempo éste, maldito,
que revuelve las horas y los años,
el sueño y la conciencia,
el ojo abierto y el morir despacio!

XI

Recién parido en el lecho de la muerte,
criatura de la paz, inmóvil, tierno,
recién niño del sol de rostro negro,
arrullado en la cuna del silencio,
mamando obscuridad, boca vacía,
ojo apagado, corazón desierto.

Pulmón sin aire, niño mío, viejo,
cielo enterrado y manantial aéreo

IX

I don't know where you went.
Your room is waiting for you.
My mom, Juan, and Jorge—
we're all waiting for you.
We've embraced one another
in sorrow, received letters, telegrams, word
that we buried you,
but your youngest granddaughter
looks for you in your room,
and all of us, without saying so,
are waiting for you.

X

This is a long, bad dream,
a dumb horror movie,
a never-ending tunnel
strewn with rocks and puddles.
What a screwed-up time this is,
mixing the hours and the years,
sleep and consciousness,
the open eye and a slow death!

XI

Newborn boy on the deathbed,
peaceful child, motionless and sweet,
new boy of the black-faced sun,
rocked in his cradle of silence,
suckling darkness, empty mouth,
snuffed-out eye, vacant heart.

Airless lung, my child, old man,
buried sky and aerial spring,

voy a volverme un llanto subterráneo
para echarte mis ojos en tu pecho.

XII

Morir es retirarse, hacerse a un lado,
ocultarse un momento, estarse quieto,
pasar el aire de una orilla a nado
y estar en todas partes en secreto.

Morir es olvidar, ser olvidado,
refugiarse desnudo en el discreto
calor de Dios, y en su cerrado
puño, crecer igual que un feto.

Morir es encenderse bocabajo
hacia el humo y el hueso y la caliza
y hacerse tierra y tierra con trabajo.

Apagarse es morir, lento y aprisa,
tomar la eternidad como a destajo
y repartir el alma en la ceniza.

XIII

Padre mío, señor mío, hermano mío,
amigo de mi alma, tierno y fuerte,
saca tu cuerpo viejo, viejo mío,
saca tu cuerpo de la muerte.

Saca tu corazón igual que un río,
tu frente limpia en que aprendí a quererte,
tu brazo como un árbol en el frío,
saca todo tu cuerpo de la muerte.

I'll become an underground cry
to cast my eyes on your chest.

XII

To die is to withdraw, to step aside,
to hide oneself a while, to quiet down,
to swim across the air, to leave one side
and secretly be everywhere at once.

To die is to forget, to be forgotten,
seek shelter, naked, in the modest heat
of God, the coiled fingers of his hand,
to grow as if, again, one were a fetus.

To die is to light up, face down in dirt,
to look upon the smoke and bones and lime
and strain to turn oneself back into earth.

To turn off is to die, is to cut time
in pieces, fast or slowly, like piecework,
and to scatter the soul in ash and lye.

XIII

Please listen, father, brother, liege and lord,
friend, tender and mighty friend of my soul,
retrieve your worn-out body; in a word,
retrieve your worn-out body from death's hole.

your heart, as strong as a river,
your carefree brow, which I learned to adore,
the trunk of your arm, which nothing could wither,
retrieve your worn-out body from death's shore.

Amo tus canas, tu mentón austero,
tu boca firme y tu mirada abierta,
tu pecho vasto y sólido y certero.

Estoy llamando, tirándote la puerta.
Parece que yo soy el que me muero:
¡padre mío, despierta!

XIV

No se ha roto ese vaso en que bebiste,
ni la taza, ni el tubo, ni tu plato.
Ni se quemó la cama en que moriste,
ni sacrificamos un gato.

Te sobrevive todo. Todo existe
a pesar de tu muerte y de mi flato.
Parece que la vida nos embiste
igual que el cáncer sobre tu omoplato.

Te enterramos, te lloramos, te morimos,
te estás bien muerto y bien jodido y yermo
mientras pensamos en la que no hicimos

y queremos tenerte aunque sea enfermo.
Nada de lo que fuiste, fuiste y fuimos
a no ser habitantes de tu infierno.

XV

Papá por treinta o por cuarenta años,
amigo de mi vida todo el tiempo,
protector de mi miedo, brazo mío,
palabra clara, corazón resuelto,

I love your silver hair, your jutting chin,
your unflinching mouth, your gaze, bright and straight,
your vast, sturdy chest, solid and certain.

I pound on your door, I'll knock till it breaks.
It seems like I'm the one who is dying:
Wake up, father, wake!

XIV

The glass you used to drink from hasn't broken,
nor has the cup, nor the tube, nor your plate.
The bed in which you died is unbroken,
and we haven't sacrificed a goat.

Everything outlives you. It's all still here,
despite your death and the cramp in my side.
Life seems to pound and crash against us, we're
besieged, like the scapula cancer rides.

We buried you, we wept you, we died you;
you're good and dead, good and screwed, depleted,
while we considered all we didn't do

and wish we had you, even sick in bed.
What you, what you and we were, would not do,
unless we all were in your hell instead.

XV

My father for thirty or forty years,
my bosom friend, there from start to finish,
guardian of my fear, my strong right arm,
plainspoken speech, determined, steadfast heart,

te has muerto cuando menos falta hacías,
cuando más falta me haces, padre, abuelo,
hijo y hermano mío, esponja de mi sangre,
pañuelo de mis ojos, almohada de mi sueño.

Te has muerto y me has matado un poco.
Porque no estás, ya no estaremos nunca
completos, en un sitio, de algún modo.

Algo le falta al mundo, y tú te has puesto
a empobrecerlo más, y a hacer a solas
tus gentes tristes y tu Dios contento.

XVI

(*Noviembre 27*)

¿Será posible que abras los ojos y nos veas ahora?
¿Podrás oírnos?
¿Podrás sacar tus manos un momento?

Estamos a tu lado. Es nuestra fiesta,
tu cumpleaños, viejo.
Tu mujer y tus hijos, tus nueras y tus nietos
venimos a abrazarte, todos, viejo.
¡Tienes que estar oyendo!
No vayas a llorar como nosotros
porque tu muerte no es sino un pretexto
para llorar por todos,
por los que están viviendo.
Una pared caída nos separa,
sólo el cuerpo de Dios, sólo su cuerpo.

you died when we were needing you the least,
when I'm missing you the most, dad, grandfather,
my son and my brother, blotter of my blood,
visor of my eyes, pillow of my sleep.

You've died, you've killed me just a little bit.
Because you are not here, we'll never be
complete again, ever, no matter what.

Something's missing in the world, and you saw fit
to reduce it further and, on your own,
make your people sad and your God happy.

XVI

(November 27)

Could you just open your eyes and look at us?
Could you just hear us?
Could you just stick out your hands for a second?

We're right here, next to you. Your birthday
is our party, old man.
Your wife and sons, your daughters-in-law
and your grandchildren—we've all come to hug you, old man.
You have to be listening!
Don't start crying like us,
because your death is just an excuse
for us to cry for us all,
cry for the living.
A fallen wall divides us,
just the body of God, just his body.

XVII

Me acostumbré a guardarte, a llevarte lo mismo
que lleva uno su brazo, su cuerpo, su cabeza.
No eras distinto a mí, ni eras lo mismo.
Eras, cuando estoy triste, mi tristeza.

Eras, cuando caía, eras mi abismo,
cuando me levantaba, mi fortaleza.
Eras brisa y sudor y cataclismo
y eras el pan caliente sobre la mesa.

Amputado de ti, a medias hecho
hombre o sombra de ti, sólo tu hijo,
desmantelada el alma, abierto el pecho,

ofrezco a tu dolor un crucifijo:
te doy un palo, una piedra, un helecho,
mis hijos y mis días, y me aflijo.

XVII

I grew used to keeping you, holding you
the way one might hold one's arm, body, or head.
You weren't different from me, nor were you
the same. You were my sadness when I'm sad.

You were, when I fell, my bottomless pit,
and when I rose, you were my strength and will.
You were the breeze, the sweat, the mishap met,
the fresh-baked loaf of bread on the table.

Chopped off from you, I stand here, half-formed
man, shadow of you, nothing but your son,
my soul dismantled, my chest an open wound,

I offer a crucifix to your pain:
a stick for you, a stone, a bracken's frond,
my sons and my days, and now I'm undone.

Parte dos

1

Mientras los niños crecen, tú, con todos los muertos,
poco a poco te acabas.
Yo te he ido mirando a través de las noches
por encima del mármol, en tu pequeña casa.
Un día ya sin ojos, sin nariz, sin orejas,
otro día sin garganta,
la piel sobre tu frente agrietándose, hundiéndose,
tronchando obscuramente el trigal de tus canas.
Todo tú sumergido en humedad y gases
haciendo tus deshechos, tu desorden, tu alma,
cada vez más igual tu carne que tu traje,
más madera tus huesos y más huesos las tablas.
Tierra mojada donde había tu boca,
aire podrido, luz aniquilada,
el silencio tendido a todo tu tamaño
germinando burbujas bajo las hojas de agua.
(Flores dominicales a dos metros arriba
te quieren pasar besos y no te pasan nada.)

II

Mientras los niños crecen y las horas nos hablan
tú, subterráneamente, lentamente, te apagas.
Lumbre enterrada y sola, pabilo de la sombra,
veta de horror para el que te escarba.

¡Es tan fácil decirte "padre mío"
y es tan difícil encontrarte, larva
de Dios, semilla de esperanza!

Quiero llorar a veces, y no quiero
llorar porque me pasas

Second Part

I

As the children grow, you and all the other dead
slowly come to an end.
I've been watching you through the nights,
over the marble, in your tiny house.
One day your eyes, nose, and ears are gone,
the next day, your throat,
the skin of your forehead splitting, collapsing,
darkly reaping the wheat of your gray hair.
You, fully engulfed in humidity and fumes,
churning out your waste, your disorder, your soul;
your flesh, ever more the same as your suit;
your bones ever more wood, the boards ever more bones.
Damp earth in place of your mouth,
putrefied air, annihilated light,
silence stretched from your head to your toe,
sprouting bubbles under the leaves of water.
(Six feet up, the Sunday flowers
wish to give you kisses, give you nothing at all.)

II

While the children grow and the hours talk to us,
you, underground, slowly burn out.
Ember, buried and alone, shadow's wick,
vein of horror for whomever scrabbles in you.

It's so easy to say "my father"
and so hard to find you, larva
of God, seed of hope!

Sometimes I want to cry, and I don't
want to, the way you move through me

como un derrumbe, porque pasas
como un viento tremendo, como un escalofrío
debajo de las sábanas,
como un gusano lento a lo largo del alma!

¡Si sólo se pudiera decir: "papá, cebolla,
polvo, cansancio, nada, nada, nada"!
¡Si con un trago te tragara!
¡Si con este dolor te apuñalara!
¡Si con este desvelo de memorias
—herida abierta, vómito de sangre—
te agarrara la cara!

Yo sé que tú ni yo,
ni un par de valvas,
ni un becerro de cobre, ni unas alas
sosteniendo la muerte, ni la espuma
en que naufraga el mar, ni —no— las playas,
la arena, la sumisa piedra con viento y agua,
ni el árbol que es abuelo de su sombra,
ni nuestro sol, hijastro de sus ramas,
ni la fruta madura, incandescente,
ni la raíz de perlas y de escamas,
ni tu tío, ni tu chozno, ni tu hipo,
ni mi locura, y ni tus espaldas,
sabrán del tiempo obscuro que nos corre
desde las venas tibias a las canas.

(Tiempo vacío, ampolla de vinagre,
caracol recordando la resaca.)

He aquí que todo viene, todo pasa,
todo, todo se acaba.
¿Pero tú? ¿pero yo? ¿pero nosotros?
¿para qué levantamos la palabra?
¿de qué sirvió el amor?

like a landslide, the way you move
like a awful wind, like a shudder
beneath the sheets,
like a slow worm traversing my soul.

If one could just say, "dad, onion,
dust, weariness, nothing, nothing, nothing!"
If I could gulp you down in a single gulp!
If I could stab you with this pain!
If with this memory-filled vigil
—open wound, heaving of blood—
I could clutch your face!

I know that neither you nor I,
nor a couple of valves,
nor a copper calf, nor a pair of wings
holding up death, nor the foam in which
the sea collapses, nor—no—the beaches,
the sand, the stone, docile in wind and water,
nor the tree, grandfather of its shadow,
nor our sun, stepchild of its branches,
nor the ripe, luminous fruit,
nor the taproot of pearls and fish scales,
nor your uncle, nor your grandchild's great-grandchild,
nor your hiccup, nor my madness, nor your shoulder blades
could understand the dark time that rushes through us
from our warm veins to the gray hair on our heads.

(Empty time, vial of vinegar,
snail recalling the undertow.)

See how everything comes, everything goes,
everything, everything comes to an end.
Even you? Even me? Even us?
Why did we bother to raise our voices?
What good was love?

¿cuál era la muralla
que detenía la muerte? ¿dónde estaba
el niño negro de tu guarda?

Ángeles degollados puse al pie de tu caja,
y te eché encima tierra, piedras, lágrimas,
para que ya no salgas, para que no salgas.

III

Sigue el mundo su paso, rueda el tiempo
y van y vienen máscaras.
Amanece el dolor un día tras otro,
nos rodeamos de amigos y fantasmas,
parece a veces que un alambre estira
la sangre, que una flor estalla,
que el corazón da frutas, y el cansancio
canta.

Embrocados, bebiendo en la mujer y el trago,
apostando a crecer como las plantas,
fijos, inmóviles, girando
en la invisible llama.
Y mientras tú, el fuerte, el generoso,
el limpio de mentiras y de infamias,
guerrero de la paz, juez de victorias
—cedro del Líbano, robledal de Chiapas—
te ocultas en la tierra, te remontas
a tu raíz obscura y desolada.

IV

Un año o dos o tres,
te da lo mismo.
¿Cuál reloj en la muerte?, ¿qué campana
incesante, silenciosa, llama y llama?

What bulwark
held back death? Where was
the black child who watched over you?

I laid slit-throated angels at the foot of your coffin
and threw dirt, stones, tears on you
so you won't climb out again, so you won't climb out.

III

The world continues on its way, time turns,
masks come and go.
Pain dawns day after day,
we surround ourselves with friends and ghosts,
at times it seems that a cable tugs at
the blood, a flower explodes,
the heart bears fruit, and weariness
sings.

Screwed on, guzzling women and drinks,
hoping to grow like plants,
still, immobile, turning
in the invisible flame.
While you, powerful man, stand-up guy,
unblemished by lies or disgrace,
warrior of peace, judge of victories
—cedar of Lebanon, oak grove of Chiapas—
you hide under the earth, burrow into
your dark and desolate root.

IV

One year, two years, three,
what do you care?
Where is death's clock? What is that bell,
silent, relentless, that tolls and tolls?

¿qué subterránea voz no pronunciada?
¿qué grito hundido, hundiéndose, infinito
de los dientes atrás, en la garganta
aérea, flotante, pare escamas?

¿Para esto vivir? ¿para sentir prestados
los brazos y las piernas y la cara,
arrendados al hoyo, entretenidos
los jugos en la cáscara?,
¿para exprimir los ojos noche a noche
en el temblor obscuro de la cama,
remolino de quietas transparencias,
descendimiento de la náusea?

¿Para esto morir?
¿para inventar el alma,
el vestido de Dios, la eternidad, el agua
del aguacero de la muerte, la esperanza?,
¿morir para pescar?,
¿para atrapar con su red a la araña?

Estás sobre la playa de algodones
y tu marea de sombras sube y baja.

V

Mi madre sola, en su vejez hundida,
sin dolor y sin lástima,
herida de tu muerte y de tu vida.

Esto dejaste. Su pasión enhiesta,
su celo firme, su labor sombría.
Árbol frutal a un paso de la leña,
su curvo sueño que te resucita.
Esto dejaste. Esto dejaste y no querías.

What unspoken voice from under the earth?
What sinking, sunken, endless cry
from the back teeth, floating in the aerial
throat, could stop fish scales?

Is this what living is for? To feel
one's arms and legs and face are borrowed,
leased to the grave, the juices
lively in the rind?
To wring one's eyes night
after night in the dark trembling of the bed,
whirl of muted transparencies,
nausea's descent?

Is this what dying is for?
To invent the soul,
God's frock, eternity, the water
in the fountain of death, hope?
To die so one can fish?
To trap the spider in a web?

You lie on a beach of cotton balls
and the swell of your shadows rises and falls.

v

My mother alone, sunken in her old age,
feeling neither pity nor pain,
wounded by your death and by your life.

This is what you left behind. Her towering passion,
her steady zeal, her somber diligence.
Fruit tree standing next to the woodpile,
her bowed dream that revives you.
This is what you left behind. What you left and didn't want.

Pasó el viento. Quedaron de la casa
el pozo abierto y la raíz en ruinas.
Y es en vano llorar. Y si golpeas
las paredes de Dios, y si te arrancas
el pelo o la camisa,
nadie te oye jamás, nadie te mira.
No vuelve nadie, nada. No retorna
el polvo de oro de la vida.

The wind passed. The uncovered well and the blighted root
were all that remained of the house.
And there's no point in crying. And if you pound
on the walls of God, and if you pull out
your hair or rip your shirt,
no one will ever hear you, no one will see you.
No one, nothing comes back. The golden
dust of life does not return.

CARTA A MI MADRE

A Teodora

recibí tu carta 20 días después de tu muerte y cinco minutos después de saber que habías muerto / una carta que el cansancio, decías, te interrumpió / te habían visto bien por entonces /aguda como siempre / activa a los 85 años de edad pese a las tres operaciones contra el cáncer que finalmente te llevó /

¿te llevó el cáncer? / ¿no mi última carta? / la leíste, respondiste, moriste / ¿adivinaste que me preparaba a volver? / yo entraría a tu cuarto y no lo ibas a admitir / y nos besábamos / nos abrazamos y lloramos / y nos volvemos a besar / a nombrar / y estamos juntos / no en estos fierros duros /

vos / que contuviste tu muerte tanto tiempo / ¿por qué no me esperaste un poco más? / ¿temías por mi vida? / ¿me habrás cuidado de ese modo? / ¿jamás crecí para tu ser? / ¿alguna parte de tu cuerpo siguió vivida de mi infancia? / ¿por eso me expulsaste de tu morir? / ¿como antes de vos? / ¿por mi carta? / ¿intuiste? /

nos escribimos poco en estos años de exilio / también es cierto que antes nos hablamos poco / desde muy chico, el creado por vos se rebeló de vos / de tu amor tan estricto / así comí rabia y tristeza / nunca me pusiste la mano encima para pegar / pegabas con tu alma / extrañamente éramos juntos /

no sé cómo es que mueras / me sos / estás desordenada en mi memoria / de cuando yo fui niño y de pronto muy grande / y no alcanzo a fijar tus rostros en un rostro / tus rostros es un aire / una calor / un aguas / tengo gestos de vos que son en vos / ¿o no es así? / ¿imagino? / ¿o quiero imaginar? /

Juan Gelman (Argentina, 1930–2014)

....

LETTER TO MY MOTHER

To Teodora

I got your letter 20 days after your death and five minutes after finding out
you'd died / a letter, you said, cut short by weariness / you'd looked well
enough then / sharp as ever / lively at 85 despite three operations for the
cancer that finally took you /

was it the cancer that took you? / not my last letter? / you read it, you
answered, you died / could you tell I was getting ready to return? / I'd enter
your room but you wouldn't let it happen / and we kissed / we embrace
and cry / and once more kiss / name / and we're together / not in these hard
irons /

you / held off death for so long / why not wait a bit longer for me? / were
you afraid for my life? / did you really care for me like that? / did I ever grow
toward your being? / was a part of your body from my childhood still lived?
/ is that why you drove me out of your dying? / like out of you before? /
because of my letter? / could you sense it? /

we haven't written much during these years of exile / in all honesty we
hadn't talked much before / from a tender age the one created by you
rebelled against you / your strict love / so I devoured rage and sadness / you
never laid a hand on me / you struck with your soul / in some strange way
we were joined /

I don't know how you can be dead / you're me / you're tangled in my mem-
ory / of when I was a young boy and suddenly grown / and I can't seem to
steady your faces into just one face / your faces are a wind / a female heat /
a male waters / I have gestures of yours within you / isn't that right? / am I
imagining it? / or do I only want to? / can't I remember? / what bloods of

¿recuerdo? / ¿qué sangres te repito? / ¿en qué mirada mía vos miras? / nos separamos muchas veces /

nací con 5.5 kilos de peso / estuviste 36 horas en la cama dura del hospital hasta sacarme al mundo / me tuviste todo el tiempo que tu cuerpo me pudo contener / ¿estabas bien conmigo adentro? / ¿no te fui dando arrebatos, palpitaciones, golpes, miedos, odios, servidumbres? / ¿estábamos bien, juntos así, yo en vos nadando a ciegas? / ¿qué entonces me decías con fuerza silenciosa que siempre fue después? / debo haber sido muy feliz adentro tuyo / habré querido no salir nunca de vos / me expulsaste y lo expulsado te expulsó /

¿esos son los fantasmas que me persigo hoy mismo / a mi edad ya / como cuando nadaba en tu agua? / ¿de ahí me viene esta ceguera, la lentitud con que me entero, como si no quisiera, como si lo importante siga siendo la oscuridad que me abajó tu vientre o casa? / ¿la tiniebla de grande suavidad? / ¿dónde el lejano brillo no castiga con mundo piedra ni dolor? / ¿es vida con los ojos cerrados? / ¿por eso escribo versos? / ¿para volver al vientre donde toda palabra va a nacer? / ¿por hilo tenue? / la poesía ¿es simulacro de vos? / ¿tus penas y tus goces? / ¿te destruís conmigo como palabra en la palabra? / ¿por eso escribo versos? / ¿te destruyo así pues? / ¿nunca me nacerás? / ¿las palabras son estas cenizas de adunarnos? /

nos separaste muchas veces / ¿eran separaciones? / ¿formas para encontrarse como primera vez? / ¿ese imposible nos hacía chocar? / ¿eso me reprochabas en el fondo? / ¿por eso eras tan triste algunas tardes? / tu tristeza me era insoportable / a veces quise morirme de eso todavía / ¿ya tenía mi pedazo de vida para ocuparme de él? / ¿como animal cualquiera? / ¿ya soy triste por eso? / ¿por tu tristeza ofende la injusticia / escándalo del mundo? /

siempre supiste lo que hay entre nosotros y nunca me dijiste / ¿por culpa mía? / ¿te reproché todo el tiempo que me expulsaras de vos? / ¿ése es mi exilio verdadero? / ¿nos reprochamos ese amor que se buscaba por separaciones? / ¿encendió hogueras para aprender la lejanía? / ¿cada desencontrarnos fue la prueba del encuentro anterior? / ¿así marcaste el infinito? /

yours do I echo? / in what glance of mine do you glance? / we were kept apart so often /

at birth I weighed 12 pounds / you spent 36 hours on that hard hospital bed until you dragged me out to the world / you kept me in as long as your body could hold / were you all right with me inside you? / didn't I stir up fury, flutters, fear, hurt, hate, enslavement? / were we okay, together like that, me in you swimming blindly? / what did you tell me then with a silent strength that always came later? / I must've been happy inside you / I must've never wanted out / you drove me out and the one driven out drove you out/

are these the ghosts I'm still haunting myself today / at my age / like when I swam in your water? / is that where I get this blindness, why I come to understand so slowly, as if I didn't want to, as if what's still most important is the dusk lowered down on me by your womb or home? / great softness gloom? / where the distant glow won't chasten with world stone or pain? / is it life with eyes closed? / is that why I write poems? / to return to the womb where every word is born? / by a tenuous thread? / is poetry a simulation of you? / your sorrows and joys? / are you ruined with me like a word in the word? / is that why I write poems? / could I ruin you that way then? / will you never be born to me? / are words these ashes uniting us? /

you kept us apart so often / were they separations? / ways to come together like the first time? / did that impossibility cause us to clash? / deep down did you blame me for it? / is that why you were so sad some evenings? / I couldn't stand your sadness / sometimes I wanted to die from it still / by then did I have my piece of life to care for? / like some kind of animal? / is that why I'm sad now? / is it your sadness that makes injustice / the world's scandal / so offensive? /

you always knew what we have between us but you never told me / was it my fault? / did I constantly blame you for driving me out? / is that my true exile? / do we blame this love sought by separation? / did it set fires to discover distance? / was each of our disencounters proof of an earlier encounter? / is that how you marked the infinite? /

¿qué olvido es paz? / ¿por qué de todos tus rostros vivos recuerdo con tanta precisión únicamente una fotografía? / Odessa, 1915, tenés 18 años, estudiás medicina, no hay de comer / pero a tus mejillas habían subido dos manzanas (así me lo dijiste) (árbol del hambre que da frutas) / esas manzanas ¿tenían rojos del fuego del pogrom que te tocaba? / ¿a los 5 años? / ¿tu madre sacando de la casa en llamas a varios hermanitos? / ¿y muerta a tu hermanita? / ¿con todo eso / por todo eso / contra / me querés? / ¿me pedías que fuera tu hermanita? / ¿así me diste esta mujer, dentro / fuera de mí? / ¿qué es esta herencia, madre / esa fotografía en tus 18 años hermosos / con tu largo cabello negriazul como noche del alma / partida en dos / ese vestido acampanado marcándote los pechos / las dos amigas reclinadas a tus pies / tu mirada hacia mí para que sepa que te amo irremediablemente? /

¿así viaja el amor / de ser a antes de ser? / ¿de ser a sido en tu belleza? / ¿viajó de vos a mí? / ¿viaja ahora / morida? / nada podemos preguntar sino este amor que todo el tiempo nos golpeó / con su unidad irrepetible / ¿para que no olvidemos el dolor? / ¿los dos niñitos del mercado de Ravelo con una gallinita en los brazos, ofreciendo barato y con gestos de madre, casi recién salidos de sus madres? / ¿por qué te apareciste en el mercado boliviano? / ¿en cada pena estás? / apagabas el sol para dormirme /

¿podés quitarme vida? / ¿ni quitártela yo? / ¿castigabas por eso? / desciendo de tus pechos / tu implacable exigencia del viejo amor que nos tuvimos en las navegaciones de tu vientre / siempre conmigo fuiste doble / te hacía falta y me echaste de vos / ¿para aprender a sernos otros? / cada mucho nos dabas un momento de paz: entonces me dejabas peinarte lentamente y te ibas en mí y yo era tu amante y más / ¿tu padre? / ¿ese rabino o santo? / ¿que amabas? / ¿más que a mí? / ¿me perseguías porque no supe parecerme a él? / ¿y cómo iba a parecerme? / ¿no me querías otro? / ¿lejos de ese dolor? / ¿por qué tan vivo está lo que no fue? / ¿nunca junté pedazos tuyos? / ¿cada recuerdo se consume en su llama? / ¿eso es la memoria? / ¿suma y no síntesis? / ¿ramas y nunca árbol? / ¿pie sin ojo, mano sin hora? / ¿nunca? / ¿saliva que no moja? / ¿así atan los cordones del alma? / ¿vos sos dolor, miedo al dolor? /

what kind of oblivion is peace? / of all your living faces why can I remember just one photo so vividly? / Odessa, 1915, you're 18, studying medicine, there's nothing to eat / and yet two apples rose to your cheeks (that's what you told me) (tree of hunger bearing fruit) / were those apples red from the pogrom's fire that was meant for you? / when you were 5? / your mother dragging the little ones from a house in flames? / your little sister dead? / in spite of all that / because of it / against it / do you love me? / did you ask me to be your little sister? / is that how you passed down this woman inside / outside me? / what is this legacy, mother / that picture of your 18-year-old beauty / with your long hair bluishblack like the soul's night / parted down the middle / the bell-shaped dress showing off your breasts / two friends sitting at your feet / you gazing at me so I'll know I love you helplessly? /

is that how love travels / from being to before being? / from being to been in your beauty? / did it travel from you to me? / is it traveling now / oh deaded one? / we can ask for nothing more than this love relentlessly striking / with its singular unity / so we don't forget the pain? / the two little kids in the Ravelo market holding a hen in their arms for a good price and with a mother's gestures, only just born of their mother themselves? / why did you show up at the Bolivian market? / are you in every sorrow? / you switched off the sun to put me to sleep /

can you take life from me? / or can I take it from you? / is that why you punished me? / I descend from your breasts / your merciless demand for the old love we shared under sail in your womb / with me you were always double / you needed me and you drove me out / so we could learn to be others? / now and then you gave us a moment's peace: then you'd let me slowly comb your hair and you'd come to me and I was your lover and something more / your father? / that rabbi or saint? / you loved? / more than me? / did you torment me because I couldn't be like him? / how could I have been like him? / didn't you want me to be another? / far from that pain? / why is what never was so alive? / didn't I ever gather up pieces of you? / does each memory burn down with its flame? / is that memory? / sum but not synthesis? / branches but never tree? / eyeless foot, hourless hand? / ever? / saliva unfit to dampen? / is that how the soul's cilices bind? / are you pain, fear of pain? /

¿qué fue lo separado? / ¿mi dedo de escribir en tu sangre? / ¿mi serte de no serte? / y vos, ¿no eras el otro? / ¿cuántas veces miraste las llamas del pogrom mientras yo te crecía, entraste al bosque donde cantaba el ruiseñor que nunca oí, jugaste con el que nunca fui? / nacimos junto a dos puertos distintos / conocemos las diferencias de la sal / vos y yo hicieran un mar desconocido con dos sales /

me hiciste otro / no sigas castigándome por eso / ¿te sigo castigando por eso? / ¿y sin embargo / y cuándo / y yo tu sido? / ¿vos en yo / vos de yo? / ¿y qué podemos ya cambiar? / ¿pudimos cambiar algo alguna vez? / ¿nunca saldé las hambres del abuelo? / los ojos claros del retrato que presidía tu cuarto / ¿qué puede el verdadero amor cambiar? / ¿o nos es de tal modo que nos empuja a ser sí mismos? / ¿para uno en el otro? / ¿resonando en las partes de la noche? / ¿como dos piedras contra el cielo? / ¿pájaro y árbol? / cuando se posa el pájaro en el árbol, ¿quién es vuelo, quién tierra? / ¿quién baja a oscuridad? / ¿quién sube a luz? / ¿qué goce pasa a llaga? / ¿te llevo en llaga viva? / ¿para que nos atemos otra vez? / ¿este sufrido amor? /

me hiciste dos / uno murió contuyo / el resto es el que soy / ¿y dónde la cuerpalma umbilical? / ¿dónde navega conteniéndonos? / madre harta de tumba: yo te recibo / yo te existo /

¿tratos de amor hay en la sombra? / ¿ya volveré a peinarte el dulce pelo / espesura donde mi mano queda? / ¿pensativa en tu aroma? / ¿gracia cuajada en lenta parecida? / ¿me quisiste imposiblemente? / ¿así me confirmaste en el furor? / ¿puerto de tardes inclinadas al que volvías tantas veces? / ¿dónde navegarás ahora sino en mí / contra mí? / ¿puerto solo? / bella de cada mar en mi cabeza / llaga de espumas / alma /

no sé qué daño es éste / tu soledad que arde / dame la rabia de tus huesos que yo los meceré / vos me acunaste yo te ahueso / ¿quién podrá desmadrar al desterrado? / tiempo que no volvés / mares que te arrancaste de la espalda / tu leche constelada de cielos que no vi / leche llena de sed / tus pechos que callaban / paciencias / caballitos que el pasado maneó / llenos

what was kept apart? / my finger from writing in your blood? / my being you from not being you? / and you, weren't you the other? / how often did you stare at the pogrom's flames while I grew inside you, enter the forest where the nightingale I never heard sang, play with the child I never was? / we were born in two separate ports / we know salt's differences / you and I they formed an unknown sea with two salts /

you made me other / stop punishing me for it / am I still punishing you for it? / and yet / and when / and am I your been? / you in I / you from I? / what could we change now? / could we have ever changed anything? / could I have ever paid off grandfather's hunger? / the clear eyes of his portrait presiding over your room / what can true love change? / or is it ours in such a way that it spurs us on to be ourselves? / one in the other? / echoing in the parts of the night? / like two stones against the sky? / bird and tree? / when a bird perches on a tree, which one is flight, which one is land? / which one descends to darkness? / which one rises to light? / what joy becomes sore? / do I bear you in an open sore? / so we can be bound together once more? / this long-suffering love? /

you made me two / one of us died with yours / the rest is who I am / and where is the umbilical bodysoul? / where does it sail with us aboard? / mother so tomb-weary: I receive you / I exist you /

does love make deals in the dark? / will I comb your sweet hair once more? / thickness under my hands? / wistful in the scent of you? / curdled grace in slow seeming? / did you love me impossibly? / is that how you bore me out in fury? / slanted evening port you went back to so often? / where will you sail now if not in me? / against me? / a lonesome port? / beauty of every ocean in my head / seafoam sore / soul /

I don't know what kind of harm this is / your burning solitude / give me the rage in your bones and I'll rock them / you cradled me I'll turn you to bone / who could disown this outcast? / time you'll never return / seas you tore from your back / your milk constellated with skies I couldn't see / milk brimming with thirst / your breasts silencing / patience / tiny horses hobbled by the past / laden with lingering steppe / crushed by my

de estepa detenida / rota por mi avidez de vos / así me alzaste / me abajaste / me amaste sin piedad / pañal feroz de tu ternura /

¿o fui yo tu cansancio? / ¿te reproché que me expulsaras? / ¿nos ata ese reproche hondísimo / que nunca amor pudo encontrar? / ¿no me quisiste mar y navegar lejos de vos? / ¿tiempo hecho de vos? / ¿no me quisiste acaso otro cuando me concebías? / ¿otra unición de esa unidad? / ¿ama total de tus dos sangres? / ¿te das cuenta del miedo que nos hiciste, madre? / ¿de tu poder / tu claridad? /

¿qué cuentas pago todavía? / ¿qué acreedores desconozco? / ¿necesito recorrer una a una tus penas para saber quién soy / quién fui cuando nos separamos por la carne / dolorosa del animal que diste a luz / sierva mía / ciega a mi servidumbre de tu sierva / pero esas maravillas donde me hijaste y te amadré / tu cercana distancia /

¿me ponías a veces delantales de fierro? / ¿me besabas a veces con pasión? / ¿y qué pasión había en tu pasión ? / ¿no podrías cesar en tu morir para decirme? / ¿no te querés interrumpir? / ¿entraste tanto en tu desaparecer? / ¿volvés al desamparo de mí? / ¿tan duro era mi amor? / ¿te di un alma y con otra te echaba a mi intemperie? / ¿no pudiste morivivirme en suave claustro / no darme de nacer? / mi nacer, ¿te habrá apagado ganas de matarme? / ¿eso me perdonabas y no me perdonabas? / ¿así peleaste con tus sombras? / ¿así me hiciste sombra tuya de otro cuerpo / me diste tu pezón / campo violeta / donde pacía un temblor? / ¿techo contra el terror? / ¿única tela de la paz? / ¿no la tejíamos los dos? / ¿en mañanas cayendo sobre el patio donde jamás hubo otra gloria? / ¿blancuras que de vos subían? / ¿rocíos de tu sangre al puro sol? / ¿lluvia de abajo interminable? / ¿yo fui animal de lluvia? / ¿te ensucié pechos con mi boca? / ¿me diste a veces leche amarga? / ¿te olvidás de las veces que no quise comer de vos? / ¿qué te venía entonces de la entraña del alma? / esos jugos, ¿no me atardecen fiero? / ¿y vos creés que estás muriendo? / ¿antes que muera yo? / ¿y se apaguen los gestos que escribiste en mi cuerpo? / ¿las dichas que imprimiste? / ¿en mi querer a las mujeres? / ¿prolongándote en ellas? / ¿que de vos me tuvieran y alejaran? /

craving for you / that's how you raised me / lowered me / loved me mercilessly / ferocious diaper of your tenderness /

or was I your weariness? / did I blame you for driving me out? / is that what binds us, the deepest blame / love could never find? / didn't you want me as sea so I might sail far from you? / time made of you? / perhaps you wanted another when you conceived me? / another unition of that unity? / absolute master of your two bloodlines? / can't you see the fear you did us, mother? / of your power / your clarity? /

what dues have I yet to pay? / what creditors have I yet to meet? / must I go over each and every one of your sorrows to know who I am / who I was when we were torn apart by the painful / flesh of the animal you gave birth to? / my servant / blind to my enslavement of your servant / still such wonders when you childed me and I mothered you / your distance near at hand /

did you dress me at times in iron aprons? / did you kiss me passionately sometimes? / and what passion was there in your passion? / couldn't you stop your dying to tell me? / couldn't you have interrupted? / were you so entranced by your disappearing? / will you ever come back to the abandonment of me? / was my love so hard? / did I give you one soul and with another throw you to my forsaking? / you couldn't give me deathlife in soft womb / couldn't give me to be born? / my birth, did it smother the urge to kill me? / did you forgive me and not forgive me for it? / is that how you struggled with your shadows? / is that how you made me your shadow in another body / you offered your nipple / field of violet / where a trembling pastured? / a roof against terror? / sole fabric of peace? / didn't we weave it together? / at daybreak dropping down over the patio where there was never any other glory? / whitenesses rising from you? / dewdrops of your blood under full sun? / unending rain from below? / was I an animal of the rain? / did I dirty your breasts with my mouth? / did you give me bitter milk at times? / do you forget the times when I refused to eat what you fed me? / what surfaced then from the innards of your soul? / those juices, don't they drag me fierce toward twilight? / and you believe you're dying? / before I die? / before the gestures you wrote on my body are smothered? / the happiness you stamped? / on my love of women? / drawing yourself out in them? / the ones who took me and kept me apart from you? /

¿qué yo habré sido para vos? / ¿cómo me habrás sufrido cuando salí de vos? / no saberte, ¿no es mi saber de vos? / yo no sé por qué cielos giraste / sé que giran en mí / nada pudiste finalmente ahorrarme / no soy sin vos sino de vos / no me reproches eso / todavía me entibia el blancor de tu nuca / y mis besos allí / siervos de esa armonía / ¿cuántas veces se detuvo allí el mundo? / ¿cuántas veces cesaste la injusticia allí / madre? / ¿cuántas veces el mundo endureció tu leche / la que me abraza / la que me rechaza / la que te pide explicaciones? / ¿ya solísima / y tarde / y tan temprano? /

y esta tarde / ¿no está llena de usted? / ¿de veces que me amó? / la voz que canta al fondo de la calle / ¿no es su voz? / ¿temblor de vientre juntos todavía? / ¿qué es este duro amor / tan suave y tuyo / lluvia a tu fuego / fuego a tu madera / llama escrita en el fuego con tu huesito último / ardor de pie en la noche? / ¿alta? / ¿qué gritás en mi alma? / pero no me gritás / tu paladar entrado a tiendas de la sombra siento frío / ¿cuántas veces sentiste mis fríos? / ¿me habrás mirado extrañada de vos? / ¿no te fui acaso el peor de los monstruos? / ¿el creado por vos? / ¿y cómo hiciste para amarme? / ¿ese trabajo dabas de comer contra tu propia oscuridad? / y cuando abrí la boca, ¿no gritaste? / ¿no se asustó tu lengua de mi lengua? / ¿no hubo un jardín de espanto en tu saliva? / ¿qué sembré / cultivé / regué con mi tu sangre? / ¿y qué te habré morido al darme a luz? / ¿y la profundidad de mis desastres? / ¿y nuestro encuentro inacabado / ya nunca / ya jamás / ya para siempre? / ¿y pedregal de vos a vos donde sangraron mis rodillas? / ¿cuando junto a mi cuna llorabas tantas cosas / y mi fiebre / y la fiebre de tu salvaje juventud? /

así mezclaste mis huesitos con tu eternidad / tus besos era suaves en noches que me dejaste solo con el terror del mundo / ¿me buscabas también así? / ¿hermanos en el miedo me quisiste? / ¿en un pañal de espanto? / ¿o me parece que fue así? / ¿dónde se hunde esta mano / dónde acaba? / ¿escribís, mano, para que sepa yo? / ¿y sabes más que yo? / tocaste el pecho de mi madre cuando fui animalito / conociste calores que no recuerdo ya / bodas que no conoceré / ¿qué subtierra de la memoria arás? / ¿soy planta que no ve sus raíces? / ¿ve la planta raíces? / ¿ve cielos / empujada? / ¿cómo vos,

what could I have meant to you? / how you must have suffered when I came out of you? / to not know you, isn't it my knowing you? / I don't know what skies you spun through / I know they spin in me / you spared me nothing in the end / I'm not without you but of you / don't blame me for it / the paleness of your nape still cools / and my kisses there / servants of this harmony / how many times did the world linger in that place? / how many times did you bring an end to injustice there / mother? / how many times did the world harden your milk? / it embraces me / it scorns me / it demands an explanation from you / now so lonely / and so late / and so soon? /

what about this evening? / isn't it awash with you? / of the times you loved me? / the voice singing at the end of the street / isn't it your voice? / womb's tremble together still? / what is this hard love? / so soft so yours / rain for your fire / fire for your wood / flame written in the fire with your last little bone / foot burning in the night? / so late? / what are you crying out in my soul? / yet you don't cry out / your tongue entering shadow's tents and I'm cold / how often did you feel my cold? / could you have watched me bewildered by you? / was I perhaps your worst monster? / the one created by you? / and how did you make yourself love me? / did you feed that labor against your own darkness? / and when I opened my mouth, didn't you cry out? / didn't your tongue fear my tongue? / wasn't there a garden of fright in your saliva? / where I planted / tended / watered with my your blood? / and what of yours did I dead when you gave birth to me? / what about the depth of my disasters? / or our unfinished encounter / now never / now ever / now always? / and what about the stony way from you to you where my knees bled? / when you cried near my cradle for so many things / and my fever / and the fever of your wild youth? /

and so you mixed my little bones with your eternity / your kisses was soft on nights when you left me alone with the world's terror / did you seek me out like that too? / did you want a brother in fear? / diapered in fright? / or does it only seem that way to me? / how far down does this hand plunge? / where does it end? / do you write, hand, so I can know? / do you know more than me? / you touched my mother's breast when I was just a little animal / you knew warmth I no longer recall / weddings I'll never know / what underground memory are you plowing? / am I a plant unfit to see its roots? / does a plant see its roots? / does it see skies / driven forth? / like

madre, me empujás? / mi mano, ¿es más con vos que mismo yo? / ¿siente tu leche o lunas de noche en mí perdida? /

¿y mi boca? / ¿cuánta alma te chupó? / ¿te fue fiesta mi boca alguna vez? / ¿y mis pies? / ¿me mirabas los pies para verme el camino? / ¿y tu ternura entonces? / ¿era tu viaje hacia mi viaje? / ¿fuiste rodeada de temor amoroso? / ¿del caminar por mí? / ¿por qué nunca supimos arreglar el dentro-fuera que nos ata? / ¿al afuerino de tu cuerpo? / tu leche seca moja mi alma / ¿ahora la soy? / ¿me es? / ¿cuáles son los trabajos del pájaro que nunca me nombrás? / ¿el que nos volaría juntos? / ¿ala yo / vuelo vos? / me obligaste a ser otro y tu perdón me muerde las cenizas / ¿acaso yo podía prolongar tu belleza? / ¿sin convertirla en cuerpo de dolor / lengua exiliada de tu nuca? / ¿y cuánto amé la ausencia de tu nuca para que no doliera? / ¿y que te devolviera? / ¿a dulzura posible en este mundo? / ¿conocida que no puedo nombrar? / ¿vientre que nadie puede repetir? / ¿lleno de maravilla, de gran desolación? / ¿pasó a río deshecho por mis pies? / ¿tan duro tu olvidar? / poderosa, ¿soy el que vos morís? / ¿ceñido de tu nombre? / ¿por qué te abrís y te cerrás? / ¿por qué brilla tu rostro en doble sangre / todavía? /

pasé por vos a la hermosura del día / por mí pasás a la honda noche / con los ojos sacados porque ya nada había que ver / sino ese fino ruido que deshace lo que te hice sufrir / ahora que estás quieta /
¿y cómo es nuestro amor / éste? /
envolverán con un jacinto la mesa de los panes /
pero ninguno
me hablará / estoy atado a tu suavísima / doy de
comer a tu animal más ciego /
¿a quién das tregua / vos? /
están ya blancos todos tus vestidos /
las sábanas me aplastan y no puedo dormir / te odiás en mí completamente
/ se crecieron la mirra y el incienso que sembraste en mí vez / dejá que te
perfumen / acompañen tu gracia / mi alma calce tu transcurrir a nada /
todavía recojo azucenas que habrás dejado aquí
para que mire el doble rostro de tu amor /

you, mother, are you driving me forth? / my hand, is it more yours than I am? / does it sense your milk or moons of a night lost in me? /

what about my mouth? / how much of your soul did it suckle? / was my mouth ever a feast for you? / and my feet? / did you watch my feet to see my way? / and what about your tenderness then? / was it your journey toward my journey? / were you surrounded by loving fear? / of walking in my place? / why couldn't we ever mend this insideout binding us? / the outsider of your body? / your dry milk dampens my soul / am I it now? / is it me? / what are the labors of the bird you've never named for me? / the one to fly us together? / I wing / you flight? / you forced me to be other and your forgiveness bites at my ashes / could I have drawn your beauty out? / without changing it to a body of pain / tongue exiled from your nape? / and how much did I love the absence of your nape so it wouldn't hurt? / so it would bring you back? / to the possible sweetness of this world? / acquaintance I can't name / womb no one can repeat / brimming with wonder, great desolation? / did it turn to a river undone by my feet? / is your forgetting so hard? / powerful one, is it me you die? / girded by your name? / why do you open and close? / why does your face flash with double blood / still? /

I passed through you toward day's beauty / through me you travel toward deep night / your eyes plucked since there was nothing to see / but that fine noise undoing what I made you endure / now that you're still /
what is our love like? / this? /
hyacinth shrouds the table for bread /
yet not one loaf
will speak to me / I'm bound to your so softness / I feed
your blindest animal /
to whom might you offer a truce? / yourself? /
all your dresses have turned white /
bedsheets bear down on me and I can't sleep / you wholly hate yourself in me / the myrrh and incense you sowed in my time have ripened / let them perfume you / go along with your grace / let my soul shoe your passing toward nothingness /
I still gather the lilies you might have left here
so I can see the double faces of your love /

mecer tu cuna / lavar tus pañales / para que no
me dejes nunca más /
sin avisar / sin pedirme permiso /
aullabas cuando te separé de mí /
ya no nos perdonemos /

Ginebra, 1984 / París, 1987

to rock your cradle / wash your diapers / so you'll
never leave me again /
with no warning / without my permission /
you howled when I tore you from me /
let's not forgive one another now /

Geneva, 1984 / Paris, 1987

De HOSPITAL BRITÁNICO

Mi madre es la risa, la libertad, el verano.

"Christus Pantokrator"

La postal tiene una leyenda: "Christus Pantokrator, siglo XIII".

A los pies de la pared desnuda, la postal es un Christus Pantokrator en la mitad de un espigón larguísimo. (1985)

"Christus Pantokrator"

Entre mis ojos y los ojos de Christus Pantokrator nunca hay piso. Siempre hay dos alpargatas descosidas, blancas, en un día de viento.

Con la postal en el zócalo, con Christus Pantokrator en el espigón larguísimo, mi oscuridad no tiene hambre de gaviotas. (1985)

"Christus Pantokrator"

La postal viene de marineros, de pugilistas viejos en ese bar estrecho que parece un submarino—de maderas y de latas—hundiéndose en el sol de la ribera.

La postal viene de un Christus Pantokrator que cuando bajo las persianas, apago la luz y cierro los ojos, me pide que filme Su Silencio dentro de una botella varada en un banco infinito. (1985)

Héctor Viel Temperley (Argentina, 1933–1987)

....

From HOSPITAL BRITÁNICO

My mother is laughter, freedom, summer.

"Christus Pantokrator"

The postcard has a caption: "Christus Pantokrator, 13th Century."

At the foot of the bare wall, the postcard is a Christus Pantokrator
halfway to the end of a very long jetty. (1985)

"Christus Pantokrator"

Between my eyes and the eyes of Christus Pantokrator there is never
a floor. There is always a pair of white espadrilles on a windy day,
coming undone.

With the postcard on the baseboard, with Christus Pantokrator on the
very long jetty, my darkness has no hunger for seagulls. (1985)

"Christus Pantokrator"

The postcard comes from sailors, from old pugilists in that narrow bar
like a submarine—of tin cans and wood—sinking into the coastal sun.

The postcard comes from a Christus Pantokrator, who, when I lower
the blinds, turn off the light, and close my eyes, asks me to film His
Silence in a bottle washed up on an endless shoal. (1985)

"Christus Pantokrator"

Delante de la postal estoy como una pala que cava en el sol, en el Rostro y en los ojos de Christus Pantokrator. (1985)

Sé que sólo en los ojos de Christus Pantokrator puedo cavar en la transpiración de todos mis veranos hasta llegar desde el esternón, desde el mediodía, a ese faro cubierto por alas de naranjos que quiero para el niño casi mudo que llevé sobre el alma muchos meses. (Mes de Abril de 1986)

Larga esquina de verano

Alguien me odió ante el sol al que mi madre me arrojó. Necesito estar a oscuras, necesito regresar al hombre. No quiero que me toque la muchacha, ni el rufián, ni el ojo del poder, ni la ciencia del mundo. No quiero ser tocado por los sueños.

El enano que es mi ángel de la guarda sube bamboleándose los pocos peldaños de madera ametrallados por los soles; y sobre el pasamano de coronas de espinas, la piedra de su anillo es un cruzado que trepa somnoliento una colina: burdeles vacíos y pequeños, panaderías abiertas pero muy pequeñas, teatros pequeños pero cerrados—y más arriba ojos de catacumbas, lejanas miradas de catacumbas tras oscuras pestañas a flor de tierra.

Un tiburón se pudre a veinte metros. Un tiburón pequeño—una bala con tajos, un acordeón abierto—se pudre y me acompaña. Un tiburón—un criquet en silencio en el suelo de tierra, junto a un tambor de agua, en una gomería a muchos metros de la ruta —se pudre a veinte metros del sol en mi cabeza: El sol como las puertas, con dos hombres blanquísimos, de un colegio militar en un desierto; un colegio militar que no es más que un desierto en un lugar adentro de esta playa de la que huye el futuro. (1984)

"Christus Pantokrator"

In front of the postcard I am like a shovel that digs in the sun, in the
Face and in the eyes of Christus Pantokrator. (1985)

I know that only in the eyes of Christus Pantokrator can I dig in the
perspiration of all my summers until I arrive from my sternum, from
noon, at that lighthouse shaded by the limbs of orange trees that I
want for the half-mute boy I bore for many months upon my soul.
(Month of April, 1986)

Long corner of summer

Someone hated me before the sun into which I was cast by my mother.
I need to be in the dark, I need to return to man. I don't want the
girl to touch me, nor the pimp, nor the eye of power, nor worldly
science. I don't want to be touched by dreams.

The dwarf who is my guardian angel sways back and forth as he comes
up the few wooden steps riddled with suns; and along the banister
of thorny crowns, the stone in his ring is a crusader climbing a hill
in a daze: small, deserted brothels, bakeries that are open but very
small, theaters that are small but closed—and above them the eyes
of catacombs, distant gazes of catacombs behind dark eyelashes at
ground level.

A shark rots twenty meters from here. A small shark—a bullet with
slits, an open accordion—rots and is my companion. A shark rots—
a fishing reel silent on the dirt floor, next to a water drum, in a tire
shop set back from the highway—twenty meters from the sun in my
head: The sun like the doors, flanked by two men in pure white,
of a military school in the desert; a military school that is no more
than a desert in a place inside this beach from which the future
flees. (1984)

Larga esquina de verano

¿Nunca morirá la sensación de que el demonio puede servirse de los
cielos, y de las nubes y las aves, para observarme las entrañas?

Amigos muertos que caminan en las tardes grises hacia frontones
de pelota solitarios: El rufián que me mira se sonríe como si yo
pudiera desearla todavía.

Se nubla y se desnubla. Me hundo en mi carne; me hundo en la iglesia
de desagüe a cielo abierto en la que creo. Espero la resurrección—
espero su estallido contra mis enemigos—en este cuerpo, en este
día, en esta playa. Nada puede impedir que en su Pierna me azoten
como cota de malla—y sin ninguna Historia ardan en mí—las
cabezas de fósforos de todo el Tiempo.

Tengo las toses de los viejos fusiles de un Tiro Federal en los ojos.
Mi vida es un desierto entre dos guerras. Necesito estar a oscuras.
Necesito dormir, pero el sol me despierta. El sol, a través de mis
párpados, como alas de gaviotas que echan cal sobre toda mi vida;
el sol como una zona que me había olvidado; el sol como un golpe
de espuma en mis confines; el sol como dos jóvenes vigías en una
tempestad de luz que se ha tragado al mar, a las velas y al cielo.
(1984)

Larga esquina de verano

La boca abierta al viento que se lleva a las moscas, el tiburón se pudre a
veinte metros. El tiburón se desvanece, flota sobre el último asiento
de la playa—del ómnibus que asciende con las ratas mareadas y
con frío y comienza a partirse por la mitad y a desprenderse del
limpiaparabrisas, que en los ojos del mar era su lluvia.

Me acostumbré a verlas llegar con las nubes para cambiar mi vida. Me
acostumbré a extrañarlas bajo el cielo: calladas, sin equipaje, con un
cepillo de dientes entre sus manos. Me acostumbré a sus vientres

Long corner of summer

Will it never end, this feeling that the devil can take what he wants from
the heavens, from the clouds and birds, just to get a look at my guts?

Dead friends who walk toward deserted handball courts on gray
afternoons: The pimp watching me smiles as if I were still able to
desire his girl.

It gets cloudy and it unclouds. I sink into my flesh; I sink into
that open sewer of a church in which I believe. I wait for the
resurrection—I wait for it to shatter my enemies—in this body, on
this day, on this beach. Nothing can stop the match heads of Time
in its entirety—and without any History they burn inside me—from
lashing me like chain mail as I lay across his Leg.

I have the coughs of old rifles at a Federal Range in my eyes. My life is
a desert between two wars. I need to be in the dark. I need to sleep,
but the sun wakes me. The sun, through my eyelids, like the wings
of gulls that scatter whitewash across my whole life; the sun like a
place that had forgotten me; the sun like pounding surf against my
limits; the sun like two young watchmen in a tempest of light that
has swallowed the sea, the sails and the sky. (1984)

Long corner of summer

Its mouth open to the breeze that carries away the flies, the shark rots
twenty meters from here. The shark vanishes, it floats over the last
seat on the beach—on the bus that rises with cold, seasick rats and
starts to split down the middle and separate from its windshield
wipers, which in the eyes of the sea were its rain.

I got used to watching them show up with the clouds to change my life.
I got used to pining for them under the firmament: silent, without
luggage, their toothbrushes in their hands. I got used to their bellies

sin esposo, embarazadas jóvenes que odian la arena que me cubre.
(1984)

Larga esquina de verano

¿Toda la arena de esta playa quiere llenar mi boca? Ya todo hambre de
Rostro ensangrentado quiere comer arena y olvidarse?

Aves marinas que regresan de la velocidad de Dios en mi cabeza: No
me separo de las claras paralelas de madera que tatuaban la piel de
mis brazos junto a las axilas; no me separo de la única morada—sin
paredes ni techo—que he tenido en el ígneo brillante de extranjero
del centro de los patios vacíos del verano, y soy hambre de arenas—
y hambre de Rostro ensangrentado.

Pero como sitiado por una eternidad, ¿yo puedo hacer violencia para
que aparezca Tu Cuerpo, que es mi arrepentimiento? ¿Puedo hacer
violencia con el pugilista africano de hierro y vientre almohadillado
que es mi pieza sin luz a la una de la tarde mientras el mar—afuera
—parece una armería? Dos mil años de esperanza, de arena y de
muchacha muerta, ¿pueden hacer violencia? Con humedad de
tienda que vendía cigarrillos negros, revólveres baratos y cintas
de colores para disfraces de Carnaval, ¿se puede todavía hacer
violencia?

Sin Tu Cuerpo en la tierra muere sin sangre el que no muere mártir;
sin Tu Cuerpo en la tierra soy la trastienda de un negocio donde
se deshacen cadenas, brújulas, timones—lentamente como hostias
—bajo un ventilador de techo gris; sin Tu Cuerpo en la tierra no sé
cómo pedir perdón a una muchacha en la punta de guadaña con
rocío del ala izquierda del cementerio alemán (y la orilla del mar—
espuma y agua helada en las mejillas—es a veces un hombre que se
afeita sin ganas día tras día). (1985)

without husbands, these pregnant girls who hate the sand piled over me. (1984)

Long corner of summer

Does all the sand on this beach hope to fill my mouth? And does all hunger for blood-stained Face hope to feast on sand and be forgotten?

Marine birds that come back from the velocity of God in my head: I don't separate myself from the clear wooden parallels that tattooed the skin of my biceps near my armpits; I don't separate myself from the only home I've ever known—it has neither walls nor roof —perched on volcanic rock of foreign brilliance in the center of deserted summer patios, and I am hunger for sands—and hunger for blood-stained Face.

But as one besieged by an eternity, can I commit an act of violence that would conjure Your Body, which is my repentance? Can I commit an act of violence alongside the ironclad African pugilist with the padded belly who is my room without light at one in the afternoon while the sea—outside—seems like an armory? Can two thousand years of hope, of sand and of dead girl, commit an act of violence? In air as damp as a store that sold black cigarettes, cheap revolvers, and colorful ribbons for costumes worn at Carnaval, even then can one commit an act of violence?

Without Your Body on earth the man who doesn't die a martyr dies bloodless; without Your Body on earth I am the back room of a shop where chains, compasses, rudders are taken apart—carefully, like hosts—beneath a fan attached to a gray ceiling; without Your Body on earth I don't know how to beg for forgiveness from a girl on the end of a scythe covered in dew from the left wing of the German cemetery (and sometimes the shoreline—foam and frozen water on its cheeks—is a man who begrudgingly shaves day after day). (1985)

Larga esquina de verano

¿Soy ese tripulante con corona de espinas que no ve a sus alas afuera
del buque, que no ve a Tu Rostro en el afiche pegado al casco y
desgarrado por el viento y que no sabe todavía que Tu Rostro
es más que todo el mar cuando lanza sus dados contra un negro
espigón de cocinas de hierro que espera a algunos hombres en un
sol donde nieva ? (1985)

Tu Rostro

Tu Rostro como sangre muy oscura en un plato de tropa, entre cocinas
frías y bajo un sol de nieve; Tu Rostro como una conversación entre
colmenas con vértigo en la llanura del verano; Tu Rostro como
sombra verde y negra con balidos muy cerca de mi aliento y mi
revólver; Tu Rostro como sombra verde y negra que desciende al
galope, cada tarde, desde una pampa a dos mil metros sobre el nivel
del mar; Tu Rostro como arroyos de violetas cayendo lentamente
desde gallos de riña; Tu Rostro como arroyos de violetas que
empapan de vitrales a un hospital sobre un barranco. (1985)

Tu Cuerpo y Tu Padre

Tu Cuerpo como un barranco, y el amor de Tu Padre como duras
mazorcas de tristeza en Tus axilas casi desgarradas. (1985)

Tengo la cabeza vendada (texto profético lejano)

Mi cabeza para nacer cruza el fuego del mundo pero con una
serpentina de agua helada en la memoria. Y le pido socorro. (1978)

Long corner of summer

Am I that crew member with a crown of thorns who can't see his wings outside the ship, who can't see Your Face in the poster nailed to the hull and torn by the wind and who still doesn't know that Your Face is greater than the entire sea when it throws its dice against a black jetty of iron stoves that waits for some men in a sun where it snows? (1985)

Your Face

Your Face like darkest blood on a soldier's plate, among cold stoves and beneath a snowy sun; Your Face like a conversation between frenzied hives on summer's plain; Your Face like green and black shadow with bleating so close to my breath and my revolver; Your Face like green and black shadow that comes down at a gallop, each afternoon, from a pampa two thousand meters above sea level; Your Face like streams of violets slowly falling from cocks bred to fight; Your Face like streams of violets that bathe a hospital in stained glass above a ravine. (1985)

Your Body and Your Father

Your body like a ravine, and Your Father's love like hard cobs of sadness in Your armpits about to tear apart. (1985)

My head is bandaged (distant prophetic text)

My head passes through the fire of the world to be born but keeps a winding stream of frozen water in its memory. And I ask it to help me. (1978)

Tengo la cabeza vendada

Mariposa de Dios, pubis de María: Atraviesa la sangre de mi frente—
hasta besarme el **Rostro en Jesucristo** (1982)—.

Tengo la cabeza vendada (textos proféticos)

Mi cuerpo—con aves como bisturíes en la frente—entra en mi alma.
(1984)

El sol, en mi cabeza, como toda la sangre de Cristo sobre una pared de
anestesia total. (1984)

Santa Reina de los misterios del rosario del hacha y de las brazadas
lejos del espigón: Ruega por mí que estoy en una zona donde
nunca había anclado con maniobras de Cristo en mi cabeza. (1985)

Señor: Desde este instante mi cabeza quiere ser, por los siglos de los
siglos, la herida de Tu Mano bendiciéndome en fuego. (1984)

El sol como la blanca velocidad de Dios en mi cabeza, que la aspira y
desgarra hacia la nuca.(1984)

Tengo la cabeza vendada (texto del hombre en la playa)

El sol entra con mi alma en mi cabeza (o mi cuerpo—con la
Resurrección—entra en mi alma). (1984)

Tengo la cabeza vendada (texto del hombre en la playa)

Por culpa del viento de fuego que penetra en su herida, en este
instante, Tu Mano traza un ancla y no una cruz en mi cabeza.

My head is bandaged

> Butterfly of God, pubis of Mary: Cross the blood of my brow—**until I kiss my very Face in Jesus Christ** (1982)—.

My head is bandaged (prophetic texts)

> My body—with scalpel birds on its brow—enters my soul. (1984)

> The sun, in my head, like all the blood of Christ against a wall of total anesthesia. (1984)

> Holy Queen of the mysteries of the rosary of the ax and of strokes far from the jetty: Pray for me who am in a place where I had never anchored with maneuvers of Christ in my head. (1985)

> Lord: From this moment on my head wishes to be, for centuries upon centuries, the wound on Your Hand as you bless me in fire. (1984)

> The sun like the white velocity of God in my head, which it breathes in and tears to the nape. (1984)

My head is bandaged (text by the man on the beach)

> Along with my soul, the sun enters into my head (or my body—along with the Resurrection—enters into my soul). (1984)

My head is bandaged (text by the man on the beach)

> It is the fault of the fiery wind that pierces its wound, at this moment, that Your Hand traces an anchor in my head and not a cross.

Quiero beber hacia mi nuca, eternamente, los dos brazos del ancla del
temblor de Tu Carne y de la prisa de los Cielos. (1984)

Tengo la cabeza vendada (texto del hombre en la playa)

Allá atrás, en mi nuca, vi al blanquísimo desierto de esta vida de mi
vida; vi a mi eternidad, que debo atravesar desde los ojos del Señor
hasta los ojos del Señor. (1984)

Me han sacado del mundo

Soy el lugar donde el Señor tiende la Luz que Él es.

Me han sacado del mundo

Me cubre una armadura de mariposas y estoy en la camisa de
mariposas que es el Señor—adentro, en mí.

El Reino de los Cielos me rodea. El Reino de los Cielos es el Cuerpo
de Cristo—y cada mediodía toco a Cristo.

Cristo es Cristo madre, y en Él viene mi madre a visitarme.

Me han sacado del mundo

"Mujer que embaracé," "Pabellón Rosetto," "Larga esquina de
verano":

Vuelve el placer de las palabras a mi carne en las copas de unos
eucaliptus (o en los altos de "B," desde los cuales una vez—sólo una
vez—vi a una playa del cielo recostada en la costa).

I want to drink back to my nape, forever, the two arms of the anchor of the trembling of Your Flesh and of the Heavens' haste. (1984)

My head is bandaged (text by the man on the beach)

Back there, on my nape, I saw the pure white desert of this life of my life; I saw my eternity, which I must traverse from the eyes of the Lord to the eyes of the Lord. (1984)

They have taken me from the world

I am the place where the Lord spreads out the Light that He is.

They have taken me from the world

An armor of butterflies covers me and I wear the shirt of butterflies that is the Lord—within, inside me.

The Kingdom of Heaven surrounds me. The Kingdom of Heaven is the Body of Christ—and each day at noon I touch Christ.

Christ is Christ the mother, and my mother comes to visit me in Him.

They have taken me from the world

"Woman I impregnated," "Rosetto Pavilion," "Long corner of summer":

The pleasure of words comes back to my flesh in the tops of some eucalyptus trees (or in the heights of "B," where once—just once—I looked out and saw a heavenly beach leaning against the shore).

Me han sacado del mundo

Manos de María, sienes de mármol de mi playa en el cielo:

La muerte es el comienzo de una guerra donde jamás otro hombre
podrá ver mi esqueleto.

La libertad, el verano (A mi madre, recordándole el fuego)

Porque parto recién cuando he sudado y abro una canilla y me
acuclillo como junto a un altar, como escondido, y el chorro cae
helado en mi cabeza y desliza su hostia hacia mis labios, envuelta en
los cabellos que la siguen. (1976)

Vengo de comulgar y estoy en éxtasis aunque comulgué con los
cosacos sentados a una mesa bajo el cielo y los eucaliptus que con
ellos se cimbran estos días bochornosos en que camino hasta las
areneras del sur de la ciudad—el vizcaíno, santa adela, la elisa.
(1982)

Por las paredes de los rascacielos el calor y el silencio suben de nave en
nave: Obsesivo verano de fotógrafo en fotógrafo, ojos del Arponero
que rayan lo que miran. Ser de avenidas verticales que jamás fue
azotado. (1978)

Después íbamos al África cada día de nuevo—antes que nada, antes de
vestirnos—mientras rugían las fieras abajo en el zoológico, subía
un sol sangriento a sus jazmines, y nosotros nos odiábamos, nos
deseábamos, gritábamos... (1978)

Instantes de anestesia, de lento alcohol de anoche todavía en la sangre
de pie de una muchacha desnuda y más dorada que la escoba:
Necesito aferrarme de nuevo a la llanura, al ave blanca del corpiño
en la pileta de lavar, detrás de la estación y entre las casuarinas.
(1984)

They have taken me from the world

Hands of Mary, temples of marble from my beach in heaven:

Death is the beginning of a war in which another man will never be
able to see my skeleton.

Freedom, summer (To my mother, reminding her of the fire)

Because I depart just when I've begun to sweat and I turn on the faucet
and lower myself as if I were beside an altar, as if I were hiding, and
the freezing water falls on my head and slides its host toward my
lips, wrapped in the tresses that come after it. (1976)

I come straight from communion and I'm in ecstasy though I took
it with the Cossacks seated at a table beneath the sky and the
eucalyptus trees that sway alongside them these muggy days when I
walk to the sand quarries south of the city—el vizcaíno, santa adela,
la elisa. (1982)

Heat and silence climb the walls of the skyscrapers from nave to nave:
Obsessive summer from photographer to photographer, eyes of
the Harpooner that stripe what they see. Being of vertical avenues
that's never been lashed. (1978)

Then we went to Africa every day as if for the first time—before
anything else, before we got dressed—while the beasts roared below
us in the preserve, a bleeding sun rose before its jasmines, and we
hated each other, we desired each other, we were screaming… (1978)

Moments of anesthesia, of last night's alcohol lingering in the blood
taken from the foot of a naked girl more golden than a broom. Again
I need to cling to smoothness, to that white bird of a bra in the
washtub, behind the station and among the casuarinas. (1984)

Tengo la foto de dos novios que cayeron al mar. Están vestidos de invierno, los invito a desnudarse. En las siestas nos sentamos junto a la bomba de agua y nos miramos: de nuevo embolsan luz los pechos de ella; él amaba a los caballos y una vez intentó suicidarse. (1978)

Necesito oler limón, necesito oler limón. De tanto respirar este aire azul, este cielo encarnizadamente azul, se pueden reventar los vasos de sangre más pequeños de mi nariz. (1969)

Y a las siestas, de pie, los guardavidas abatían la sal de sus cabezas con una damajuana muy pesada, de agua dulce y de vidrio verde, grueso, que entre todos cuidaban. (1982)

I hold the photo of two lovers who fell into the sea. They're dressed
for winter, I ask them to take off their clothes. During siestas we sit
beside the water pump and stare at each other: light collects in her
breasts again; he loved horses and one time he tried to kill himself.
(1978)

I need to smell lemon, I need to smell lemon. The tiniest blood vessels
in my nose could burst from breathing in so much of this blue air,
this sky so viciously blue. (1969)

And, at siesta time, the lifeguards stood up and rinsed the salt from
their heads with a cumbersome demijohn of thick green glass,
heavy with fresh water, that they took turns refilling. (1982)

De ARBOL DE DIANA

II

Éstas son las versiones que nos propone:
un agujero, una pared que tiembla…

IV

AHORA BIEN:

Quién dejará de hundir su mano en busca del tributo para la
pequeña olvidada. El frío pagará. Pagará el viento. La lluvia
pagará. Pagará el trueno.

a Aurora y Julio Cortázar

VI

ella se desnuda en el paraíso
de su memoria
ella desconoce el feroz destino
de sus visiones
ella tiene miedo de no saber nombrar
lo que no existe

VII

Salta con la camisa en llamas
de estrella a estrella,
de sombra en sombra.
Muere de muerte lejana
la que ama al viento.

Alejandra Pizarnik

(Argentina, 1936–1972)

From DIANA'S TREE

II

These are the versions put forth to us:
a pinhole, a wall that trembles…

IV

NOW THEN:

Who will no longer dig his hand deep in search of tribute for the
forgotten girl. The cold will pay. The wind will pay. The rain
will pay. Also the thunder.

For Aurora and Julio Cortázar

VI

she undresses herself in the paradise
of her memory
she's unaware of the ferocious destiny
of her visions
she fears not knowing how to name
what doesn't exist

VII

She leaps with her shirt in flames
from star to star,
from darkness to darkness.
She dies of a faraway death
the woman who loves the wind.

VIII

Memoria iluminada, galería donde vaga la sombra de lo que
    espero.
No es verdad que vendrá. No es verdad que no vendrá.

IX

Estos huesos brillando en la noche,
estas palabras como piedras preciosas
en la garganta viva de un pájaro petrificado,
este verde muy amado,
este lila caliente,
este corazón sólo misterioso.

X

un viento débil
lleno de rostros doblados
que recorto en forma de objetos que amar

XI

ahora
      en esta hora inocente
yo y la que fui nos sentamos
en el umbral de mi mirada

XIII

explicar con palabras de este mundo
que partió de mí un barco llevándome

VIII

Illuminated memory, gallery where the shadow of what I wait
for wanders.
It's not true it will come. It's not true it won't come.

IX

These bones brilliant in the night,
these words like precious stones
in the living throat of a petrified bird,
this beloved green,
this hot lilac,
this heart alone mysterious.

X

a weak wind
full of folded faces
I cut into the forms of objects to love

XI

now
        at this innocent hour
I and the one I was sit together
at the threshold of my gaze

XIII

explain with words of this world
that bore of me a boat elsewhere

XIV

El poema que no digo,
el que no merezco.
Miedo de ser dos
camino del espejo:
alguien en mí dormido
me come y me bebe.

XV

Extraño desacostumbrarme
de la hora en que nací.
Extraño no ejercer más
oficio de recién llegada.

XVI

has construido tu casa
has emplumado tus pájaros
has golpeado al viento
con tus propios huesos

has terminado sola
lo que nadie comenzó

XVII

Días en que una palabra lejana se apodera de mí. Voy por esos
días sonámbula y transparente. La hermosa autómata se
canta, se encanta, se cuenta casos y cosas: nido de hilos
rígidos donde me danzo y me lloro en mis numerosos
funerales. (Ella es su espejo incendiado, su espera en
hogueras frías, su elemento místico, su fornicación de
nombres creciendo solos en la noche pálida.)

XIV

The poem I don't speak,
the one I don't deserve.
Fear of being two
the way of the mirror:
someone in me asleep
eats and drinks me.

XV

Strange weaning
off the hour of my birth.
Strange to never again practice
the skill of newly arrived.

XVI

you've built your house
you've feathered your birds
you've beaten the wind
with your own bones

you alone ended
what nobody began

XVII

Days in which a distant word takes hold of me. I go through
    those days sleepwalking and transparent. The lovely
    automaton sings to herself, she enchants herself, she tells
    herself stories and things: nest of rigid threads where I
    dance and cry for myself in my many funerals. (She is
    her blazing mirror, her hope in cold bonfires, her mystic
    element, her fornication of names growing alone in the pale
    night.)

XVIII

como un poema enterado
del silencio de las cosas
hablas para no verme

XIX

cuando vea los ojos
que tengo en los míos tatuados

XX

dice que no sabe del miedo de la muerte del amor
dice que tiene miedo de la muerte del amor
dice que el amor es muerte es miedo
dice que la muerte es miedo es amor
dice que no sabe

a Laure Bataillon

XXII

en la noche

un espejo para la pequeña muerta

un espejo de cenizas

XXIII

una mirada desde la alcantarilla
puede ser una visión del mundo

la rebelión consiste en mirar una rosa
hasta pulverizarse los ojos

XVIII

like a poem buried
in the silence of things
you talk to not see me

XIX

when you see the eyes
I have tattooed on mine

XX

she says she doesn't know of the fear of the death of love
she says she's afraid of the death of love
she says that love is death it's fear
she says that death is fear it's love
she says she doesn't know

To Laure Bataillon

XXII

in the night

a mirror for the small dead girl

a mirror of ashes

XXIII

a view from the sewer
can be a vision of the world

rebellion involves gazing at a rose
until your eyes shred

XXV

(exposición Goya)

un agujero en la noche
súbitamente invadido por un ángel

XXVII

un golpe del alba en las flores
me abandona ebria de nada y de luz lila
ebria de inmovilidad y de certeza

XXVIII

te alejas de los nombres
que hilan el silencio de las cosas

XXIX

Aquí vivimos con una mano en la garganta. Que nada es
    posible ya lo sabían los que inventaban lluvias y tejían
    palabras con el tormento de la ausencia. Por eso en sus
    plegarias había un sonido de manos enamoradas de la
    niebla.

a André Pieyre de Mandiargues

XXX

en el invierno fabuloso
la endecha de las alas en la lluvia
en la memoria del agua dedos de niebla

XXV

(*Goya exhibition*)

a pinhole in the night
invaded suddenly by an angel

XXVII

one strike of dawn in the flowers
abandons me drunk on nothing and lilac light
drunk on immobility and certainty

XXVIII

you withdraw from the names
that spin the silence of things

XXIX

We live here with a hand at our throats. Those who invented
    rains and wove words with the torment of absence they
    already knew that nothing is possible. Because of this their
    prayers held the sound of hands in love with fog.

To André Pieyre de Mandiargues

XXX

in the fabled winter
the endecha of wings in the rain
in the water's memory the fog's fingers

XXXI

Es un cerrar los ojos y jurar no abrirlos. En tanto afuera se
    alimenten de relojes y de flores nacidas de la astucia. Pero
    con los ojos cerrados y un sufrimiento en verdad demasiado
    grande pulsamos los espejos hasta que las palabras
    olvidadas suenan mágicamente.

XXXII

Zona de plagas donde la dormida come
        lentamente
su corazón de medianoche.

XXXIII

alguna vez
        alguna vez tal vez
me iré sin quedarme
        me iré como quien se va

                        a Ester Singer

XXXIV

la pequeña viajera
moría explicando su muerte

sabios animales nostálgicos
visitaban su cuerpo caliente

XXXV

Vida, mi vida, déjate caer, déjate doler, mi vida, déjate enlazar
    de fuego, de silencio ingenuo, de piedras verdes en la casa
    de la noche, déjate caer y doler, mi vida.

XXXI

It's closing your eyes and swearing not to open them. In the
    meantime outside they're nourished on clocks and flowers
    born of duplicity. But with eyes closed and a sorrow that's
    really too much we press the mirrors until the forgotten
    words magically sound.

XXXII

Zone of plagues where the sleeping woman eats
                slowly
her midnight heart.

XXXIII

sometime
        sometime maybe
I'll leave without staying
        I'll leave like someone who's going

                                    To Ester Singer

XXXIV

the small traveler
died explaining her death

wise nostalgic animals
visited her hot body

XXXV

Life, my life, let yourself fall, let yourself hurt, my life, let
    yourself be bound by fire, by naive silence, by green stones
    in the night's house, let yourself fall and hurt, my life.

XXXVI

en la jaula del tiempo
el dormido mira sus ojos solos

el viento le trae
la tenue respuesta de las hojas

a Alain Glass

XXXVII

más allá de cualquier zona prohibida
hay un espejo para nuestra triste transparencia

XXXVIII

Este canto arrepentido, vigía detrás de mis poemas:

este canto me desmiente, me amordaza.

XXXVI

in the cage of time
the sleeping woman looks at her eyes alone

the wind brings her
the tenuous response of the leaves

To Alain Glass

XXXVII

beyond any prohibited zone
there's a mirror for our sad transparency

XXXVIII

This remorseful song, watchtower of my poems:

this song denies me, it gags me.

ENTONCES, EN LAS AGUAS DE CONCHÁN

(Verano 1978)

Entonces en las aguas de Conchán ancló una gran ballena.
Era azul cuando el cielo azulaba y negra con la niebla.
Y era azul.
Hay quien la vio venida desde el Norte (donde dicen que hay muchas).
Hay quien la vio venida desde el Sur (donde hiela y habitan los leones).
Otros dicen que solita brotó como los hongos o las hojas de ruda.
Quienes esto repiten son las gentes de Villa El Salvador,
pobres entre los pobres.
Creciendo todos tras las blancas colinas y en la arena:
Gentes como arenales en arenal.
(Sólo saben el mar cuando está bravo y se huele en el viento).
El viento que revuelve el lomo azul de la ballena muerta.
Islote de aluminio bajo el sol.
La que vino del Norte y del Sur
y solita brotó de las corrientes.
La gran ballena muerta.
Las autoridades temen por las aguas:
la peste azul entre las playas de Conchán.
La gran ballena muerta.
(Las autoridades protegen la salud del veraneante).
Muy pronto la ballena ha de podrirse como un higo maduro en el verano.
La peste es, por decir,
40 reses pudriéndose en el mar
(ó 200 ovejas ó 1000 perros).
Las autoridades no saben cómo huir de tanta carne muerta.
Los veraneantes se guardan de la peste que empieza en las malaguas de la
    arena mojada.
En los arenales de Villa El Salvador las gentes no reposan.

Antonio Cisneros

(Peru, 1942–2012)

THEN, IN THE WATERS OF CONCHÁN

(Summer 1978)

Then a great whale anchored itself in the waters of Conchán.
It was blue when the sky blued, and black under fog.
And it was blue.
Some saw it come from the North (where they say there are many).
Some saw it come from the South (land of lions and ice).
Others say it sprouted like a mushroom, or like leaves of rue.
People tell of it in Villa El Salvador,
poor among the poor.
All raised behind white hills, and in the sand:
People like quicksand in the sand.
(The only sea they know is fierce, is a smell on the wind)
Wind riffling the blue back of the whale's corpse.
Aluminum islet under sun.
That came from the North and from the South
and sprung alone from the tide.
The great dead whale.
Water spooks the authorities:
blue stink along the beaches of Conchán.
The great dead whale.
(The authorities protect the health of summerfolk).
Soon the whale will rot like a ripe summer fig.
The stench, let's say:
40 putrid cattle in the sea
(or 200 sheep or 1,000 dogs).
The authorities don't know how to flee so much dead flesh.
The summerfolk ward off a stink that starts with sea nettles on damp sand.
In the sandlands of Villa El Salvador, the people never rest.

Sabido es por los pobres de los pobres
que atrás de las colinas flota una isla de carne aún sin dueño.
Y llegado el crepúsculo
no del océano sino del arenal
se afilan los mejores cuchillos de cocina y el hacha del maestro carnicero.
Así fueron armados los pocos nadadores de Villa El Salvador.
Y a medianoche luchaban con los pozos donde espuman las olas.
La gran ballena flotaba hermosa aún entre los tumbos helados.
Hermosa todavía.

Sea su carne destinada a 10000 bocas.
Sea techo su piel de 100 moradas.
Sea su aceite luz para las noches
y todas las frituras del verano.

They know, the poorest of the poor,
that past the dunes a fleshy island floats without a keeper.
As twilight comes
from sand, not from the sea,
they've sharpened the best kitchen knives, the master butcher's ax.
And Villa El Salvador's few swimmers swam out, armed.
At midnight fought the whirlpools where the waves spumed.
The great whale beautiful, heaved by the frigid swells.
Beautiful still.

May 10,000 mouths receive that meat.
May that skin roof 100 houses.
May all that oil fuel the nights
and frying pans of summer.

EL GUARDIÁN DEL HIELO

Y coincidimos en el terral
el heladero con su carretilla averiada
y yo
que corría tras los pájaros huidos del fuego
de la zafra.
También coincidió el sol.
En esa situación cómo negarse a un favor llano:
el heladero me pidió cuidar su efímero hielo.

Oh cuidar lo fugaz bajo el sol…

El hielo empezó a derretirse
bajo mi sombra, tan desesperada
como inútil.

    Diluyéndose
dibujaba seres esbeltos y primordiales
que sólo un instante tenían firmeza de cristal de cuarzo
y enseguida eran formas puras
como de montaña o planeta
que se devasta.

No se puede amar lo que tan rápido fuga.
Ama rápido, me dijo el sol.
Y así aprendí, en su ardiente y perverso reino,
a cumplir con la vida:
yo soy el guardián del hielo.

José Watanabe

(Peru, 1946–2007)

GUARDIAN OF ICE

We met in the land-wind,
the ice-vendor with his rickety cart
and I
who chased after birds fleeing the
harvest fire.
And the sun was there.
Under the circumstances, how could I deny a simple favor?
The vendor asked me to watch his ephemeral ice.

Oh, to nurture what perishes under the sun!

The ice began to melt
in my shadow, desperate
and inept.

    Thinning down,
it revealed svelte, primeval beings
which for the slightest instant took on solidity
like quartz crystal
then were just as soon forms pure
as a mountain or planet
wiped away.

What is so short-lived cannot be loved.
Love faster, the sun told me.
So I learned, in its perverse and ardent world,
to comply with life:
I am the guardian of ice.

VIDA

Un pájaro vuela, galopa un caballo;
un gato trepa por un álamo;
un pez nada río arriba.
Las plantas cuando crecen
lentamente se mueven,
si extienden sus ramas,
si hunden las raíces en la tierra
y cuando abren sus flores.

El pájaro huye si se quiebra una rama.
El perro acude al escuchar la voz del amo.
Los peces vienen en masa
cuando se echan migas en el agua.
El animal salvaje, por ejemplo el puma,
olfatea de lejos a su presa.
Y la sensitiva cierra sus hojas
si casi se la toca.

Las aves se alimentan de insectos,
semillas, peces o alimañas.
Los animales pacen o se devoran.
El hombre es omnívoro.

El pez y el pájaro cubren a la hembra
en el viento o en el agua.
El perro se monta sobre la perra.
El hombre se tiende sobre la mujer
y entra por sus piernas entreabiertas.

Gonzalo Millán (Chile, 1947–2006)

LIFE

A bird flies, a horse gallops;
a cat climbs a poplar tree;
a fish swims upstream.
Plants, as they grow,
sway gently,
spread their branches,
sink their roots in the ground
as well as when they flower.

Birds take flight at the snap of a branch.
Dogs heed their master's voice.
Fish surface together
when crumbs are thrown on the water.
Wild animals, the puma, for example,
sniff their prey from a distance.
And the sensitive plant folds its leaves
at the slightest touch.

Birds feed on insects,
seeds, fish, or vermin.
Animals coexist or devour one another.
Man is omnivorous.

Male fish and birds cover the female
in wind or water.
The male dog mounts the female dog.
Men lie on top of women
and enter between their parted legs.

Los árboles se fecundan con el viento.
El pez raja la ova;
el pájaro triza el huevo y deja el nido,
y uno echa plumas y el otro escamas.
El animal nace con pelaje de las entrañas.
La planta arranca de la semilla
y echa al aire corteza y vellos.
El hombre sale del vientre
desnudo y cubierto de sangre.

El lagarto cría nueva cola
si pierde la antigua,
y los cangrejos si pierden pinzas y patas
echan pinzas y patas nuevas.
Las heridas de hombres y animales cicatrizan;
los huesos quebrados sueldan solos.

Se desgastan las células,
los órganos, los tejidos.
Disminuyen las fuerzas vitales.
La muerte es el fin de la vida.

Trees pollinate one another on the wind.
Fish split open the egg,
birds hatch and leave the nest;
one grows feathers while the other grows scales.
Animals are born from the bowels with hair.
Plants burst from seeds
and shoot bark and blooms into the air.
Man leaves the womb
naked and covered in blood.

Lizards grow new tails
when they lose their old ones,
and when crabs lose their pincers and legs
they grow new pincers and legs.
Wounds on men and animals scar over;
broken bones mend on their own.

Cells, organs, tissues wear out.
Life forces wane.
Death is the end of life.

ABOUT THE TRANSLATORS

HAROLD AUGENBRAUM ("You Don't Hear Dogs Barking") is the author of six books on U.S. Latino culture; he's a translator of literary works such as Alvar Núñez Cabeza de Vaca's *Chronicle of the Narváez Expedition* and the Filipino novelist José Rizal's *Noli Me Tangere* and *El filibusterismo*, out with Penguin Classics. He edited *The Collected Poems of Marcel Proust* and coedited the *Norton Anthology of U.S. Latino Literature* and has been awarded various prizes including a Raven Award from the Mystery Writers of America for distinguished service to the mystery field.

ANNA DEENY ("The Fugue," "From *Diana's Tree*," "Not Anymore") is a poet, literary critic and the translator of poetry by Raúl Zurita, Mercedes Roffé, Marosa di Girogio, and Nicanor Parra, among others. She teaches Latin American literature at Harvard University.

The poet CLAYTON ESHLEMAN ("From *Spain, Take This Cup from Me*") has translated *The Complete Poetry of Cesar Vallejo, Watchfiends and Rack Screams,* by Antonin Artaud, *The Collected Poetry of Aime Cesaire* (with Annette Smith), and, with Franisek Deak and Michel Heim, *A Night with Hamlet,* by Vladimir Holan (in *Conductors of the Pit*). His most recent collection of poetry is *Anticline.* He is also the founder and editor of *Caterpillar* magazine and *Sulfur* magazine; *A Sulfur Anthology* will appear in 2014.

MICHELLE GIL-MONTERO ("Guardian of Ice") is a poet and translator of contemporary Latin American writing. Her translations include *Poetry After the Invention of America: Don't Light the Flower* by Andres Ajens, *Mouth of Hell, The Tango Lyrics,* by Maria Negorni, and *This Blue Novel,* by Valerie Mejer. She lives in Pittsburgh and is Assistant Professor of English at Saint Vincent College.

CARMEN GIMÉNEZ SMITH ("The Old Man's Song") is the author of *Milk and Filth* and the editor of *Beyond the Field: New Latin@ Writing.* She teaches creative writing at New Mexico State University and is the publisher of Noemi Press.

KATHERINE M. HEDEEN ("Letter to My Mother") is the NEH Distinguished Teaching Associate Professor of Spanish at Kenyon College. Her book-length translations include collections by Juan Bañuelos, Juan Calzadilla, Marco Antonio Campos, Juan Gelman, Fayad Jamís, José Emilio Pacheco, Víctor Rodríguez Núñez, and Ida Vitale. She is editor of the Latin American Poetry in Translation Series for Salt Publishing and was a 2009 NEA Translation Project Fellow.

JEN HOFER ("Soliloquy of the Individual," "Prayer for Marilyn Monroe") is a poet, translator, social justice interpreter, teacher, and cofounder of the language justice and literary activism collaborative Antena. Her translations, which have won awards from the Academy of American Poets and Pen American Center, can be found at Action Books, Counterpath Press, Kenning Editions, Les Figues Press, Litmus Press, Ugly Duckling Presse, and University of Pittsburgh Press. She lives in Los Angeles, where she teaches poetics, translation, and bookmaking at CalArts and Otis College.

STUART KRIMKO ("From *Hospital Británico*") is the author of two collections of poetry, *The Sweetness of Herbert* and *Hymns and Essays;* and the translator of *The Last Books of Héctor Viel Temperley* and *Belleza y Felicidad: Selected Writings of Fernanda Laguna and Cecilia Pavón*.

EVAN LAVENDER-SMITH ("The Old Man's Song") is the author of *From Old Notebooks* and *Avatar*. He lives with his wife, Carmen Giménez Smith, and children in Las Cruces, New Mexico.

VÍCTOR RODRÍGUEZ NÚÑEZ ("Letter to My Mother") has published twelve books of prize-winning poetry along with numerous editions of his selected poems, the most recent being *Cuarto de desahogo*. He is also an accomplished scholar, cultural journalist, editor, and literary translator. He divides his time between Gambier, OH, where is a professor of Spanish at Kenyon College, and Havana, Cuba.

ALASTAIR REID ("Conjectural Poem") is a poet and major translator of Latin American writers such as Jorge Luis Borges and Pablo Neruda, both of whom were his friends. He has recently collaborated with Mexican poet Pura López Colomé on a bilingual anthology of poems and recordings, *Resonance: Poetry in Two Languages*. Born in Scotland, he lives in New York City.

MARK SCHAFER ("A Few Words on the Death of Major Sabines," "Life") is an award-winning translator, visual artist, and lecturer in Spanish at the University of Massachusetts Boston. He has translated the poetry of David Huerta and Gloria Gervitz; fiction by Belén Gopegui, Virgilio Piñera, Alberto Ruy Sánchez, and Jesús Gardea; and essays by a wide range of Latin American authors.

JACK SCHMITT ("From *The Heights of Macchu Picchu*") was a Professor of Spanish and Portuguese at California State University, Long Beach, and a translator of *Canto general,* by Pablo Neruda, and *Anteparadise,* by Raúl Zurita, among other major works.

ROWAN SHARP ("When You Love What Do You Love?" "Then, in the Waters of Conchan") is a poet and translator who lives in Providence and New Orleans. Recent work appears in *Jai-Alai* and *Natural Bridge.*

ILAN STAVANS ("You Don't Hear Dogs Barking") is Lewis-Sebring Professor in Latin American and Latino Culture at Amherst College. He has translated Emily Dickinson, Elizabeth Bishop, and Richard Wilbur into Spanish; Borges, Neruda, and Rulfo into English; Isaac Bashevis Singer from Yiddish; Yehuda Amichai from Hebrew; and *Don Quixote of La Mancha* into Spanglish. An anthology of his work in English, *The Essential Ilan Stavans,* is available, along with one of his work in Spanish, *Lengua Fresca.*

ELIOT WEINBERGER ("From *Altazar*") is an essayist, occasional political journalist, editor, and translator. He has published two complete translations of *Altazor,* the most recent from Wesleyan University Press.

ABOUT THE EDITORS

RAÚL ZURITA, winner of the Chilean National Poetry Prize, is one of the most vital voices in contemporary Latin American literature. Coming out of the Chilean avant-garde (and, through his grandmother, out of the Italian tradition for poetic sequences), Zurita's work is nevertheless incredibly intimate and often shocking in its emotional immediacy and clarity. He is the creator of massive landscape poems bulldozed into the Atacama Desert and poems skywritten over New York. Arrested and tortured by the Pinochet dictatorship, Zurita has, in his life as in his work, transformed rage and pain into transcendent compassion. Among his many books in Spanish are the Dantesque trilogy *Purgatorio, Anteparaíso,* and *La Vida Nueva.* Other important books include *Zurita* and *El día más blanco.* His books in English translation include *Purgatory, Dreams of Kurosawa, Song for His Disappeared Love,* and *INRI.*

FORREST GANDER's most recent translations include *fungus skull eye wing: selected poems of Alfonso D'Aquino, Panic Cure: Poetry from Spain for the 21st Century,* and *Watchword* by Pura López Colomé. His 2012 book *Core Samples from the World* was a Pulitzer Prize and National Book Critics Circle Award finalist. He is the Adele Kellenberg Seaver Chair of Literary Arts and Comparative Literature at Brown University.

ACKNOWLEDGMENTS

Thanks to the Poetry Foundation, Señor I. Kaminsky, Fred Courtright.

Unless otherwise specified below, the rights in any English translations included in this book remain with the individual translators.

And thanks to:

Katerina Seligmann, superlative editorial assistant, and to the great company of translators: Anna Deeny, Clayton Eshleman, Forrest Gander, Michelle Gil-Montero, Katherine Hedeen & Victor Rodriguez Nuñez, Jen Hofer, Stuart Krimko, Valerie Mejer, Evan Lavender-Smith & Carmen Giménez Smith, Mark Schafer, Jack Schmitt, Rowan Sharp, Ilan Stavans & Harold Haugenbraum, and Eliot Weinberger. Special thanks to Esther Allen. Raul Zurita and Forrest Gander would like to thank Valerie Mejer for her incredible assistance in making this book possible.

Jorge Luis Borges, II ["What can I hold you with?"] from "Two English Poems" from *Selected Poems 1923–1967,* edited by Norman Thomas di Giovanni. Copyright © 1968, 1969, 1970, 1971, 1972 by Emecé Editores S.A. and Norman Thomas di Giovanni. Spanish from *Obras Completas* © 1995 by Maria Kodama. Used by permission of The Wylie Agency, LLC. "Conjectural Poem," translated by Alastair Reid, from *Selected Poems,* edited by Alexander Coleman. Spanish "Poema Conjetural" from *El Otro, El Mismo.* Copyright © 1999 by Maria Kodama. Translation copyright © 1972, 1999 by Alastair Reid. Used by permission of The Wylie Agency, LLC, Viking Penguin, a division of Penguin Group (USA) LLC, Penguin Group (Canada), Penguin Group (UK) Ltd., Random House Mondadori, and Alastair Reid through the Colchie Agency, New York.

Ernesto Cardenal, "Prayer for Marilyn Monroe," translated by Jen Hofer. Reprinted with the permission of the translator. "Oración por Marilyn Monroe" from *Oración por Marilyn Monroe y otros poemas* (Medellin: Ediciones La Tertulia, 1965). Reprinted with the permission of the author.

Antonio Cisneros, "Entonces, en las Aguas de Conchán" from *Crónica del niño Jesús de Chilca* (1981). Reprinted with the permission of the Estate of Antonio Cisneros. "Then, in the Waters of Conchán," translated by Rowan Sharp. Reprinted with the permission of the translator.

Pablo De Rokha, "The Old Man's Song," translated by Carmen Gimenez Smith and Evan Lavender-Smith. Reprinted with the permission of Carmen Giménez Smith and Evan Lavender-Smith. "El canto del macho anciano" from *Mis grandes poemas: antologia* (Santiago: Editorial Nascimento, 1969). Reprinted with the permission of Patricia Tagle, Director, Pablo De Rokha Foundation.

mayor Sabines" from *Algo sobre la muerte del Mayor Sabines*. Reprinted with the permission of Judith Sabines.

Héctor Viel Temperley, "Christus Pantokrator," "Long corner of summer 1-5," "Your Face," "Your Body and Your Father," "My head is bandaged 1-6," "They have taken me from the world 1-4," and "Freedom, summer" from "Hospital Británico" from *The Last Books of Héctor Viel Temperley*, translated by Stuart Krimko. Copyright © 2011 by Stuart Krimko. Reprinted with the permission of Sand Paper Press, Key West. "Christus Pantokrator," "Larga esquina de verano 1-5," "Tu rostro," "Tu Cuerpo y Tu Padre," "Tengo la cabeza vendada 1-6," "Me han sacado del mundo 1-4," and "La libertad, el verano" from "Hospital Británico" from *Crawl y Hospital Británico*. Reprinted with the permission of the Estate of Héctor Viel Temperley.

César Vallejo, "III," "V. Spanish Image of Death," "VI. Cortege After the Capture of Bilbao," "VII," "IX. Short Prayer for a Loyalist Hero," "XII. Mass," and "XV. Spain, Take This Cup from Me" from "Spain, Take This Cup from Me" from *The Complete Poetry, César Vallejo*, edited and translated by Clayton Eshleman. Copyright © 2007 by The Regents of the University of California. Reprinted by permission of the University of California Press.

Idea Vilariño, "Not Anymore," translated by Anna Deeny. First published in *Hotel Lautrémont: Contemporary Poetry from Uruguay*, edited by Roberto Echavarren and Kent Johnson (London: Shearsman Books, 2011). Reprinted with the permission of the translator. "Ya no." Reprinted with the permission of Ana Ines Larre Borges/Estate of Idea Vilariño.

José Watanabe, "Guardian of Ice," translated by Michelle Gil-Montero. Reprinted with the permission of the translator. "El guardián del hielo" from *Poesia completa* (Pre-Textos, 2008). Reprinted with the permission of Pre-Textos, Valencia.

NOTE

Readers may note a relatively small number of women included in this book's selection. Besides the extraordinary Gabriela Mistral, Alejandra Pizarnik, and Idea Vilariño, there were other notable women who wrote, with double merit, in a time of adverse conditions and in a world dominated by men; Blanca Verela, in Peru, for example, and Olga Orozco, in Argentina. But the greatest explosion in writing by women happened in the late twentieth century, and continues today, when women are writing much of the most innovative, profound, and groundbreaking poetry of our time. If this was an anthology of more recent work, the gender proportions would have been reversed.

—RZ

POETRY
FOUNDATION

Harriet Monroe Poetry Institute
POETS IN THE WORLD SERIES

PUBLICATIONS

Ilya Kaminsky, *Poets in the World* series editor, 2011–2013, HMPI director

Another English: Anglophone Poems from Around the World, edited by Catherine Barnett and Tiphanie Yanique (Tupelo Press)

Elsewhere, edited by Eliot Weinberger (Open Letter Books)

Fifteen Iraqi Poets, edited by Dunya Mikhail (New Directions Publishing)

"Landays: Poetry of Afghan Women," edited by Eliza Griswold (*Poetry* magazine, June 2013)

New Cathay: Contemporary Chinese Poetry, edited by Ming Di (Tupelo Press)

Open the Door: How to Excite Young People about Poetry, edited by Dorothea Lasky, Dominic Luxford, and Jesse Nathan (McSweeney's)

Pinholes in the Night: Essential Poems from Latin America, edited by Raúl Zurita and Forrest Gander (Copper Canyon Press)

Seven New Generation African Poets, edited by Kwame Dawes and Chris Abani (Slapering Hol Press)

Something Indecent: Poems Recommended by Eastern European Poets, edited by Valzhyna Mort (Red Hen Press)

The Star by My Head: Poets from Sweden, edited and translated by Malena Mörling and Jonas Ellerström (Milkweed Editions)

The Strangest of Theatres: Poets Writing Across Borders, edited by Jared Hawkley, Susan Rich, and Brian Turner (McSweeney's)

Katharine Coles, HMPI inaugural director

Blueprints: Bringing Poetry into Communities, edited by Katharine Coles (University of Utah Press)

Code of Best Practices in Fair Use for Poetry, created with American University's Center for Social Media and Washington College of Law

Poetry and New Media: A Users' Guide, report of the Poetry and New Media Working Group (Harriet Monroe Poetry Institute)

Poetry is vital to language and living. Since 1972, Copper Canyon Press has published extraordinary poetry from around the world to engage the imaginations and intellects of readers, writers, booksellers, librarians, teachers, students, and donors.

WE ARE GRATEFUL FOR THE MAJOR SUPPORT PROVIDED BY:

THE PAUL G. ALLEN
FAMILY FOUNDATION

Lannan

THE MAURER FAMILY
FOUNDATION

WASHINGTON STATE
ARTS COMMISSION

Anonymous
John Branch
Diana and Jay Broze
Beroz Ferrell & The Point, LLC
Janet and Les Cox
Mimi Gardner Gates
Gull Industries, Inc.
on behalf of William and Ruth True
Mark Hamilton and Suzie Rapp
Carolyn and Robert Hedin
Steven Myron Holl
Lakeside Industries, Inc.
on behalf of Jeanne Marie Lee
Maureen Lee and Mark Busto
Brice Marden
H. Stewart Parker
Penny and Jerry Peabody
John Phillips and Anne O'Donnell
Joseph C. Roberts
Cynthia Lovelace Sears and Frank Buxton
The Seattle Foundation
Dan Waggoner
Charles and Barbara Wright
The dedicated interns and faithful
volunteers of Copper Canyon Press

To learn more about underwriting Copper Canyon Press titles,
please call 360-385-4925 ext. 103

The Chinese character for poetry is made up of two
parts: "word" and "temple." It also serves as press-
mark for Copper Canyon Press.

The interior and cover are set in Monotype's digital
version of Bulmer, originally cut by William Martin
in 1790. Headings set in Brown Gothic, designed
by Nick Shinn in 2000. Book design and composi-
tion by VJB/Scribe.